The
Age
of the
Image

The
Age
of the
Image

REDEFINING LITERACY IN

A WORLD OF SCREENS

Stephen Apkon

Farrar, Straus and Giroux ■ New York

Farrar, Straus and Giroux
18 West 18th Street, New York 10011

Printed in the United States of America
First edition, 2013

Library of Congress Cataloging-in-Publication Data
Apkon, Stephen.
   The age of the image : redefining literacy in a world of screens / Stephen Apkon.
      p.   cm.
   Includes bibliographical references.
   ISBN 978-0-374-10243-2 (alk. paper)
   1. Visual literacy.   2. Visual communication.   3. Visual perception.   I. Title.

   LB1068 .A75 2013
   370.15'5—dc23

                                                      2012037556

Designed by Abby Kagan
Illustrations by Robin Richesson

www.fsgbooks.com
www.twitter.com/fsgbooks • www.facebook.com/fsgbooks

10   9   8   7   6   5   4   3   2   1

To Dora Apkon

[In the future] illiteracy will not be defined by those who cannot read and write, but by those who cannot learn and relearn.

—ALVIN TOFFLER

■ CONTENTS

FOREWORD BY MARTIN SCORSESE   XI

INTRODUCTION   3

ALL THE WORLD'S A SCREEN   15

WHAT IS LITERACY?   37

THE BRAIN SEES PICTURES FIRST   75

THE EVOLUTION OF THE AUDIENCE   102

THE BIG BUSINESS OF IMAGES   136

GRAMMAR, RHYTHM, AND RHYME IN THE AGE

   OF THE IMAGE   158

TEACHING A NEW GENERATION   210

THE SHARPENING PICTURE   242

NOTES ON SOURCES   255

ACKNOWLEDGMENTS   259

When I was young, the division between words and images was as wide as the ocean. Pictures—moving or still, painted or photographed—were something you looked at, period. Words, you read. End of story.

At a certain point, early on, I started to understand that there was a language of images; I should say, I understood it without knowing it or articulating it. I couldn't have told you the difference between a close-up and a tracking shot, and it was a while before I realized that there was such a thing as editing. But all the same, I had an intimation of *something*—varying levels of emotional intensity, tonal inflections, the understanding that the eye of the audience was being *directed* through the story with shifts and modulations of scale and depth, light and shadow, rhythm and color, nuances in behavior and body language. In other words, I had a growing understanding that every element in a film *counted*. I was not alone.

As I grew older and became interested in movies and how they were made, I looked at some of the books that had been written about their history. People were still grappling with movies, which, after all, were just a half a century old. Film history was a matter of movie stars and Hollywood lore, and a succession of milestones— *The Great Train Robbery* to *The Birth of a Nation* to *Greed* to *The Jazz Singer* to *Citizen Kane* and so on. Filmmaking itself seemed *very* distant and forbidding—big, costly, cumbersome, and out of reach of mere mortals like us. The books about how to make your own movies were, I'm sorry to say, a little sad—the stills that illustrated close-ups and wide shots and "expressionistic lighting" were depressingly drab, and the point of view was often extremely pedantic—close-ups were "emotional," cross-cutting "built tension," tracking shots were "mysterious."

Hovering above it all was a strange antagonism between literature and film. Movies were dismissed and vilified within the world of high culture—theater and the novel were superior art forms, while cinema was a toy, a diversion that "left nothing to the imagination." It was "frivolous" while all the other arts were "serious"—in fact, it wasn't an art at all because it was "collaborative." The image was ephemeral but the word was forever. I know that old prejudices die hard, but I'm amazed that this particular prejudice, still with us, is taking so long to give up the ghost.

Then there was television. If movies were vulgar and "escapist," TV was even less substantial, a droning amusement, an ongoing distraction. Needless to say, it wasn't something that you needed to "read"—you supposedly just turned it on, sat and watched, and then turned it off.

In the early sixties, everything changed in movies with the introduction of lightweight 16mm cameras and portable sound equipment, coupled with the examples of Cassavetes's *Shadows* and Godard's *Breathless* and avant-garde films like Anger's *Scorpio Rising* and Bruce Conner's *Cosmic Ray*. And all around the world, filmmakers were telling stories in new, radical ways. I've referred to this moment in cinema many times, and the older I get the more powerful it becomes in my memory. One of the most interesting and exciting aspects of that time was the very clear division between the people who got it and the people who didn't. This was *not* a matter of being hip. Believe me, those of us who spent our days and nights in movie theaters were far from hip. It was actually a matter of knowing that movies were *not* there to be consumed and forgotten when the lights came up, but *read* and attentively and lovingly returned to and studied, in exactly the same way you would read a novel or a play. We would look at what Bergman was doing side by side with the new Pasolini film and then walk into a showing of the new Kurosawa film, our memory of one illuminating and enriching our experience of the other, which paved the way in turn for the new Antonioni and the new Satyajit Ray and so on. And at the same time, the late critic Andrew Sarris was showing us the glories of Hollywood cinema. Here was someone who told us it's not only okay to love John Ford and Alfred Hitchcock—they are *giants*, and it's time to do what the French have already done and recognize them as such. Many of the old masters were still making movies at the time, so *The Man Who Shot Liberty Valance* and *The Birds* were also part of the great endless conversation, in which every film ever made became a subject *and* a participant.

We take all this for granted now, but half a century ago it was brand new—not to mention extremely threatening to the people who *didn't* get it. Movies-as-novelty was easy to cope with, but cinema-as-*art-form*? Unthinkable. Certain films and filmmakers were the acid test. I'm thinking of Andy Warhol, Sam Fuller, and Jean-Luc Godard, to take three extremely different examples. A rock critic once wrote that if you didn't like the Rolling Stones then you didn't like rock 'n' roll. At the time, we probably would have said that if you watched the work of these three filmmakers and didn't recognize its beauty and mystery and eloquence, then you didn't like cinema. Now, I think I'd phrase it differently: if you held on to the idea of moving images as something to be consumed and forgotten, you would be blind to cinema in general and maybe to Warhol and Fuller and Godard in particular.

And blind to the growing sophistication of television and advertising. After the famous example of Nixon's five o'clock shadow in the televised presidential debate of 1960, politicians and performers started to pay more attention to the way they presented themselves on TV. Television ads were carefully designed to hit you where you least expected it, which meant that the advertising industry was always changing, adapting to every new wrinkle in the culture, refining its understanding of the visual down to the millisecond. I remember a lot of worry about TV and what it was doing to the culture, but the culture had already changed. We needed to prepare ourselves. We need to stop worrying about it and start *reading* it.

In 2012, moving images are absolutely everywhere—movies, TV, video games, YouTube, streaming services, taxi cabs, subway ads, electronic billboards, and on and on. For someone of my generation, the most astonishing aspect of this development is that many of these images were created by nonprofessionals, shot with smartphones and cameras of all shapes, sizes, and levels of expense. The need for visual literacy has only become more urgent. In fact, it has become *necessary*. This wonderful book, written from the unique perspective of someone who loves cinema *and* who is passionate about education, helps put this need in perspective. Steve Apkon starts with the cave paintings and takes us all the way to YouTube and beyond, by way of Gutenberg and Edison and Hitchcock, and in so doing he helps us to clearly understand the *continuity* between word and image, as opposed to the divide. In the process he redefines the word *literacy* to include *all* the means by which we communicate today.

I first met Steve when I visited the Jacob Burns Film Center for a screening of *Gangs of New York* in 2001. Over the past decade, the Film Center has grown into an exciting and thriving independent theater as well as a creative and educational hub. Steve and his team have created a broad curriculum that links critical viewing to film production, with visual storytelling at the core.

The Age of the Image lays out the tools we need to cultivate our awareness of and attention to every message and every gesture, artistic or opportunistic, expressed in print or in pixels. It's not just a plea for literacy, but a wonderful road map and guide for how it can be taught and nurtured.

The
Age
of the
Image

This book is the culmination of more than a decade of thought and work, yet its origins lie in my childhood.

When I was five years old, we moved to a new house in Framingham, Massachusetts. There were already three kids, with another to come, and we needed more space. We even had the luxury of a garage, and my parents had some very different ideas for this structure.

My mother was not happy when my father's idea won out. He was an engineer by trade, but his true love was photography. The garage would become a darkroom.

We would all take turns sitting with my father as he sorted through strips of negatives, holding each up to the light to find which one he would work with that day. The lights would be extinguished, and he would turn on an enlarger that would cast an image on a blank piece of paper held down by four black metal strips that framed the image.

Then came a series of liquid baths. At my father's elbow, under the red glow of a "safe light," we would slowly watch the image emerge. No matter how many times I witnessed this—like a young boy who knew the illusionist's tricks but was still mesmerized—the magic never ceased.

I was given my first camera a few years later. It was a simple point-and-shoot, but it meant that I could join my father on his photography expeditions. He went to oddly dull places to find subjects, but I remember them vividly—a town dump, an abandoned industrial area, along a creek, or often just down some new street we hadn't explored yet—camera dangling around my neck at the ready. I would look for the first thing that caught my novice eye, and soon my roll of film would be finished and I'd be ready to move on.

My father would be engaged in something altogether different. He'd be looking in all directions, as if hunting for big game and not wanting to disturb it. Every once in a while something would catch his eye and he would stop and lower his bag to the ground and take out his equipment. I could never quite figure out where his eye was drawn, as his subjects could range from a small corner of a building; to a piece of old metal or rope he found lying in the street; or even a dirty, broken old doll with an eye missing that some little girl's parents had discarded in the dump.

My father had trained his eye to see beauty in the mundane. He was a keen observer of the world and saw story in the smallest or most obscure of images.

I later went on to Georgetown University and Harvard Business School, but nothing in my education, nothing I ever learned, would prove as helpful to me or my sense of the world's inner workings as those walks around the neighborhood to film ordinary junk—to look closely and find the story within.

Every generation for the last two centuries has seen a shift in basic technology—whether in transportation, health care, the preservation and preparation of food, or another facet of what at each moment could be called "modern living." For my generation, growing up in the 1960s and '70s, it was television. And while I had lots to do as a kid, including a daily paper route, we were drawn to the television like particles to a nucleus.

For my parents, who grew up in the golden age of radio, television was a novelty. For us it was an appliance. I never knew life without it, and turning it on to see images broadcast to this little box was as natural as opening the refrigerator to grab a cold drink.

The term might not have arisen until more recently to describe today's teenagers, but we were the first real generation of *screenagers*.* All we had initially was a small black-and-white television with rabbit ears antennae, which we had to manipulate back and forth to get better reception, but it was enough to captivate our imaginations. I remember my father going up on the roof to install a directional antenna, which gave us more clarity of images and a few more channels, and I remember our first color television, when I was about five years old. (The black-and-white was moved up to my parents' room.) We consumed everything we could get our eyes on.

We also took small steps into the world of creating images. We were capturing home movies with a silent Super 8 camera. Then we would gather with grandparents and extended family several times a year, unfold and slide open a portable screen, thread the tiny film reels through the projector, shut off the lights, and squeal in delight at the well-worn family movies. We watched these images as artifacts of past events even though we weren't constructing narrative stories with them.

Whatever we learned in school couldn't match the stimulation

---

* The term *screenagers* first appeared in Douglas Rushkoff's *Playing the Future*, which looks at the first generation of children growing up with access to personal computers.

of what we were watching on television. Movies were seen largely as entertainment and escape. We assumed television had "always been there," but our parents knew life without it, and our schools and teachers weren't quite sure what to do with it.

I don't remember much of anything that came from formal classroom learning—our public system in Framingham was indistinguishably average—but I do remember what happened when the teacher asked for volunteers to go fetch the audiovisual cart. Every hand would instantly shoot up.

This was well before middle school, when we would learn that this job was for geeks and we were too cool to volunteer. Back then, we were excited to maneuver the cart through the hallways, and we relished the fact that this meant a mini-vacation for the class. Unlike our other lessons, AV time usually meant we had reached the end of a lesson a bit early, or that there were a few days to kill at the end of a semester and the teacher was done teaching.

There was never any explanation of the film we would be viewing, and rarely any substantive discussion afterward. If there was, it was relegated to what happened in the film and whether we'd liked it, as opposed to talking about the structure, the language it used to construct narrative and meaning, or anything else along those lines. Film wasn't treated as a text, to be studied in an academic way, but rather as a show, something to be tasted and swallowed and then moved on from, a lot like a bowl of popcorn: enjoyable, but with very little nutrition.

I don't believe it was out of negligence on our teachers' part, or that of the school system. They simply didn't have the tools to begin to talk about this kind of storytelling. Teachers were still unprepared to talk about film and television was quite new and constantly evolving, and they didn't know how this media would come to dominate our communication channels. We were all just feeling our way and letting the "experts" do the work.

A few decades later, when my oldest daughter, Talia, was born, my wife and I were soon faced with the decisions faced by most parents: when to place her in front of a screen and start feeding her media. Even without access to a screen, her world was already a visual one, just as with countless generations before her.

In her first months, she would open her eyes and see these massive heads smiling down at her, cooing and making silly faces. While her skull was still soft enough to allow for continued brain growth, her mirror neurons were ready to fire almost on day one. We would smile; she would smile. We would open our eyes and mouths as if surprised, and she would do the same. She took in and understood the world through her primary senses, but mostly through her eyes. And then she would be the one smiling in order to trigger *our* mirror neurons and provoke *our* responses, as she unconsciously moved from consumer to creator.

When she got a little bit older and could hold her head up and then sit, we spent countless hours reading her picture books such as *Stellaluna* or *The Velveteen Rabbit*. She would study each of the pictures as we read, often asking us to pause so she could really soak in the images on the page. She could construct her own story through the images, which were much more open to interpretation than the words.

This kind of "visual reading," the ground upon which reading is built, is sadly dismissed in favor of just words when our children get to school. Picture books give way to books with fewer and fewer illustrations. Ultimately, the image becomes an afterthought, with much sacrificed along the way. We spend countless hours on letters and words, but hardly anything on the images.

I don't recall the exact moment it happened: the first time we placed her in front of a screen. My favorite leisure position as a young father was supine on the couch, watching a Red Sox game, with my daughter on my chest—although the truth is that this usually just put her to sleep. As she was our first child, we were able to carefully monitor her consumption of media (as opposed to our third child, who, with two older, then television-loving older siblings, saw a lot more), but once school started and she was off at friends' homes, the fight was essentially over. I began to think about the exposure of our kids to media and understood that ultimately this was a wave we couldn't hold off, but rather one we would need to help our children prepare to navigate.

In just the three decades it took for me to grow from teenager to parent of three children, screens had permeated our environment. If screens were a novelty to my parents, and mere appliances to us, they are appendages to our children. The two televisions and one Super 8 camera of my youth gave way to a current inventory of no fewer than four televisions, two desktop computers, five laptops, two portable DVD players (none mounted in cars), five phones with screens, an iPad, an iPod touch, and four other mp3 devices, all sporting screens enabling us to view an endless array of video, many of which can access countless hours of streaming media.* We also have several generations of digital video cameras to capture images, and editing software that either comes native to the computers or is available for a few hundred dollars at most and that supplies the kind of editing power that a few decades earlier would have cost hundreds of thousands of dollars.

Lest you think we are an aberration, look at your own surroundings and take inventory. If you live in the average U.S. home, you are housing more televisions than you are people. When you add in the other screens, you will no doubt well tilt the

---

* We also have a few projectors, although I didn't include them in the inventory, as they are more particular to my work—and it was getting just a little embarrassing.

balance toward screens and away from people. This is a growing trend throughout the world. The global population of approximately 7.0 billion people in 2012 possesses more than 3.5 billion televisions and computer screens—and that is before we get to counting up smartphones and other screened devices. In fact, in the last quarter of 2011, the birth of iPhones alone (at a rate of 4.37 per second) exceeded the birth of human babies on this planet (which came in at a rate of 4.2 births per second).

And once you step outside your home, almost regardless of where that is, you encounter a deluge of more screens. Grocery checkout lines, retail stores, gas stations, airports, airplane seats, and taxicabs are all adding innumerable screens to their environments in an effort to capture your attention. Whether you are in a yurt in the Mongolian desert or a penthouse apartment in New York City, you are likely exposed regularly to visual communication. We are awash in a world of screens and moving images.

Visual media are redefining what it means to develop the tools of literacy to understand a changing world—with regard not just to the reception of information but also to its expression. If you were born anytime before the late 1980s, you, like me, grew up in a world where there were many consumers but very few storytellers. To get a visual story into the hands of the world, you had to be either a television executive or a big, powerful Hollywood studio head. It required enormous power and capital and squadrons of underlings to produce and distribute what amounted to a very expensive piece of media. But now, thanks to the introduction of digital movie cameras that can literally fit into our pockets (and some of which double as phones, music devices, or even computers) and the advent of widespread file sharing offering easily accessible distribution channels, those old empires have fallen.

In 1998, I began to talk publicly about the concept of a nonprofit organization with a dual mission in film programming and education, and found a receptive audience in a group of committed community members and talented core staff who joined up along the way. In June 2001, we opened the Jacob Burns Film Center in Pleasantville, New York.

We show more than four hundred films a year from more than fifty countries, have welcomed hundreds of guests, and have learned about cultures through the stories people share on the screen. On the education side, we are squarely focused on what it now means to be "literate" in a world dominated by visual media, and this has been the main focus of our work over the past decade. Along the way we have also opened a twenty-seven-thousand-square-foot Media Arts Lab, which both supports our existing programs and provides a laboratory in which we develop new curricula and programs aimed at introducing these concepts of visual literacy into classrooms.

From the beginning, we realized we were up against some entrenched bias in public school classrooms. I wasn't surprised. Most students of today's generation receive the same lame treatment of movies in the classroom that I had—movies is still a fallback device when the teacher is too busy or too lazy to teach. But today's students have the added burden of standardized testing, which has left little room for creativity or the other elements of a well-rounded education.

We wanted the teachers who came to our Media Arts Lab to think differently about the visual texts brought into their classrooms. The material needed to be not in addition to, but *in the service of* the work the teachers were already required to do. As new literacies emerge, they don't negate more traditional forms of literacy, but rather embrace them wholly.

For its first program, the Media Arts Lab had the good fortune of connecting with Anne Marie Santoro, who, in addition to spending time as a master third-grade teacher in the Bronx, spent a decade as the director of education for Children's Television Workshop, the creators of *Sesame Street*. Under Anne Marie's leadership, we created a program that used the language and tools of a filmmaker to help third-grade students improve their writing skills. The program was based on the notion that there are three primal components to the experience of media—what we see, what we hear, and what we feel (or what emotional response we have to the text). All three together help develop empathy toward and a connection with a character or story, which informs children's social and emotional development. All good storytellers, in whatever media, are first keen observers of the world around them. They see nuance and story in the small details of life, and they possess the skills to convey these observations in compelling ways.

See Hear Feel Film was introduced into schools in September 2001. We weren't certain how it would be accepted—by teachers or by students. The program dealt with sophisticated material: wide shots, medium shots, close-ups, and extreme close-ups, and we even talked about mise-en-scène*—*with third-graders*; and they understood it all instinctually. Barely old enough to read complex sentences, these kids could "see" what we meant when we talked about these things.

One of the first films we showed, an animated film called *Trompe l'oeil*—French for "tricks the eye"—follows a worm digging through what seems to be dirt. As the camera pulls back, we realize that he is busy hollowing out an apple for his home. We assume we have the picture; then the camera pulls out again and we see that the apple is within a larger, bucolic countryside setting.

---

*Mise-en-scène refers to all the physical elements in the frame, including set design, props, costumes, lighting, and even actors.

One more pullback reveals something else, and we gradually realize that what we thought we were looking at is actually something quite different. The apple is one of a bunch of apples in a bowl on a kitchen table, sitting in front of a painting of a bucolic landscape hanging on the wall beyond. The sound of heels walking across the floor tells us that someone is coming. The camera draws our eyes to the knife on the table. When the screen goes black and we hear metal against wood, we understand that the apple is being sliced. An entire story told in four minutes, without dialogue, bedazzles us with a literature of its own.

Students love this little film, and are thrilled when we later hand them a writing journal wrapped in a cover that is imprinted with an image of the apple from the film and invite them to write their own stories about it. Even those who had never handed in a complete paragraph, let alone a story, became loquacious about what they had seen. Students would show up for their next sessions with entire journals filled and asking for more. They were consuming media more critically, seeing the cuts and camera angles and story structure. They were also reading and writing with more excitement.

This method of learning actually goes back to an oral tradition, and I could see it awakening an atavistic impulse in our kids—what you might call the roots of nonverbal emotional intelligence. We explained how nuances and gestures conveyed unspoken meanings, often more powerful than the text. We see the visual text and we understand subtext. The difference between what a character is saying and what he or she is thinking (based on action or posture) can be immense, and the skill at being able to see it, and also reproduce it, is literacy.

Over the past eleven years, we have developed courses that have reached more than a hundred thousand children in pre-K to grade-twelve classrooms, in boys' and girls' clubs, at homeless shelters, and even in the local prison system as part of a young offenders program. We have also worked with adult learners eager to tell their own stories or to acquire these skills to further their opportunities at work. We have seen what works and have watched people flourish as they acquire a new level of literacy.

This book is an outgrowth of this work and of a decade of trying to understand the unique power of these media and how to harness their power most effectively. From pure entertainment to international activism, individual image makers are seizing the tools of creation and distribution to reach audiences of millions in a way that wasn't possible before. The commonality of these videos is the literacy that sustains their construction and their messages, and which allows an audience to derive meaning.

Literacy is always a response to emerging technology. While conservative elements in a society often fear and resist change, the transformation is usually painless, especially, in the case of visual media, for those who embrace the notion of literacy evolving to reflect our human desire for the most direct, unmediated modes of communication. The power of visual media has been with us from the beginning of our species, as we are physiologically constructed to consume and find meaning from images in a way that transcends other forms of communication. With today's visual technology, our work lives will be changed forever, and soon it will be as unfathomable not to know how to make a video as it is not to know how to send an e-mail. The vocabulary of Hollywood is becoming the vocabulary of Main Street. We must embrace these powerful tools, not only to ensure American viability and competitiveness, but also to realize the opportunity they offer to make us more effective and valuable as employees, managers, and leaders.

Don't be intimidated. Finding your way in this world is easier than you think; in fact, you've been living in it and absorbing its rituals for as long as you have been alive. You will be surprised by how the codes of this new literacy are available to you—in some sense, how they have *always* been available to you—and how, with practice and some guidance, you can find your own voice.

At the Jacob Burns Film Center we have a custom of screening new works from emerging visual storytellers for their families and communities. As one of our faculty members, Joe Summerhays, has said, "When you see these young filmmakers being honored, not only for their unique vision, but also for the sheer persistence it takes to collaborate and execute these visions, it is as if you can actually see their DNA being transformed."

In a book called *The Storytelling Animal*, Jonathan Gottschall explains how we are consumed with and driven by narrative. We have evolved from a species that transmitted stories to one another orally, sitting around a campfire; to one that invented and propagated the use of alphabets and printed texts in order to share stories; to one that has given birth to the tools of creation and distribution of visual images as we strive to tell more and more compelling stories. It is not hyperbole to say that our society's cultural and storytelling DNA is being transformed—whether we accept it or resist it.

After each revolution, political or cultural, we can look back and see the elements that came together to make it possible and even inevitable. Those who understand and prepare for these revolutions thrive, and those who don't are left behind. We are at one of those moments with regard to the ways in which we participate in society, democracy, and the global economy, and visual images and story are at the heart of this historic change. This book is a guide to how to understand the elements that have brought us here and how to seize the power they offer.

We often look for signs of systemic change in the highest of places, yet it is often in the most profane of places that we find the fuel for this change.

So it seems appropriate that a look at the shape of literacy in the twenty-first century can be gleaned in a visit to a set of ratty industrial warehouses at the edge of downtown Los Angeles, in a neighborhood favored by filmmakers for its moody alleys and car-chase venues.

Inside a drafty space that bears the most charitable appellation of "office," a stout young man in a T-shirt and flip-flops named Freddie Wong, along with several of his friends from the University of Southern California, thinks of new ideas for simple Internet videos that millions will watch.

Wong's first breakout success played off the video game Guitar Hero, in which the player makes exaggerated riffs on a plastic guitar in order to score points and keep an electronic "crowd" cheering. Some of the nation's more exuberant players were in the habit of videotaping themselves jamming on the fake guitars and uploading this footage to YouTube, the massive file-sharing site that had been launched only a year earlier.

Those who were paying attention noticed a commonality in the really popular clips: they emphasized ridiculous quasi–rock star poses, and the cameras zoomed in on the player's face while ignoring the game unfolding on the screen.

This emerging trope seemed ripe for parody. Wong enlisted a few friends; borrowed a motorcycle, donned a black leather jacket, a red sequined shirt, and medieval chains; and preened like a vain thug. "What's up, Internet?" he said. "My name's Freddie and I've come from a long hard day of rocking faces and doing jumps with my sweet bike here to come and *rock you*." A flunky removes the jacket from Wong's shoulders like an obedient valet. Wong sneers that the chains on his chest are there to keep his soul tied down; otherwise, it would fly off and "impregnate women."

Then comes an utterly ridiculous set piece in which Wong's exaggerated licks on the fake guitar are kept in time with the scoring of the game, run as a split screen. Wong does a relatively average job on the scoring, but he acts throughout as though he were supremely pleased with himself. And then, in an unexpected coup de grâce, he smashes the plastic guitar, punk-style, with a triumphant "Yes!"

The performance was designed to be ludicrous—which it was—but the larger purpose was to engage the Internet's boisterous hive of largely anonymous users who watch, criticize, and share amateur videos. It didn't matter that the strap of the guitar was accidentally hanging on Freddie the wrong way, or that the lighting was crude. The video was smart and it was literate and it shared a set of in-gestures with the audience. Within a few weeks, it received more than a million hits on YouTube, as friends e-mailed it through the exponential matrix of social connections. Wong has since duplicated this success many times over.

"Gamer Commute," for example, which received more than nine million views within two months, begins with a shot of Wong waking up in an ordinary bedroom and making a choice of clothes from an electronic menu—glasses, gray T-shirt, flip-flops, cargo shorts. Three guns fly toward him and embed themselves in his body with a metallic click. He then gets into his Toyota, and after taking it up to the speed limit on an ordinary Los Angeles street, he climbs on top of the roof of the moving car and fires a pistol in the air. All of this was achieved with green screens and special effects. The video ends with Wong coming into his ordinary-looking office cubicle and sitting down with a bored expression, resigned to the mundane workday. The video builds upon a foundation of cultural knowledge, and then leaves an unstated moral conclusion: that the gaming world contains far too many thrills and blood spatters to be sustainable in the dreary existence of working life.

One wonders how many of the nine million clicks "Gamer Commute" received were made from cubicles such as the one Wong occupies at the video's end.

Freddie Wong's success on YouTube was anything but a random accident. He did not make a video and just throw it against the wall of the Internet to see if it would stick. In fact, his career has been built not so much on creative randomness as on deliberate calculation, in much the same way Jack Kerouac wrote *On the Road* not as a freewheeling, spontaneous howl of beatnik joy, but rather as a shrewd attempt to write a bestseller that would embody the rambling spirit of the late 1950s. Like Kerouac, Wong found cultural receptivity, and he has done more to uncrack the nebulous market "science" behind effective amateur filmmaking than just about anybody working today.

This inquiry into the base code of successful videos started when Wong was still an undergraduate at USC. He wrote a thesis called the "10^6 Project," its name implying a force with exponential power. "Why do videos go viral?" he asked. "What kind of content goes viral? And what are the strategies and techniques utilized to promote them?" Wong and his classmate and partner Brandon Laatsch started looking closer at the videos that had gone viral, and at the core factors in their doing so.

"They repeat a formula," Wong said. "The success of videos was seen as this random force, but when you have an enormous body of people doing the same thing, that element of randomness disappears."

Herein lies a paradox: watching videos on the Web is usually a solitary experience, but Wong tapped into a social gold mine. People who watch homemade videos love to pass them on to their friends. It is a way to have a connection with others and even to claim a little credit for the creativity of the filmmaker, because it is you who first noticed and laughed at his brilliance; the humor accrues to the sharer. People take a social risk when they e-mail a link to a Web video to friends, or call them over to the laptop. "You're putting yourself out there," says Wong. So it had better be amusing.

The factor he is aiming for, then, is what, for newspapers, used to be called the "Hey, Martha" factor: the quirky, indescribable story that would persuade a reader to toss the Metro section over to his wife and say, "Hey, Martha, you have to read this." Enjoying the story together and then talking about it, even arguing about it, become as much a part of the experience as the viewing. So in Wong's case, the maker's imperative is to provoke a specific response in the viewer, namely, "What will make me want to show this to other people?"

This medium of exchange is critical in an era when our choices of what to watch are so easily driven by the recommendations of our friends, which usually come in the form not of spoken plaudits but of a forwarded e-mail. This is the way we share literacy in this century.

Henry Jenkins, a professor of communication at the University of Southern California, writes about this in a book called *Spreadable Media: Creating Meaning and Value in a Networked Culture*, written with Sam Ford and Joshua Green. Jenkins says the act of forwarding a video link both gives an inherent sense of added value to the product and instantaneously creates a mini-community.

"Rather than seeing circulation as the empty exchange of information stripped of context and meaning, we see these acts of circulation as constituting bids for meaning and value," Jenkins writes with his coauthors. "We feel that it very much matters who sends the message, who receives it, and most importantly, what messages get sent."

In short, context matters in these mini-communities. Freddie Wong, too, noticed a contextual factor at work in videos that were truly successful in eliciting page clicks. The sound and the dialogue needed to be only basically intelligible, as they were likely to be competing with other sounds. And for that reason, sound element didn't matter nearly as much as the visual components. The filmmaker's credo that "plot matters" holds true more than ever, but plot must be expressed in a way that can be seen. It lends itself to a more physical type of acting—almost a mimetic method that dates to the silent era of movies at the turn of the twentieth century.

"You have to assume that these videos are being played on laptops, tablets and cell phones with tiny speakers" says Wong. "And that there's going to be noise and other distractions in the room. And so you have to make it visually interesting in order to cut through the static noise and draw the proper attention to the central message of the video."

The new era of the digital peep show has something else in common with the brief films of the silent era. Like those early films, today's videos are meant to be international in their appeal. The early film studios in Patterson, New Jersey, were cranking out three-minute reels that could be understood in Paris and Buenos Aires as well as in New York. Short films with limited dialogue are more easily appreciated, and therefore more likely to be watched and shared in nations where English is not widely spoken. Visuals are not hampered by the constraints of tongue; they work in most any culture—which is why Freddie Wong has a following in Croatia.

Thus stripped of most traditional linguistic elements, the short film has to move fast, but it must strive not to confuse the viewer with too many moving objects or jarring cuts. The format of a short online video is subject to a concept called "dropoff," in which the viewer simply gets bored and stops watching. Conventional Hollywood movies longer than ninety minutes and shown to a captive paying audience in a theater have the luxury of padding out the material or slowing down the story to draw out the narrative experience. Video shorts do not enjoy that luxury; viewers can "walk out" with a simple click.

This isn't to say that filmmakers succeed when they aim for the lowest common denominator. The video has to demonstrate a balance between accessibility and sophistication.

The Harvard scholar Marjorie Garber, in her landmark book *The Use and Abuse of Literature*, lays out the tricky question of what distinguishes a piece of literary writing from the merely everyday. Garber postulates that a text ought to draw upon some of the foundational works that came before it, if even in shadow—the myth of the flawed hero, a Homeric sea journey, a pair of doomed lovers. The work also ought to have a quality of openness to it, a certain ambiguity that leaves the author's intentions at least partly in the dark, so that the "meaning" of the text might be pleasingly unclear and the conclusion left for the reader to draw from his own experiences.

This is a hard thing to get right, and Wong's videos meet both standards of Garber's literacy test. He draws upon a body of work that is familiar to most of his viewers: the world of video games, in which certain tropes (the car chase, the first-person shooter, and the explosions of colorful blood in simulated combat) are recognizable and even shopworn to the audience. Wong's videos take these standards and apply them to ridiculous scenarios so that the "fish out of water" quality might itself be the locus for the joke, and for the narrative pleasure of the audience, who is acquainted with the in-references.

Wong is not alone in tapping old literary veins with new visual technology. Just across town from him live two transplanted New Yorkers, brothers Benny and Rafi Fine, who have produced several narrative Web series and their own sort of talk-show format called *Kids Watch Viral Videos* (which evokes memories of Art Linkletter's 1960s television program *Kids Say the Darndest Things*). The Fine brothers' videos have garnered millions of hits, and Benny and Rafi have become celebrities in the Web video world, complete with squealing fans. On a recent trip to London, they were spotted by a group of young teens who trailed them down the sidewalk until they had the courage to approach them and gush over their videos. While the Fine brothers are not exactly the Beatles, their videos have recognition and panache. And they are hard at work creating new pieces while meeting with corporations that want to hire them to create videos that feature the companies' products.

When a mysterious person who called herself "wigoutgirl" posted the video "Bride Has Massive Hair Wig Out" on the Internet, it spread like angry lice, reaching 2.8 million viewers in a few weeks. The home video, shot by an unseen bridesmaid, shows a freaked-out bride on her wedding day who has just received a bad haircut. She grows progressively more upset, then seizes a pair of scissors and begins cutting it all off—a scenario that perhaps fed directly into every woman's worst nightmare. Most men laughed at the distaff drama of it, but the scene was compelling, and lent itself to multiple watchings and sharings.

Turns out, the video was not documentary footage but a scripted set of images filmed in a real hotel suite. The shampoo company Unilever had done it as a publicity stunt—but a clever one. The footage has been viewed over twelve million times, essentially because it is a well-constructed piece of drama that transfixes the viewer with a story that almost everyone can relate to.

There is big money to be made in creating literate visual stories, even if they are somewhat silly. You don't need to be highbrow to be literate.

Among the more than three billion videos watched each day on sites such as YouTube, there is undoubtedly a lot of garbage. But in what medium is there not? Of all the paintings hanging on walls of museums around the world, there is a small subset that I'd like to hang on my own walls. In every medium there is a wide range of content, and a difference in taste among consumers. We must never assume that an appeal to the masses represents illiteracy. In fact, it implies a high degree of literacy. And in the new century, that increasingly means visual media.

The language of the modern cinema is only about a century old, and it continues to develop. Some of its conventions will never change, yet it has suddenly become relevant not just to passive moviegoers, but also to ordinary citizens, who can now "write" in a way that was once reserved for the elite.

Freddie Wong's guitar stunt would have been impossible even seven years ago. There was no giant information commons of video files, no YouTube or Vimeo. His creations definitely would have gotten some laughs among his friends, but they would never have gotten such instant traction in the world at large. The proliferation of devices that allow us easily and proficiently to capture moving images, the introduction of inexpensive and accessible editing tools, and at the same time the emergence of distribution sites such as YouTube, which made its debut in 2005, have changed the game forever.

Today more than forty-eight hours of fresh video is uploaded to YouTube every minute, which translates to eight years of content added every day. To put that in perspective: each month, there is more video added to the site than the collective output of the three major television networks since their founding after World War II. There are more than eight hundred million unique visitors watching videos each month on YouTube, with more than 70 percent of this traffic coming from outside the United States. We are part of a global visual conversation. The medium of television itself is moving quickly away from the polished network-produced shows and into more renegade do-it-yourself programming, where the rules are being rewritten.

"With more and more people being connected, the economics are improving, so it makes sense that storytellers of all kinds would want to come to us," YouTube's global head of content, Robert Kyncl, told a reporter. "The more connected devices we get, the more this system will open up . . . We'll take the couch potato, sure. But what we're really after is the couch potato who is willing to get up and lean in and get engaged."

Meanwhile, newspapers are dwindling rapidly as they lose their perch as the world's most trusted medium of news and information. According to the Pew Research Center's Project for

Excellence in Journalism, there were about sixty-two million paid newspaper subscriptions in 1990. What a difference twenty years and the Internet have made: by 2010, that number had fallen (and it continues to fall) to about forty-three million, and several old lions such as the *Seattle Post-Intelligencer*, *The Ann Arbor News*, the *Rocky Mountain News*, and the *Tucson Citizen* had gone out of business entirely.

Those papers that want to survive are struggling to find ways to make their copy accessible and relevant on the Web. Big stories now routinely come with video components. Schools of journalism are racing to re-create themselves lest they remain trapped in a world of print that no longer exists in the way it did even ten years ago.

What we are now seeing is the gradual ascendance of the moving image as the primary mode of communication around the world: one that transcends languages, cultures, and borders. And what makes this new era different from the dawn of television is that the means of production—once in the hands of big-time broadcasting companies with their large budgets—is now available to anyone with a camera, a computer, and the will. "Hollywood will always bring great content," Chad Hurley, the head of YouTube, told *Forbes*, "but amateurs can create something just as interesting—and do it in two minutes."

The rate of change has been dizzying. The first job I ever had was delivering daily newspapers: the *Boston Globe* in the morning and the *South Middlesex News* in the afternoon. Those papers and the Big Three networks of ABC, CBS, and NBC were the primary links we had then to the larger world of information. We depended on them to tell us the truth. As one of the few places where corporate marketing departments could reach their target consumers, these media outlets commanded the advertising revenues that kept them profitable and allowed them to develop teams of reporters who could take their time pursuing a story. We had no other alternatives for our news. The networks and the papers represented a wall of information with very few cracks.

Now the spread of mini-publishing presses and mini-television studios has turned that wall into rubble. There are no longer limited outlets of information, and consequently there is diminished consensus on what constitutes the most important events of the day. Now there is only a bewildering array of choices for the reader/viewer—and a tremendous opportunity for those who seek to tell their own stories and hurl their own papers onto the porches of the world. Now the new media presents each of us with the power—even beyond that of print—to tap deeply into the well of obscurity and bring forth a message, an idea, an image, that was heretofore unknown or unimagined.

Even in the midst of an economic crisis (in fact, maybe even *because* of it) the Arab entrepôt of Dubai is opening the Mohammed Bin Rashid School for Communication, to teach students the basics of film and new media storytelling in Arabic. "This is the first time in the Arab world you have a school of communications teaching the indigenous population in their indigenous language how to work within their own countries," the school's new dean, Ali Jaber, told *Variety*. "It is only when you tell your own stories to your own people that you'll be able to tell them to others."

The grammar of violence is a particularly powerful means of communication unleashed by this new visual potency. Napoleon once said he feared three hostile newspapers as much as a thousand bayonets. The image is a tool of revolutionaries as well as counter-revolutionaries.

During the protests surrounding the disputed 2009 elections in Iran, a woman named Neda Agha-Soltan was hit in the chest by a sniper's bullet as she stepped from a car that belonged to her singing instructor. She bled to death almost immediately. In almost any other circumstance, she would have been known in the public consciousness only as one of an estimated ninety-eight people killed during the upheaval in Tehran and in the months afterward—a statistic instead of a person. But a man with a video camera happened to be standing nearby and filmed the fifty-two horrifying seconds of her shooting and death in the street, as her friends tried to stop the bleeding. That image became one of the signal facts—yes, *facts*—about the uprising that took place around that election stolen by Mahmoud Ahmedinijad. It was reproduced in thousands of propaganda videos and distributed immediately.

Neda has become the "Marianne" of Iran, the symbol of the people's yearning for liberty that once was captured in oils by Eugene Delacroix in his painting *Liberty Leads the People*, and is now captured without warning by a cell phone camera and spread around the world in the space of a day. We see her as she actually died on Karekar Street, wearing sneakers and jeans, saying her last words: "It burned me." In this instance, and in many others, the video form of expression has become a global vernacular for expressing reality.

Even the most radical organizations understand the power of visual media. In 2001, Al Qaeda reversed a decade-long Taliban prohibition on video as it created its own production company, As-Sahab, in order to spread its message and recruit new members. Headed up by the media-savvy disaffected American Adam Gadahn, the company once produced close to a hundred videos a year deep in the mountains bordering Afghanistan and Pakistan. Its reach, though, is global.

Evan Kohlmann, the director of the international consulting firm Flashpoint Partners, which follows terrorist activity, had respect for the skill of the As-Sahab productions, even if he finds their content despicable. "It's actually amazing," he said. "You're talking about very, very high-quality video subtitling. You're talking about

English translations. Graphic sequences have been done showing rockets being fired into an American flag, and having the American flag exploding into pieces. And it, you know, these are very high-quality videos. They're very dramatic. They get passed around like baseball cards. They're being distributed in formats that you can even watch on your cell phone. So it shows us there are dedicated teams of individuals working on this. And that they're spending quite a bit of time on this."

In this instance, and in many others, the video form of expression has become the preferred method for expressing a point of view to an international audience, where a spoken language is not always held in common by interested parties. The Mohammed Bin Rashid School for Communication is in partnership with the Annenberg School for Communication and Journalism at the University of Southern California. Elizabeth Daley, the Annenberg School's founding executive director and current dean of the USC School of Cinematic Arts, goes even further in her assessment about the historically transformative powers of visual media.

Daley likes to draw an analogy between our current state of linguistic history and that of Italy in the fourteenth century, where, cloistered behind monastery and university walls, scholars lectured in Latin while, in the streets and marketplaces, people spoke, joked, bargained, and yelled in vernacular Italian dialects.

"The corresponding argument today," she writes, "simply put, is that for most people—including students—film, television, computer, and online games and music, constitute the current vernacular."

If you take this metaphor to its logical end point, written speech fades away, like Latin, to mere ceremony and obscurity, whereas video becomes the only mode of future semiosis. Instead of sending e-mails, we'll be sending videos.

This is not, however, an obituary for the printed word. There will never be a "death" of words on paper (or on screens or some other delivery mechanism), or an end to the sequentially ordered sentences that define how we transmit and preserve ideas. That form of expression will never cease to be relevant. I am choosing to use it right now, and you are choosing to receive it this way, from this book. More than this, the literacy of images shares a mutually reinforcing relationship with the literacy of words. The two are forever entangled.

Reading is so often a sensual experience, contingent on the ability of the reader to form pictures and shadows along with the writer. This works on the creative end, too. William Faulkner once wrote that the whole idea for *The Sound and the Fury*, arguably one of the greatest novels ever to come from the American South, derived from a single, puzzling image that he could not get out of his mind: a boy in the branches of a tree, peering into a girl's bedroom through a window. First came the mind movie, then came the novel.

Yet we are breaking away from the past in one critical way that makes Elizabeth Daley's point worth considering. The unstoppable rise of visual expression as a popular means of conveying truth is going to require a new discernment on the part of the reader/viewer: a combination of skepticism and incisiveness that assesses the value of the image-based argument rather than the spoken. It is a sensual kind of literacy.

We have to understand that writing ultimately charts back not to the eyes but to the ears. The building blocks of text are merely repurposed symbols of the spoken word.

Thirty thousand years ago, humans learned to transmit feelings and ideas to one another through a series of animal grunts and whines; these sounds grew more complex as the ideas grew more complex, and eventually our tribal units accepted certain whines as the common understanding of a concept. The utterance was a way to store and catalog experience for later retrieval. These ideas were eventually expressed as graven symbols: first letters, and then words assembled from those letters, atomizing and alienating the sign from its original home in the realm of grunts.

Images are traced to a different home, and also a different method of acquiring knowledge. They are more primal and less filtered. And we have a more emotional relationship with those messages. Sound-writing is primarily an intellectual exercise. Seeing is more libidinal. Naked images bring us back to some atavistic forest in our species' memory, where beauty dapples the branches but killers lurk in the shadows. Delight and fear are intermingled.

We get a perverse and uncomfortable feeling when, for example, we see Neda Agha-Soltan struck in the chest by a sniper's bullet and watch the life leave her eyes in less than thirty seconds. It twinges a chord of sympathetic pain; it makes us imagine what it would feel like to see an innocent friend or relative suffer the same inexplicable fate. Ultimately, the image reminds us of our own precarious existence.

Yet understanding the larger meaning of the Neda Agha-Soltan death video is impossible without knowing the background on the state of affairs in Iran, and why people were out protesting that day against Ahmedinijad and the stolen election. A broader conception is necessary, and text is an important element in supplying that context, even if that text is delivered as spoken word in the form of a voice-over to the images. Without it, you have only a meaningless act of violence. With the text and the accompanying context, the image becomes a powerful indictment of the sitting Iranian government and its callous treatment of its own citizens. The image does not live in isolation. The emotion it provokes has to be anchored in a larger conceptual and cultural understanding.

When ex-soldier Joe Cook and his father set out to shoot a

video entitled "Dear Mr. Obama," they relied on the public's knowledge that many soldiers were returning from war in Iraq and Afghanistan missing limbs that had been blown off by IEDs. This allowed them to craft an intimate message from Cook to then-candidate Barack Obama, admonishing him not to abandon the U.S. troops. When it came time for Cook to walk away in the video, the camera provided the most jarring nonverbal message: Cook's leg was missing—and we understood the context. This contextual understanding is a function of multiple forms of texts, including print, visual, and oral texts, each utilizing its particular strengths to create a foundation for deeper understanding.

When a filmmaker can tap into reserves of experience-based, image-based, and text-based knowledge already present inside the viewer, a bit of neurological necromancy takes over. One simple image becomes like an electric cord plugged into an existing grid of knowledge acquired through reading, listening, or experiencing, all of which make the image brighter and more immediate, pouring a surge of intellectual electricity into a rebus that fills the eye and dominates the discussion. The image touches us in a way that speech cannot; it becomes the handle for carrying the whole luggage. It brings a superbly human dimension into the picture.

Accomplishing this trick is a key element of visual literacy, not just unconsciously on the part of the viewer, but also for the one making the film. There is an implied contract between filmmaker and viewer that what is being shown is not only an accurate depiction of what is inside the camera's frame, but an accurate *distillation* of the larger story outside it.

Here's a personal story that helps explain what I mean. We live not far from the town of Armonk, New York, where an apple orchard and farm stand stood for decades. My wife and I for years had been in the habit of dropping by for a dozen apples or a jug of cider whenever we drove down that road, and so we were dismayed to hear that the family that owned the orchard was selling it off to a condominium developer. This is not an uncommon fate for agricultural land in this part of New York State, as everyone around here is aware, and the slipping-away of the bucolic character of the landscape is a subject you hear a lot of at every regional zoning meeting. I certainly don't begrudge any of the parties involved their desire to make a buck. The farmer was making a reasonable business decision, as was the condo builder. Nobody is a bad guy here. But it does spell the loss of that orchard.

My son was particularly attached to this place and wanted to make a short film about the change that was imminent. So I took him out there to film on a day when the developer was setting up a sales office for McMansions next to the apple trees that would shortly be uprooted. We all happened to be sitting in the fellow's office as he explained what was happening. "We're going to make this place beautiful," he said. "We're calling it Cider Mill."

Behind the guy's shoulder was a window that looked out onto the farmhouse yard, and you could plainly see a bulldozer ripping down one of the structures. His words were given a new visual layering. And the viewer could immediately understand the irony: they were building the very *opposite* of a cider mill; in fact, they were destroying the mill in order to create a simulacrum.

We were not trying to create a "gotcha" moment, or make the developer look bad. But that ten-second moment represented a marriage of sound-based knowledge and an eye-based event that illustrated a home truth about the place where we live. All in all, an effective piece of film. Like Freddie Wong's compression of reality, it worked because it was literate.

When you tell a good visual story, you are creating a mysterious chain of events in the viewer's mind with every electronic visual choice you make, and the final truth and beauty of it depend largely on the degree of literacy brought to its creation.

We have seen a historical-change moment like this before. Television was introduced to the American public right after World War II, and by 1968 its influences had sunk so deep into the culture that a new way of understanding it had to be developed.

An academic named John Debes was particularly out in front on this. With the help of the Eastman Kodak company, he convened a seminar dedicated to what he called "visual literacy"—the idea that comprehension of what we see in movies, photography, and television is as vital a skill as that of reading the written sentence. Being visually literate, said Debes, enables the viewer "to interpret the visible actions, objects, symbols, natural or manmade, that he encounters in his environment."

This idea coincided with a similar movement in "media literacy," a more politicized discipline of the 1960s that encouraged citizens to be more insightful consumers of what they were absorbing from radio and television. The effects of American political demagoguery, it was thought, would be easier to understand if the listener-viewer had a more sophisticated understanding of how a message was constructed. The anthropologist Edmund Carter said, "The new mass media—film, radio, TV—are new languages, their grammar as yet unknown. Each codifies reality differently, each conceals a unique metaphysics."

We Americans fell in love with that reality. In 1945, fewer than ten thousand televisions populated our homes. Only fifteen years later, that population had grown to almost sixty million. Today there are well over a quarter of a billion sets in the United States, with almost 97 percent of all households owning at least one set. (This is actually down from 98.9 percent, as fewer people now rely on television to get their visual fix.) But that doesn't tell even half the story, as our computers, tablets, personal entertainment devices, and cell phones stream an endless array of content. And that content is available not just when we choose to watch. There are screens at our restaurants and retail stores, at our offices and gas stations, and even in our cars and airplane seats. It took less than thirty years for the science fiction of Ridley Scott's *Blade Runner* to become reality, and in cities like New York, Tokyo, and Seoul, skins of buildings have been turned into screens, and visual media has become an essential part of the vocabulary of architecture. The Grand Indonesia tower, a fifty-seven-story building in Jakarta, is wrapped in more than sixty thousand square feet of screens. In an interview with a trade publication, the architect Darryl Yamamoto says that "up to now architecture has been about fitting buildings into three-dimensional space. The inclusion of video screens completely covering a building's surface changes that equation of how a building occupies that space. In a sense, video-screen coverage on a building surface places it in a fourth dimension where pictorial and iconic imagery now becomes a representational feature of how the building presents itself." Moving images increasingly occupy our public spaces and add to the ever-expanding body of visual data we are steeped in.

The time has come to rebuild the idea of "visual literacy"—not to overthrow it, but to expand it. We must now take into account what is technologically inevitable in the twenty-first century: the proliferation of messages that are increasingly divorced from their written foundations and increasingly married to the wordless visual pathways of knowledge that have been the human birthright since before we were even human.

We have now reached a point in our romance with the electronic image where it has moved in to stay, and all of us will be called upon to be not just consumers but producers. Listening to the story and judging it is no longer enough. We now have to start *telling the story ourselves*, all of us, if this is to be a literate society.

The medium is ripe not just for entertainment and frivolity. It has a powerful social effect that we cannot ignore. Those in power have much to fear from it, just as Napoleon said he feared newspapers more than bayonets.

One of the founding intellectuals of the media literacy movement was Marshall McLuhan, a Canadian professor whose book *Understanding Media: The Extensions of Man* made clear the distinction between what he called "hot media" and "cool media." This had nothing to do with temperature or style. It had to do with the level of participation required by the receiver. The more the medium filled up the frame of reality (as in a photograph or a movie), the more it was "hot," and the experience was more passive. If the medium was a bit starker, and called upon the viewer to fill in his or her own mental spackle (as with a cartoon, a discussion, or a snippet of jazz), the more it was "cool"—that is, an experience that asks for a bit more intellectual participation, a little more cognitive presence.

By this definition, videos on YouTube and elsewhere are mostly hot, because all we have to do is click and watch. But the larger field of possibility they open is truly breathtaking because of the newfound ease of creating one's own moving images and adding them to the growing body of society's collective dialogue. Only the very talented and the very lucky could manage this in McLuhan's time because of the huge commercial barrier (represented by publishers, movie studios, magazine editors, and television stations) that stood between the creator and the market, and the creative barrier presented by the lack of access to affordable tools of creation.

Those barriers are now falling fast. The experience of media is growing less and less passive.

When German playwright and author Bertolt Brecht wrote a famous essay called "Radio as an Apparatus of Communication" in 1932, he was not imagining the distribution of image-driven media through the television and now the Internet. Still, he understood well the importance of being proficient not just in listening but also in speaking, and that communication is, eventually, a two-way street of dialogue as opposed to monologue, even within mechanically mediated forms of communicating.

> It is purely an apparatus for distribution, for mere sharing out. So here is a positive suggestion: change this apparatus over from distribution to communication. The radio would be the finest possible communication apparatus in public life, a vast network of pipes. That is to say, it would be if it knew how to receive as well as to transmit, how to let the listener speak as well as hear, how to bring him into a relationship instead of isolating him. On this principle the radio should step out of the supply business and organize its listeners as suppliers. Any attempt by the radio to give a truly public character to public occasions is a step in the right direction.

Brecht was living in the golden age of cinema, but he focused on the radio because it was one of the most dominant forms of communication available in his day. Today the vast majority of our information is delivered through visual media: the television, the cinema, the Internet, and the screens that surround us where we work, shop, socialize, and learn.

Update Brecht's observation for changing technology and we're essentially reading about the Internet and the ease of sharing the enormous power of the wordless icon, the thing that has no alphabetic expression. I can only imagine that Brecht would have smiled at the dramatic explosion of video-sharing outlets such as YouTube, whose slogan implores its billions of users to "Broadcast Yourself."

The manipulation of video is shortly to become a global language, and its seductive powers will be on display for all to see. But it is morally neutral. It can be used for good and evil and everything in between.

The most pertinent question now facing us is not how can we resist this revolution in thought, but how can we respond with the maximum amount of thoughtfulness, energy, and smarts? How will we present ourselves to the world?

How literate will we be?

◼ WHAT IS LITERACY?

*Language . . . is rather like a code; it is a way of representing
actual things and events in the perceived world.*
　　　　　—DAVID ABRAM, *The Spell of the Sensuous*

The word *literacy* finds its roots in the eighteenth-century word
literatus, which quite literally means "one who knows the letters."
But it has come to refer to much more than the ability to read an
alphabet or other script.

We think of it today as meaning "proficiency"—or, more
broadly, the ability to comprehend and to express or articulate.
Literacy goes beyond merely reading and writing, and denotes
the ability both to decode or encode words and to infer deeper
meaning or to express more complex thoughts. It has come to mean
the ability to comprehend and have facility with those areas that are
deemed critical to our being full participants in the world, and its
definition has been extended to include "environmental literacy,"
"financial literacy," and many more disparate ideas.

But a more limited definition is helpful when we talk about
communication. Literacy is the ability to express oneself in an

effective way through the text of the moment, the prevailing mode of expression in a particular society. Literacy follows language. To be literate, in other words, is to be conversant in the dominant expressive language and form of the age.

Languages evolve in substance as we add words to our vocabulary constantly, and even grammatical conventions shift over time. They also change in form and in the medium in which they are communicated, as a function of many forces, including the economics of production and distribution. The evolution of language and literacy can be best understood not through these technological lenses, however, but rather through an emotional lens.

The inescapable fact is that man is a fundamentally social, yet in some ways isolated, animal, and language is in response to this. We all yearn to be seen and understood by those around us. This has pragmatic reasons—we need cooperation as a species in order to hunt and grow food and fight enemies. We need to coo the sounds of seduction that attract mates. We need to sound alarms and cry in sadness and shriek in combat. But language also has reasons of the soul, which are more mysterious. We don't know where we come from, we have only suspicions about where we're going, and our existence is often a puzzle.

Each of our major religions is based on the belief that we have been given "words" of the divine immanent presence, handed down through Buddha, Moses, Jesus, or Muhammad and captured in our religious texts and oral traditions. Native American peoples and other tribal cultures throughout the world share the importance of archetypal stories passed from generation to generation in their traditions. The major themes of religion and spirituality have also been the primary source of art and literature throughout the centuries, as we construct stories to communicate our deepest needs and ideas to one another—what I consider a deeply spiritual urge, whether we realize it or not.

We are all striving for unmediated communication: I want you to be in my body for a moment and hear the notes of a piece of music in just the way I hear them, or see the injustice of a particular moment, or feel the beauty of a sunset, or experience the deep sadness at the loss of a loved one. While this is impossible, we have created stories and text and language to help us communicate those sensations.

It is no accident that some of the greatest leaps forward in our existence as a species have been a result of finding new ways to bring information and story to one another. Our never-ending search for this elusive pure communion has driven technology. Paint, the alphabet, the press, the camera, the television, the semiconductor, the satellite—all these derive from that hunger and scratching we were born with: to reach out, to share, and to connect.

With each progression of language, text, and technology, we strove to move closer to this ideal of unmediated communication—to express ourselves more fully and more emotionally. This led to the emergence of spoken language, the explosion of print media, and the exponentially accelerated wave of radio, television, and the Internet. But the combination of moving image, spoken word, text, and music—plus the way that combination shoots like a needle straight into the cerebral cortex—makes the movie the most powerful and compelling text we have yet created.*

True literacy is always a two-way transaction. We don't just consume; we produce. We don't just read; we write. The ability to

---

* The phrase "moving image" refers not only to the trick of the mind created by a series of fluttering images, but also to the embedded emotion it exposes. There can be little wonder that Hollywood sells approximately $7.5 billion worth of tickets each year. We sit with strangers in the dark, but we seek to put a balm on what is deep inside: this desire to hear a story that makes us feel less lonely and more connected—and just to feel.

receive information is always the first part of the literacy equation that is necessary for the masses, and then the ability to *express* information generally follows, as we strive to quench our desire to communicate. The root of *communicate* is to commune.

Another example from religion: the scholar Maimonides wrote that all faithful Jews were required to study the Torah—which necessitated a high degree of receptive literacy—while only a few were required to be *sophers*, or writers. The holy books were meant to be read by everybody in society, not just the elite. And then it also became important for everyone in this society to be able to communicate through written language. This is the pattern with virtually every form of communication known to what we call civilization. The priests can't have all the power. In order for the full measure of human creativity to be unlocked, the literate power has to be spread around.

We will not have arrived at that point until a critical mass of citizens is capable both of seeing and critiquing what is put in front of them with some level of sophistication, and of creating their own versions of reality with the same means as the elite. Sometimes the tail takes a long time to catch up with the head. Even though the *process* of people becoming literate in new texts and technologies is generally a slow one, what has always remained constant is the motivation to grasp new literacies, for these literacies speak to an urge at the very center of our human biological drive. This is an inevitable force.

The economics of both production and distribution of moving image–based texts has favored expression by a few and consumption or reception by many. We have experienced limited access to this language as an expressive tool, which has curtailed the need for true literacy. This has all changed.

We now stand at a point in technological history where we don't have to simply sit in the dark anymore consuming others' stories—at least not in terms of the moving image. Nearly a century and a half after the development of the world's first ultra-primitive "movie," the power to make and share movies with the world is at a point of transformation, and is in the hands of everyone with a few cheap pieces of equipment and a good idea.

This moment of democratic transformation has happened with nearly every advance in mediated communication since the dawn of consciousness. And while the elite have typically viewed such transformation as a threat and have tried to suppress broad change, it has never been anything to be afraid of.

The power of the motion picture lies in the recesses of the human heritage. It is simultaneously a return to the most primal of experiences and a natural progression of the evolution of human communication. The British author Margaret Barber wrote in her posthumously published 1902 book of meditations, *The Roadmender*, "To look backward for a while is to refresh the eye, to restore it, and to render it the more fit for its prime function of looking forward." To begin to understand the evolution of communication and literacy requires a brief historical journey.

Any look at the historical arc of literacy, even an abridged one, must begin with the most basic of communications between people: that of the mouth sounds that carry a shared meaning.

We began as a species with a common understanding of a sound or a gesture. Language was a way to turn the howls and grunts of the other human into a rational system for passing information that had heretofore been expressed only in movements, facial gestures, and simple actions. *I am hungry. I am hurt. Let's get some water. I would like to mate with you. I am angry.* In this sense, the formation of words that expressed abstract information was the first step away from the purely visual means of communication.

The philosopher David Abram has written about the uncanny similarity between the register of human voices and their audible roots in the time before language. "If, for instance, one comes upon two human friends unexpectedly meeting for the first time in many months, and one chances to hear their initial words of surprise, greeting and pleasure, one may readily notice, if one pays close enough attention, a tonal, melodic layer of communication beneath the explicit denotative meaning of the words—a rippling rise and fall of the voices in a sort of musical duet, rather like two birds singing to each other." We are not as far removed from the primitive nature of sight and sound as we would like to believe.

We formed words and language as vessels to carry story, and at some point early in our existence on this earth, storytelling became essential to the nature of man. At our core, we are story animals. Oral storytelling had structure, cadence, and rhythms. It was almost song. It enabled us to pass along memorized text and information, but also to convey emotion. There is no doubt that the invention of fire or the wheel had profound impacts on humankind—but perhaps nothing has had as great an impact as language and story. We have created nations, cultures, and wars and have made peace through story. It is impossible to imagine anything more important or profound in the human existence.

In many ways, the power of film and filmic language is rooted most deeply in this oral storytelling tradition, as we receive information encoded not only within the actual words, but also in the deeper insights delivered by the nuance of gesture, facial expression, body language, intonation, and other auditory and visual cues. There are evident limitations to oral storytelling as our sole communication mode—especially in regard to reach and the specificity of memory. Thus we were compelled to address some of these constraints with a new technology: the written word.

Nobody knows when the practice of writing, or recording (or

encoding), story first emerged. Writing was another type of technology that, while scratching one human itch, also drew us farther away from how our brains had been constructed. The Neanderthals, our distant biped cousins who died out twenty-eight thousand years ago, used to make little carvings out of bone and ivory, another step toward synthetic representation of abstract ideas. They were already skilled at chipping flint stone to fashion arrows, and some of the more artistic of them must have found the time to engrave stone for obscure reasons, perhaps religious in nature, or perhaps as jewelry to attract mates. One of these carvings, found in a French cave, looked like a crude version of a human face. It is not exaggerating to say this may have been history's first recorded instance of literature. People are always looking to the biology of other people, and themselves, in the creation of art, which is also the way they organize the world.

Think, for example, about our number system. Mathematics is based on powers of ten. But there is nothing magical about this number that makes it the repository of the advanced digits. Most historians believe that the advanced method of counting that was first developed in India and then appropriated by the Arabs (hence the term *Arabic numerals*) uses a ten count because of the ten fingers on the human hand. There is a biological source for some of the most intrinsic communication systems we know.

Some of the very first complex examples of mediated communication were painted on the walls of caves, in what is now Spain and France, nearly thirty-five thousand years ago. That figure staggers the mind, and yet it is such a brief flash in geologic time. Anthropologists still aren't sure of the intended purpose of these figures, painted with a mixture of ash, manganese, and ochre. They were mostly of animals such as bison and deer, and curiously, in rare instances only, of humans. Were these cave dwellers painting the animals with a sense of worship? Were the hunters bragging about the size of their prey? Was it supposed to be a primitive guide to the stars, which were a constant source of fascination to ancient peoples?

A French priest and anthropologist named Henri Breuil theorized that the drawings were meant to conjure the animals themselves out of their hiding places—a hoped-for effect that he called "hunting magic." Oddly enough, though these artists ate a lot of reindeer—their bones are scattered about the floor at the complex at Lascaux like so many takeout wrappers—no reindeer are pictured on the walls. Generally speaking, these people depicted what they *weren't* eating, and the presence of so many of these drawings over the course of thousands of years suggests that there may have been some friendly competition to outdo both their neighbors and even their ancestors. This was a startling new technology—the reduction of the physical world to a representation. It was the first example of the distancing effect of the natural to the artificial.

The French philosopher Voltaire called writing "the painting of the voice," and I think he gets this right not just because of the physical rendering of something abstract, but also because of the range of tones and colors that painting implies. It is one thing to draw a picture of a sun over water, but quite another to make us see it as it looked—to convey the impression of wave motion and the magnificent hues of the light on the water.

We struggle to derive meaning in these drawings and to understand their true intent, yet at one point it is highly likely that the language in which those drawings were produced provided deep meaning to both the painter and the viewer. Both were "literate" in a language that we have lost. In these lost primitive societies, moreover, the painters were almost certainly an elite class, and the access to the cave paint was restricted. They possessed the ability to "write"—they were the broadcasters of the tribe—while

many more were able to "read" and interpret the depictions of animals upon the wall. This is certainly consistent with how other
literacies and technologies emerged. Cave paintings, like books
and videos, were produced by few, but they were viewed by all.

In the 2011 documentary movie *Cave of Forgotten Dreams*,
Werner Herzog uses the camera to take us into the Chauvet caves
in the South of France, where tourists are no longer able to visit.
We see extraordinary paintings, including a series of almost super-
imposed images of a bison lunging forward as it turns its head toward the viewer, as if preparing for an impending collision. This
series of images functions almost like an animated zoetrope or
storyboard.

There is a moment toward the end of the film when Herzog
asks Jean-Michel Geneste, director of the Chauvet Cave Research
Project, what constitutes humanness, and Geneste responds,
"With the invention of figuration, it's a way of communicating
between humans and with the future—to evoke the past, to
transmit information that is very better than language." As he
points to the camera in Herzog's hands, he concludes, "And this
invention is still the same in our world today with this camera."
Technology continues to evolve, but the steady core is our human
desire to communicate story.

The religio-artistic emanations on the cave walls were matched
by an innovation that took place in sunlight in around the year
3000 B.C., as the Sumerian kingdoms near the Persian Gulf, what
is today Iraq, began to use pictorial symbols to represent certain
dealings among them. These symbols were usually carved into wet
clay tablets using a reed called a stylus, and the symbols looked
like little boxes and triangles and dots. These were meant to represent concepts such as "ships" and "coins" and "corn." The script was
called cuneiform, and it was used as an accounting system for mer-
chants and a propaganda tool for scriveners of the local strongman.

Then, as now, being able to "write" and be literate in the latest technology signified wealth or power, or both.

The clay tablets shattered and were too heavy to carry for long distances. In approximately the same period, the Ancient Egyptians, possibly influenced by the Sumerian script, developed their own writing system. The term *hieroglyphic* (sacred symbols), later coined to describe this form of writing, was a tool of control for the priests and the elite.

An advance in technology soon made the skill of writing lighter and more flexible, and it came because of a strange-looking marsh plant called papyrus. The plant grew in stalks up to nine feet tall, along the banks of the Nile; its leaves looked like that of a palmetto tree, and could be cut into long strips and hammered into sheets that were as near to waterproof as anyone was likely to get in the ancient world. Papyrus was good for making the skins of boats, and it also turned out to be good at retaining the marks from a primitive type of ink made from ashes, fat, and water. Symbols scratched with an ink-soaked quill upon papyrus became useful for keeping records of business accounts and for circulating the laws of the pharaohs—not to mention spreading news of the accomplishments of the royal court.

Papyrus was the YouTube of its day: it was light, cheap, easily passed around, and widely recognized. But while it could be used effectively within the range of a shared language, it was not a technology that could carry a message beyond the tongue of a localized society. If you couldn't read Egyptian hieroglyphs, the message would be worthless to you.

The value of papyrus would change radically because of the introduction of a tool we now take for granted—you're using it right now—one that may have had more effect on the course of humanity than almost any other innovation: the alphabet. The practice of using a written symbol to stand for a particular sound from the human mouth represented a cognitive leap forward that had transformative effects on humanity. It allowed portions of "words" to be transferred and reassembled into new words. The distance between the name of something and what it represented was growing wider.

Scholars believe that the alphabet originated in Phoenicia (centered in what is today Lebanon) around 1700 B.C., and was spread by traders who spoke a Semetic dialect and used the system of substituting symbols for mouth sounds as an international marketing language for the various cultures with whom they dealt across the Mediterranean—notably Greeks, Cretans, and Anatolians. This primitive system had no room for vowels, and thus used only consonants. In it, one can see the infancy of the Greek alphabet and the shape of our own Roman letters.

Here was one of the most remarkable things about this new technology, what the Hebrews called the *aleph-beth*: its components were derivative of the natural phenomena they were presuming to represent. The very first letter is rendered like a modern *A* tipped on its side. This conforms to the old Hebrew word for "ox," which was rendered as a head with horns, such as that possessed by an ox. The visual roots in the Semetic tongue go deeper— David Abram also points out that the word *mem*, or "water," was pictured as a series of ripples as though on a pond. The actual word for water in Hebrew is *mayim*, which is spelled *mem-yud-mem*. The *mem* does look like a wave, and the *yud* is a simple half-slash that separates the *mems*. We know it today as the letter *m*, but the waves can clearly be seen inside the letter.

The alphabet emerged like this, as an intellectual appropriation of the natural world, pictographs that had been virtually harvested from the earth. And it was still more: the moveable type of the mind. Words could be scrambled, recast, reassembled, and reinterpreted. A guttural sound from the mouth could have a stable meaning that could also be reconstructed in a new tongue for the hearing of new people. It was the first international technology. Ideas and stories could be captured and shared, across communities and across time.

Yet this came at a cost. In a remarkable book called *The Alphabet versus the Goddess*, published in 1998, a heart surgeon named Leonard Shlain lays out a systematic theory of understanding the methods by which humans absorb images. The sensual visual experience of the wordless image is primarily absorbed in the right brain, which governs acts such as nurturing and caring for others, which are prototypical feminine values. Lines of alphabetic text, disconnected from their sites of representation and marching in logical rows, speak more to the mathematical, rational, and even nationalistic portions of our consciousness—the prototypical masculine values.

As written text ascended, Shlain argues, so, too, did the patriarchal and militaristic aspects of humanity, with a consequent loss to the status of women and the holistic sensuality of icon worship, hence the "alphabet" and "goddess" dichotomy set up in his book's title. "Any form of writing dramatically changes the perceptions of those who use it," he writes. "In cuneiform and hieroglyphic based cultures, the changes manifested as a slippage of right-brain feminine values below conscious awareness . . . Upon learning the alphabet, both women and men turned away from the worship of idols and animal totems that represented the *images* of nature, and began paying homage to the abstract *logos*."

The masculine interchangeability of the alphabet was key to the building of transoceanic commerce, and with it, the seeds of imperial conquest. To have command over the means of expression that crossed the seas was to ensure oneself a career in Phoenicia or in any of the port settlements where people did business. The Greeks later added vowels to their version of the alphabet, making the decoding of words more accessible, but literacy still remained the domain of the rich and priestly classes there. During the Roman Empire, to know how to read Latin was a skill reserved for copyists and clerks; it was considered useless, if not dangerous, for anyone of the peasant class to possess the tools of written communication.

Even then, there was anxiety about what directions writing would take humans as a civilization. One of the first recorded ruminations about this "potion for memory and wisdom" was between Socrates and a philosopher named Phaedrus, taken down by Socrates's pupil Plato around 370 B.C. Socrates notes the potentially dangerous aspects of writing and compares a writer to a farmer who grows words only for his own amusement. Writing would never replace the experience of listening to "the living, breathing discourse of a man who knows, of which the written one can be fairly called an image." Yet the advantages written text offered in terms of recording messages to be delivered across both time and geography were compelling advances. The anxiety about this new technology mirrors our own sense of disquietude about a return to the image.

The Romans were enthusiastic users of parchment. What might be called the world's first newspaper, or at least a public broadcast, was the *Acta diurna* ("Daily Acts"), which began publication at some point after 131 B.C. Julius Caesar, with his taste for fame, was a particularly avid proponent. The sheet was a regular summary of the doings of the Senate, official announcements, dates of festivals, announcements of births and deaths, and notices of auction, and was posted on message boards where citizens would congregate. The "Daily Acts" were also carved on stone or wood.

What would eventually make these texts available to a mass

audience across geographies, of course, was printing with moveable type. Block-letter printing was done in China as early as the 800s, using clay type, but this was a laborious process, and complicated by the forty-thousand-some ideograms in the Chinese vocabulary. European monks also figured out how to carve a printing plate out of wood, smear it with ink, and press it upon a page to make an imprint. But carving these plates was an arduous task.

A goldsmith living near Mainz, Germany, named Johannes Gutenberg developed a better way. He knew how to fashion small-bit tools, and around 1440 he developed an ingenious system of setting cast metal letter pieces into a screw press similar to that used to squeeze olive oil and apple cider. This produced in two days what it took a single copyist a year to produce by hand. The most popular book Gutenberg printed, naturally, was the Bible (and the twenty-one complete Gutenberg Bibles that survive are among the most valuable books in the world). From Mainz, the technology spread rapidly throughout Europe, and going into business as a town printer then was akin to starting up an Internet company today. The more ambitious printers also saw themselves as apostles of a new era of mechanized intelligence.

"I exhort the unlearned, by reading to be more skillful, and to purge that swinelike grossness that maketh the sweet marjoram not to smell to their delight," said printer Richard Tottel in 1557. Naturally, he had this printed.

Twenty million books were in circulation by the end of the fifteenth century—a remarkable figure, considering that the world itself held about five hundred million people, only a small percentage of whom had access to books or were literate. (Just fifty years before, books had been as rare and as precious as sapphires.) The writings of a young firebrand preacher named Martin Luther were big-selling items, and the Protestant Reformation washed in on a cascade of ink and threatened the hegemony of the Roman Catholic Church. Pamphlets attacking corrupt church practices, lampooning bishops, and arguing about minor points of scripture were printed up with amazing speed and distributed at markets—a strange precursor to the flame wars of the Internet, as people respond to one another with increasing hostility and contempt. It was seemingly all that people could talk and argue about.

The Bible went out in German and English and other vernacular languages, the tongues of the people, deposing Latin as the language of the privileged. By 1550, an Italian writer named Anton Francesco Doni complained of "so many books that we do not even have time to read the titles." A present-day visitor to YouTube's teeming archives might feel the same way. What was needed was curation—a method to organize and separate the really important stuff from the dross. The printers themselves began to favor certain titles and authors over others, based on their propensity to sell. Thus was the market-driven nature of publishing established: bestsellers tend to beget the same.

The Gutenberg press not only brought mass-produced media into the world, but also had a profound impact on the culture of communication. The era of print began to chip away at the culture of *orality* that had been the center of human communication ever since the time when grunts and howls were molded into standardized sounds to be understood by a collective. Testimony in courts began to shift from what you told an illiterate magistrate to what kind of printed affidavit you might secure from a witness. It was no longer enough to know how to communicate orally—to listen and speak the language; it was now important to be able to read.

A taste of the fear that surrounded this new invention might be gleaned from an exchange from Victor Hugo's *The Hunchback of Notre Dame*, written in 1831 but set in the Paris of the 1480s, when Gutenberg's radical technology was infecting every area of

society and encouraging young people to spend their hours playing with its possibilities.

> Meanwhile, the sworn bookseller of the university, Master An-
> dry Musnier, was inclining his ear to the furrier of the king's
> robes, Master Gilles Lecornu.
> "I tell you, sir, that the end of the world has come. No one
> has ever beheld such outbreaks among the students! It is the ac-
> cursed inventions of this century that are ruining everything,—
> artilleries, bombards, and above all, printing, that other German
> pest. No more manuscripts, no more books! Printing will kill
> bookselling. It is the end of the world that is drawing nigh."
> "I see that plainly, from the progress of the velvet stuffs," said
> the fur-merchant.

Hugo was writing fiction, of course, but he was spot-on in his
depiction of the fear that came along with this leap forward in
literacy. This was fear not just of the strength of the Catholic
Church—hence the sly reference to the "German pest" Luther—
but the worry that the new technology would destroy economies
and corrupt the youth. Shortly after the first books came rolling
off Gutenberg's press, the archbishop of Mainz demanded that
permission be obtained before any new book could be printed,
though Gutenberg himself had allies within the Church. Within
fifty years, the Catholic Church set up its *Index of Prohibited Books*,
and the Pope ordered that all books that questioned his authority
be burned. The man who first translated the Bible into English,
William Tyndale, was himself burned at the stake. The awesome
power of the press ensured that the agonized rebellion of the renegade priest Martin Luther would be played out not inside a
sealed council room but in the open air, where everyone could see.
People could make up their own minds about the question of

ecclesiastical authority—did it come from the Church or from the printed magic of the Bible? Luther himself called the printing press "God's highest and extremest act of grace, whereby the business of the gospel is driven forward." The Lutheran Church in Sweden decided that everyone in its ranks should be able to read the Gospels for themselves, and as the critic John Freeman has noted, the literacy rate in that nation was 100 percent within a century. Britain saw a similar shift, albeit slower, from 10 percent of men to about 95 percent in the space of four hundred years.

Still, even the Protestants looked with occasional despair and regret on the word-churning beast they had helped bring into the world. It could foment rebellion and sedition, and it was extremely hard to suppress a book. The chief censor for the British king Charles II, Sir Roger L'Estrange, was led to ask publicly "whether more mischief than advantage were not occasioned to the Christian world by the invention of typography." He might as well have been trying to hold back a raging sea.

There was one major part of the world almost completely untouched by Gutenberg's marvelous innovation, though. The Islamic world of the fifteenth century was indifferent and even directly opposed to mass production of printed material. It was not as if the Arabic culture lacked for interest in science or discovery—quite the opposite. Baghdad had been a legendary center of learning in the eighth century, where the works of the great Greek philosophers were translated onto scrolls. The library at the Moorish city of Cordoba had an equally impressive collection, dwarfing the holdings of even the most well-stocked monastery libraries in Europe. Yet the printing press was seen as a destabilizing force within Muslim nations, according to Gutenberg biographer John Man, because of the oral beauty of the Quran, which was meant to be heard recited out loud rather than read from a page, its central repository being that of a living human performance rather than a frozen set of marks on a page. Those who cannot speak Arabic are said to miss the exquisite nature of the rhymes and the verbal dynamics of the Quran. "Imams would not willingly have done themselves out of a job by allowing people direct access to knowledge," wrote Man. Hierarchies remained in place in those societies, while the old monarchies of Europe would soon begin to teeter.

The religious books that rolled out of the print shops in Europe were supplemented by newsbooks. Especially in England, with a navy that extended the reach of Britannia across the water, these reported on high business culture, and were highly serious accounts of foreign dealings. One example was the 1590 issuance *Credible Reportes from France and Flanders*, from the printer John Wolfe. Like the religious pamphlets of the sort that had circulated around Europe during the Reformation, these were thicker and of higher quality, often illustrated with woodcuts of exotic scenes or battles. They also bore a secular message, aimed more at the pocketbook than the soul. It wasn't long before the campaigns of the Thirty Years' War made the king nervous, and he instituted a newsbook blackout for at least six years.

The real precursor to the modern newspaper, though, and perhaps even to the Internet, was something called a "broadside," whose origin was almost a matter of accident. Printers who had paper left over after they were done printing books—where the real money was—made use of this waste by printing handbills and advertisements on one side only so that they could be affixed to street side walls. Broadsides were meant to be used and thrown away—the equivalent of chalk on the sidewalk, or a "tweet" from a local retailer.

Yet a man named Nathaniel Butter grew rich from printing up broadsides and the crude antecedents of what we would call a newspaper. Butter and his partner, Nicholas Bourne, had been clever, persuading the king that "nothing dishonorable to princes in amity with his Majesty should pass the press." Butter had already had a place in history as the publisher of the first edition of Shakespeare's *King Lear*, thus giving textual expression to what had been an oral art form. Butter stayed one step ahead of the king's censors, with an art form that had been perfected in Venice the previous century, where those who published newssheets often did so underground and anonymously. These broadsides of the seventeenth century were the equivalent of the funny and sometimes serious videos that people are today uploading to YouTube and Vimeo.

By 1702, the printing press was speedy enough, and the public hunger for information great enough, that an entrepreneur named Edward Mallet sensed a market for the first newspaper to be published daily. The *Courant* was a digest of news from abroad, presented without commentary, because, Mallet wrote, he was "supposing other people had sense enough to make reflections for themselves." The *Courant* was a success, yet, in an appeal to the more ignoble of instincts, the high-minded refrain from commentary soon went by the wayside as daily papers of varying quality sprang up for business and competed with readers with all manner of crime, politics, and noise. These sheets were read, discussed, and laughed about in coffeehouses all over England, and out of this robust culture came some distinguished literature. Richard Steele and Joseph Addison are best known today for their sharp and smart philosophical essays in *The Tatler* and then *The Spectator*, which helped inculcate England with a sense of middle-class optimism and manners. The American printer Benjamin Franklin said he loved Addison and Steele, and patterned some of his earliest writings around theirs. It would soon become impossible to be a rising person in American or British business without being literate in these newspapers—not just being able merely to read them and decode the words, but also to discern the values and structure that created them.

The first newspaper in the United States was what we might today call a partisan rag. Benjamin Harris started a feisty digest called *Publick Occurances Both Foreign and Domestick*, on September 25, 1690, and it so offended the governor of Massachusetts that it was ordered shut down after only one issue, with a stern warning from the authorities that nobody could "set forth anything in Print" without permission.

This didn't last long. Information became an obsession in the colonies—particularly news that concerned the abuses of the English king—and anyone who set up a print shop was in an excellent position to use the waste paper to print up a digest of events and commentary, religious and otherwise. Franklin, the paragon of a useful eighteenth-century man, drew his main income from printing, and found time to publish *The Pennsylvania Gazette* on the side. The rabble-rouser Tom Paine helped rally support for the fledgling revolution through a cheap pamphlet he called *Common Sense*. Most of the critical debates surrounding governance of the new independent country were carried out in the inky sheets of these papers. James Madison thought enough of these early newspapers to publish the Federalist Papers, one of the most persuasive defenses of a strong constitution ever seen, in the *New York Packet*.

The medium flourished in the early nineteenth century, as receptive literacy moved toward participative literacy. Free education for the poor was seen as an American birthright. By 1852, New York State had made it a requirement for every child to attend school, either private or public, and other states followed suit. By the end of the nineteenth century, the idea that society would teach a person to read was so ingrained in the national mindset that Mark Twain called a free public education one of the crowning glories of America. The growth of the U.S. Post Office made it cheap to send a letter—three pennies in 1852—and the act of writing lengthy narratives to distant friends became a habit and a means of everyday artistry with words.

Yet the southern landowners who depended on a captive population of human beings to plant and harvest their crops could not afford to have the enlightenment of literacy spreading amid the bunkhouses. As early as 1740, the colony of South Carolina made it a crime for anyone to teach a slave to read and write. If they could communicate with one another over distances, it was reasoned, slaves might become aware of their numerical strength and rise up against their masters. Notably, however, many Christian denominations encouraged the teaching of Bible reading among slaves, and many southern states imitated South Carolina's policy only to the point of forbidding writing, which was seen as the real threat. By the time of the Civil War, only about 5 percent of the slave population had picked up the tools of writing, through sympathetic preachers or owners or housemistresses.

One of those was Frederick Douglass, who later told his story in *Narrative of the Life of Frederick Douglass.* At a pivotal moment in his childhood, he had been taught to read and write the ABCs by the wife of his new master, Hugh Auld.

"Just at this point of my progress," Douglass writes,

> Mr. Auld found out what was going on, and at once forbade Mrs. Auld to instruct me further, telling her, among other things, that it was unlawful, as well as unsafe, to teach a slave to read . . . "Now," he said "if you teach [him] to read, there would be no keeping him. It would forever unfit him of being a slave." These words sank deep into my heart, stirred up sentiments within that lay slumbering, and called into existence an entirely new train of thought. It was a new and special revelation, explaining dark and mysterious things, with which my youthful understanding

had struggled, but struggled in vain. I now understood what had been to me a most perplexing difficulty—to wit, the white man's power to enslave the black man. It was a grand achievement, and I prized it highly. From that moment, I understood the pathway from slavery to freedom.

In the context of slave owners and slaves, literacy was about access to education, information, and power. The slave owners understood this, and it remains true today. Literacy is the gateway to full participation in society, and as the nature of the texts we communicate in evolves, so does our need to find room for new ways of communicating.

Literacy would soon take on a broader definition than just words. A quarter century after the Civil War, a technological leap would happen in the realm of imagery.

Artists had known for hundreds of years about an effect called camera obscura (Latin for "dark room"), in which a darkened chamber with a small aperture can cast the image of whatever is outside the chamber against an interior wall of the chamber, upside down but highly detailed. The Chinese scientist Mo Ti wrote about this in 470 B.C. He called it a "locked treasure room." The image could be preserved if an artist with an ink pen or brush simply painted over the light shadows with the appropriate colors. Leonardo da Vinci used a camera obscura—and there the technology remained, until 1825, when Nicéphore Niépce coated a plate inside a camera obscura with bitumen dissolved in lavender oil and exposed it to the light. A hazy image appeared on the plate. Photography was born. Niépce later partnered with a man named Louis Daguerre, and together they developed the pysautotype, a process that also used lavender oil. After Niépce's death, Daguerre developed a different process by coating silvered copper plates with silver iodide. He named the process the daguerreotype.

A new frontier, of sorts, was crossed a half century later by the New York *Daily Graphic*, which pioneered the use of photos in newspapers. Mechanics at the paper made a zinc plate bearing the lithographic imprint of a photo that contained deeper areas where the photo was dark and shallow areas where the photo was light, all to hold the proper amount of ink. The process, called photoengraving, wasn't perfect, but the *Graphic* debuted its work on March 4, 1880, with a photo of snow-covered dilapidated buildings it called "A Scene in Shantytown, New York." No story accompanied this photo; the image said it all.

Though they purported to depict life "as it really is," mass-produced photographs had the power to create noble images out of quotidian subjects through the use of framing and tricks of lighting. They also had enormous power to convey the gruesome nature of war. Susan Sontag wrote in her critical work *On Photography*,

> One's first encounter with the photographic inventory of ultimate horror is a kind of revelation, the prototypically modern revelation: a negative epiphany. For me, it was photographs of Bergen-Belsen and Dachau which I came across by chance in a bookstore in Santa Monica in July 1945. *Nothing I have seen*—in photographs or in real life—ever cut me as sharply, deeply, instantaneously. Indeed, it seems plausible to me to divide my life into two parts, before I saw those photographs (I was twelve) and after, though it was several years before I understood fully what they were about.

But as powerful as still images could be in conveying information and story, moving images would far surpass this. The critical leap, in terms of moving from still photography to moving images—for which a San Francisco photographer named Eadweard

Muybridge would later be famous—took place at the Palo Alto stock farm owned by Leland Stanford. Muybridge carefully rigged a series of cameras at the side of a track to be triggered with threads stretched across a dirt path. He then transferred the sequential images to glass disks and mounted them on a lamplike fixture called a zoopraxiscope, a version of which would later be called a zoetrope. The effect of seeing still images fluttering before the eyes at a rapid speed created motion in the mind's eye—the illusion of moving life itself, though the means for producing it were as still as any inanimate object could be.

Muybridge's books of photos, *Animals in Motion* (1899) and *The Human Figure in Motion* (1901) depict motion in an extraordinarily granular and time-frozen way. This is especially so for his set of 1884 photos from the Philadelphia Zoological Garden, which show, in vivid frame-by-frame sequence, a tiger attacking a buffalo, and display how the tiger's body moves at the exact point of attack. Shuffle these photos rapidly before the eye and you have the illusion of motion—a replication of life perhaps no different from cave paintings—but one that got into the taproot of the visual brain like nothing seen before.

The flutter of film was a brilliant piece of visual deception, and one for which the public had already been prepared because of the new speeds afforded by the locomotive. Several early zoetrope viewers remarked on how similar these two new technologies seemed: one moved the body; the other moved the brain. A Muybridge biographer, Rebecca Solnit, put it this way:

> The sight out the railroad window had prepared viewers for the kinds of vision that cinema would make ordinary; it had adjusted people to a pure visual experience stripped of smell, sound, threat, tactility, and adjusted them to a new speed of encounter, the world rushing by the windows; had taken them farther into that

world than they would have ever gone before, broadening many horizons at the same time it made the world itself a theater of sorts, a spectacle. Photography had adjusted them to moving freely in time, to a past that was retrievable and a world in which even the things over the horizon were visible, to a world that had become vastly more accessible, but only as monochromatic images.

In the same way, the sixty years of the disembodied shapes and shadows appearing on television screens in our homes have adjusted us to accept the vast new proliferation of moving images that are suddenly accessible through the deepest catalog yet known to man. The shift in view from the railroad window to the still photograph, radical as it may have been, was a passive action for everyone but the well-equipped photographer back in Muybridge's day.

And the means of production would stay in the hands of the wealthy and the experts. The reason people always look grim and never smile in photos from the late nineteenth and early twentieth centuries isn't because their lives were necessarily grim. On the contrary: they laughed just as much as people in this century. Having a photo taken was such an expensive and formal process for most people that to take it frivolously would have been a social faux pas. Also, the long exposure time on the photographic plates of the day meant that portrait subjects had to remain absolutely still for up to a minute, lest the image be blurred. The chairs in some photographers' studios even had metal rods and braces sticking out the top so that people could fix their heads in place lest the photo come out blurry.

The motion picture camera as we know it was not invented out of nowhere and had no singularly identifiable "father." Like the internal combustion engine, the hot air balloon, and the railroad itself, it was a giant collective effort. The early pioneers of image machines had known about the trick of the eye that allows a fast-flickering set of photos effectively to mimic motion, though Muybridge was the first to give it a concrete demonstration. As the historian Irving Fang has pointed out, Muybridge had no way of knowing that it would become "a means of storytelling that would entertain, enthrall and influence billions of people around the world."

An inventor in France took note of Muybridge's trick of the eye and invented a device he called a "photographic revolver"—a single camera that took multiple shots in a short period of time to create a loop of card-flipping images. It was a crude and unwieldy gadget, but it attracted the attention of Thomas Edison, who thought it might make a nice addition to the phonographic sound machines he was busy marketing to the public—though the images projected against the wall would be secondary to the aural experience. Edison put an apprentice, W.K.L. Dickson, to work in his New Jersey lab, and the result was a highly efficient photo gun, which Edison called a kinetograph. The kinetograph could produce a series of photo negatives that could be arranged in a machine against an electric light and rapidly flipped for up to thirty seconds while music played. These peep shows, known as nickelodeons, quickly attracted customers in London, Paris, and New York in the late 1890s, and became a sensation among both the wealthy and the working class. They marked the democratization of the moving image—available for the first time not just to the rich, but also to the poor.

This was no actor reciting lines on a stage in a live theater. This was a distant representation of humanity that nonetheless commanded fascination—a cave painting that moved. The first movies were what we might consider documentaries. They depicted scenes from real life: waves crashing on the beach, a train rushing down a set of tracks. One of the most famous early comedies was *Fred Ott's Sneeze*, an odd seven-second set piece featuring all the excitement of a mustachioed comedian sneezing in an exaggerated fashion. Some of the earliest audiences famously recoiled from these startling images, fearing they would get wet from the waves or the sneeze, or struck by the train. Their shock must have been comparable to that of a nation that had never seen ink on a scroll.

The possibilities of this fantastic light machine captured the imagination not just of viewers but also of small businessmen, who immediately recognized that the pictures were only going to get bigger and that the public thirst for this new medium was only going to grow—even though Thomas Edison was vigorous in protecting his patent and trying to keep competitors from copying his machine. He was not entirely successful. The nickelodeons would move from peep show parlors to large, dark rooms where the flickering images were broadcast against a wall, and where customers were eager to pay a modest fee for the privilege of watching the electric shadows among strangers. These films were more cinema of spectacle than story.

The medium of film would allow for trick photography, and was used to great effect in William Kennedy Dickson's 1895 Edison Studios film *The Execution of Mary Queen of Scots*, to simulate a beheading, in a still very believable style. Wes Craven's and Tobe Hooper's horror film tropes can be traced back to these early images. Special effects were also at work in presenting that Hollywood favorite, the vehicle crash. The film historian Charles Musser has noted that when Edison unveiled his new projector, the Vitascope, he promised to take the cinema of spectacle a step further in a scene that would foreshadow countless movie scenes, including Steven Spielberg's teenage impulses as rendered in J. J. Abrams's *Super 8* a century later. A *New York Times* article reported:

> Mr. Edison is working hard for the absolute perfection of his machine, and at the same time is arranging for the securing of pictures the like of which, in other than inertness, the public has

never seen. He has bought, for about $5,000, two ancient, but still serviceable locomotives and several dozen flat cars. He has built about a quarter of a mile of railroad track in a secluded spot, not far from his laboratory. In a few weeks he will start a train from each end of the track, and will run them to a crash. The engines and cars will be manned, just as trains are in active service, and all the incidents of a train wreck will be caught by machines stationed at short intervals near the track.

Perhaps aware that the Bible was the first bestseller of the Gutenberg era, Edison arranged the production of another blockbuster film. Said the *Times*: "Machines have been sent to Rome, and in a short while the entire stage at Koster & Bial's will be occupied by a realistic representation of Pope Leo XIII, saying mass in the Sistine Chapel."

Cinematic language took another step forward in France. Georges Méliès, a French magician and filmmaker, was in the audience at the first public screening of the film *La sortie des usines Lumière* (*Workers Leaving the Lumière Factory*) on December 28, 1895, and he was smitten like a young boy tasting ice cream for the first time. As an illusionist, he could easily imagine the possibilities of this new medium, and he got his hands on the technology as quickly as he could. In his early work, he played with special effects and began to understand how the camera and the director could create different experiences for the audience. Most of these early films were single-take shots, or crude sequences, but in 1902, Méliès brought his newfound skills together in *Le voyage dans la lune* (*A Trip to the Moon*). This would be his masterpiece, and one of his great contributions to the language of cinema we speak today.

The story itself is not much—certainly something that science-fiction writers from the days of Gilgamesh could have envisioned—but the visual language of cinema brought it to life in a magical way. Méliès used the camera to have things vanish and transform as he had learned to do in other films, but here he tried something else as well. He arranged thirty different shots into a sequence that leapt off the page and onto the screen in a transformative way, and that foreshadowed the rich world of science-fiction imagery given to us over the last century.

Méliès knew that his fortune lay in satisfying the growing American appetite for dazzling stories, and he made plans to exhibit the film all over the United States. One of Edison's employees managed to steal a copy of the film, and the company distributed it for free in perhaps the first act of movie piracy. The film was a hit with audiences, and made an impression on Edwin Stanton Porter, an electrician and director for the Edison Manufacturing Company.

Porter had spent several years as a projectionist, and in fact was arrested for creating a public nuisance when he projected the first known commercial, a pitch for Dewar's Scotch, on a large canvas hung across an intersection at Herald Square in 1897 (a harbinger of things to come in today's Times Square). Porter saw how Méliès used a variety of shots to create a narrative, and late in 1902, in what was the first real "mash-up," he appropriated an array of previously shot Edison film footage in *Life of an American Fireman*.

The film presented a sequence of images—from a fire chief asleep at his desk in the firehouse, dreaming (with the dream appearing in a vignette on the wall) of a woman putting her child to bed; to a close-up of the lever in a fire alarm box being pulled; to the sleeping quarters in the firehouse as the firemen seemingly react to the alarm and jump out of their beds and slide down the fire pole; to an exterior shot of firemen coming down a pole to jump on their horse-drawn fire carriages. The sequence progresses until the firemen have rescued the woman and daughter in dramatic fashion.

The public was hooked on the intoxicating attraction of these image-based stories. These were the images that humans had always known, since the cave paintings in France, but here they were given new, electric life with light and motion.

One of the pioneering businessmen to understand film was the son of Ukrainian immigrants, Louis B. Mayer, who worked in his family's scrap metal business in Boston before buying a ramshackle burlesque theater in the suburb of Haverhill and turning it into that most modern of showpieces, a theater with a screen—which he rechristened the Orpheum. Soon he and a partner, Nathan H. Gordon, owned a chain of cinemas across New England, yet Mayer realized that the commercial possibilities would be even greater if he financed the creation of the movies themselves.

The mild climate and gentle light of Southern California had already created a small nucleus of filmmakers in the sleepy Los Angeles suburb of Hollywood, which also had the benefit of plenty of cheap labor and being far away from Edison's patent investigators and trust enforcers. Longer pictures with more frivolous and clearly fictional themes could be more economically shot under a binding contract, and movie companies provided ready access to everything from the costumes to the cameras to the actors themselves. This was the root of the studio system.

These powerful early studio chiefs—among them William Fox, Adolph Zukor, Samuel Goldwyn, and the Warner brothers—understood that while the *means* for creating a film were necessarily time-consuming and expensive, the *capacity* to watch and understand a movie was extremely democratic and appealing. It required much less mental effort than reading a book.

The basic vocabulary of film could be appreciated even by those of limited education, especially among the unemployed and the laborers in America's fields and factories, for whom going to a ten-cent picture show was a treat and a luxury, and a way to savor the exciting new expression of a "movie," whose visual style appealed to the optic nerve. The barrier of high culture was not an impediment; even the illiterate could be reached, because the form of "literacy" being used was accessible and even intrinsic to all humanity.

Hollywood today is routinely accused of shoveling out reams of tasteless crap, and I don't necessarily disagree, but a crucial antecedent must be understood. The studios were more interested in attracting viewers than in creating high art, in much the same way that the pamphleteers of the seventeenth century were trying to appeal to the widest possible audience. For this reason, this new method of writing had to continue to evolve. You might say that the tubload of crap had a higher purpose. This was a mass medium in a way that transcended what was possible with print.

Marshall McLuhan has noted that the basic language structures of new technology are usually derivative of what immediately preceded them, and it is no accident that Hollywood's founding class had its roots in either vaudeville or live theater. The studio chiefs hired directors who could assemble the moving images in ways that spoke to the core sensibilities of viewers.

One of the most important of these early practitioners was a man named David Wark (or D. W.) Griffith, the son of a Confederate Army colonel who tried to make it as a Broadway actor before being offered a job at the American Mutoscope and Biograph Company as a director of short motion pictures—creations barely advanced from the crude peep shows that featured fake Indian attacks or actors kissing each other. Griffith brought things to a new horizon.

The silent movie actress Lillian Gish called Griffith "the father of film," and Charlie Chaplin said he was "the teacher of us all." Perhaps James Agee said it best when he said of Griffith, "To watch his work is like being witness to the beginning of melody, or the first conscious use of the lever or the wheel; the emergence, coordination, and first eloquence of language; the birth of an art: and to realize that this is all the work of one man."

This sounds like hyperbole, and Griffith wasn't a perfect man, but most scholars agree that the laudatory words aren't far off in at least one integral way. The ways in which film is a literate medium have their alphabetic roots in what D. W. Griffith figured out at the beginning of the century.

Griffith presciently understood the camera as the "viewer's eye," the only source of information that the viewer was going to have, and from which an effective emotional punch might be levied. He played with the ideas of wide shots to show larger landscapes and to establish place within the story, and close-ups for intimacy and to see the characters' expressions, and he began to develop the kinds of shots that have become inherently understandable to us as part of a common vocabulary.

He also began to use the process of editing a film, or combining different shots in order to advance a narrative. One of his most important innovations was the intercut, or cross-cut. You've seen this a million times: the juxtaposition of one scene with another to imply that both events are happening at the same time, and will eventually converge; or the back-and-forth cutting between shots of characters, which creates the viewer's experience of a two-sided conversation.

While Griffith advanced cinematic language and grammar, a Russian professor took this emerging language to the next level of development with an astounding discovery.

The magic of editing finds its roots in the 1920s, in the University of Moscow workshops of Lev Kuleshov. He showed the connection of two wholly unrelated images seen in succession creates a new meaning that didn't exist before. He created the simplest of experiments to test his theory. He filmed a close-up of the actor Ivan Mozzhukhin, who was essentially expressionless, and then separately filmed a bowl of soup, a young girl, and an old woman in a coffin. He put this all together in one piece, interjecting the same shot of the actor in front of each of the objects and then showed it to audiences, "which marveled at the sensitivity of the acting" as Mozzhukhin seemingly looked at each of the objects.

In other words, they perceived a change in the actor in reaction to each of the objects that in actuality was nonexistent. Based on the images, the audience was actively reading and constructing a narrative that wouldn't have been supported by each image alone. This was akin to the development of ancient writing systems that could be understood across distances.

Classical Hollywood cinema embraced the concept of continuity editing, where the transition of both sound and images is constructed in a way that we do not feel the break, or cut between shots. The idea has been to allow (or even seduce) the audience to experience the story as one moment of unmediated, direct, personal, and immersive reality. If a filmmaker is telling a story, as for a novelist, the narrative won't necessarily be linear and continuous. In fact, if there is more than one character, there will likely be multiple things going on in multiple places that are all relevant to the plot. Continuity editing makes use of tools that are unique to this kind of media in order to hide these ellipses, or breaks in time or place. Elements of images can be matched with elements of other images to connect completely unrelated clips in ways that are almost unnoticed by the audience.

A movie's sound is used to blur these transitions, as when we hear sound bridging two moments joined together by a cut and we experience them as being one continuous moment. Harold and Carl Kress, the only father-and-son team to win an Oscar for film editing (for *The Towering Inferno*)—Harold won one alone for *How the West Was Won*—said it most simply: "We don't want the audience to know it's a film." In large part, audiences have been the object of media makers' manipulations (*manipulations* not necessarily meant to be pejorative), and we are often not the slightest bit aware of it.

All you need to do is watch one advertisement, especially a political one, to understand how this language is being used to persuade us to buy or to vote. Look at the happy and bright images that surround the candidate, and the darker ones that are chosen to surround his opponent. Very loud, very compelling statements and emotional connections are being telegraphed through these images.

This simple but profound concept is the basis for editing in film language, and one of the keys to becoming a literate writer with visual media. It is also the filmic equivalent of watching images emerge on light-exposed, emulsion-covered photographic paper sitting in the liquid bath of a darkroom. In a word, magic.

Language—and hence, literacy—isn't a static thing. Each year, we add a collection of new words to our dictionaries, yet the core of our language remains relatively constant, as do the essential structure, grammar, and syntax of our sentences and written texts.

This is true not only in our spoken and written languages but also in the language of visual storytelling that has emerged in the last century. When a filmmaker introduces a new concept and it takes hold, it is essentially added to our vocabulary and is there for future visual storytellers—including you and me—to draw upon. The emergence of this filmic language bears a strong resemblance to the emergence of human alphabetic language more than 3,500 years ago, and to the visual leaps made by the painters of the caves in France.

We all have "libraries" in our minds that we access in a fraction of a second. Sigmund Freud tried to explore this in a 1935 essay called "A Note Upon the 'Mystic Writing Pad.'" He asked the reader to think about a tablet with sheets that have surfaces like film. When we write on the top sheet with a stylus, the writing seems to disappear. But if we lift the sheet and look closely we can see indentations. That second sheet is like our subconscious. Each time we open our eyes and take in new information about the world, it seems as if it is being written on a clean slate, but in actuality, it is in conversation with the traces of everything we have taken in before it. Freud thought that "consciousness arises in the perceptual system *instead* of the permanent traces." How we feel about any given work of art, then, is the result of an unseen dialogue between the present stimulus and all that we have read or seen before it. This happens with everything we consume, and increasingly this is delivered in visual portions.

The cinema of spectacle is available to anyone down at the corner multiplex. The animalistic flashing of quick cuts resembles the moving legs of the deer. The images are like individual words; the clips and the cuts are like sentences that express a particular meaning and then are broken off to limit that meaning. Sequences of films that show, for example, a woman drinking poison in her tea, or a train arriving at a station while the sheriff tries to gather a posse—these are like paragraphs of visual expression.

The language that will govern the next century's primary method of expression was cast in the previous century, and its tropes and conventions settle easily onto brains whose ancestry is still in a completely different, and more primitive, region of human development. We have the capacity both to appreciate the goddess and to understand the alphabet, as Leonard Shlain might have put it, and filmic language speaks to both. That is why it is so effective, and why it, instead of text, has emerged as the means of choice when it comes to communication. One hundred years after its founding, film language is in a new moment of flowering.

That filmic "grammar" developed in the 1910s got even more democratic as the science of photography became a subject of play for electricians who were especially interested in the way that a substance called selenium reacted to an electric current.

A Scottish inventor named Alexander Bain was able to duplicate the strokes of a metal brush at a distance via a selenium wire in 1842. What would happen if those same electric currents could be sent through the vacuum of a glass tube? It turned out that an image from a camera tube could be sent remotely to be broadcast via a receiving tube. By 1926, Bell Laboratories was sending short movies a distance of up to five miles, and within thirteen years, the technology had advanced to the point where it was being demonstrated at the 1939 World's Fair in New York under the banner THE WORLD OF TOMORROW.

By the end of 1950, and with family life retreating to the privacy and isolation of the suburbs, the number of television sets in the country was nearly ten million. And the basic film vocabulary of the movies was altered, though not displaced. As McLuhan said, new mediums tend to use, and then ultimately transform, the medium they replace.

Sixty years later, this is the case with the digital revolution. The medium has co-opted the basic "language" of cinema and television, while also bringing in its own visual elements and conventions. Success in this medium rises and falls based on the ability of the filmmaker to understand this language, which has a proven power to delight, engage, and influence a wide audience.

Fluency in this language does not come at birth, however. It comes through repeated exposure to certain film tropes and conventions that have long been a part of the media diet of the West.

In 2010, researchers from the Knowledge Media Research Center in Germany and Istanbul University examined how the vocabulary of visual language develops when they traveled to a small mountain village south of Isparta, Turkey. There they found a population of adults who were fully sighted, had seen photographs, but hadn't seen moving images beyond what their eyes had captured in real life. The residents had recently been provided with electricity, but many had not had any access to movies or ever seen a television broadcast. Such a pristine population—"video virgins," as it were—were prime candidates for research into the mind, research that could be conducted only once.

When people in this town were first shown a movie, they weren't able to follow the story at all. They hadn't been exposed to the language of visual storytelling. It was as if someone were to speak to us in a language we have never heard. They couldn't derive meaning or narrative out of what seemed to be disconnected and unrelated images.

As the university researchers related in their study, published in December 2010 in the journal *Psychological Science*, the movie showed the outside of a house and then a second shot of a woman sitting on a couch inside the house. But the video virgins weren't able to connect these images. They couldn't understand that the point of that short sequence was that the woman was sitting inside the house depicted in the first shot. This was true for other kinds of cinematographic techniques, those that we, as video-saturated Westerners, seem to understand innately. The "computer program" or syntax that drives the story in movies or other moving images didn't exist for them.

Understanding film is a form of literacy, even if we don't recognize it as such. When we started reading as children, we began with letters and then words; then we moved on to the simplest of picture books; and then early readers, and eventually more sophisticated texts. At each step, we picked up vocabulary, grammar, sentence structure, and more tools of decoding meaning. These descended onto our minds like magic. This learning process continues at every age. Each time we pick up a newspaper, book, or other printed text, we have the opportunity to encounter new words or new ways of expressing ourselves through the printed word.

The reason we are able to understand a written piece of communication so quickly is that we have built up a sophisticated knowledge of language while reading or listening to someone speak. As we hear each word, we have already distilled the possibilities of the next word or words, just as an experienced chess player can anticipate his moves five moves ahead. We know that when we read or hear the verb in a sentence, all the other verbs are not likely possibilities for the next word and that the universe of possibilities is limited.

Whether we are aware of it or not, we read not just as readers or receptors of information, but also as "writers one day," consciously or subconsciously processing and storing that information about how to tell a story when the time comes for us. When we read or consume movies, we prime ourselves as future imitators.

If you were able to go back and reconstruct a personal history of your parallel development as a reader and a writer, you would no doubt see that the level of sophistication of your reading was generally one step ahead of your writing. In the case of visual texts, however, until recently, most of us haven't had the opportunity to be creators of visual stories, but we have spent extraordinary amounts of time watching. And the information from our consumption is still there to be mined.

We're not starting off in a remote Turkish village. We know how this is done. But it helps immensely to understand the basic components of what generally works as visual syntax. That "language" is only about a hundred years old, but its roots are dendritic and they are located deep in the cerebral cortex.

■ THE BRAIN SEES PICTURES FIRST

Sight is by far the most trusted of our senses, and the one that has the greatest impact on our conception of reality. Our eyes are the gateway to enormous volumes of data and information, and it is no accident that up to 85 percent of the brain is dedicated to processing and making sense out of the visual stimulation that flows in at an astonishing rate. The eye and the brain evolved together as a working unit.

This concrete biological reality is the biggest part of the reason communication with images is going to get even stronger in the coming decades. Put simply, we are primed to be drawn toward visual media (whether television, YouTube, video games, or home-made movies) because our limbic systems, the deep-set instinctual region of our brains, are already aware in ways that we are not about the amount of information that can be soaked up just from letting images play over the surface of the eyes.

First of all, communicating with images is quicker than with words. Images hit the brain in a shockingly brief sequence of events. Neuroscientists now know that the brain begins to categorize and make sense of an image within 150 milliseconds of the first glimpse. Patterns of light and shadow flow through the cornea and are refracted and then projected as an inverted image against the retina at the back of the eye. The image is translated into ganglionic cells, which transmit it directly, via the optic nerve, into two regions of the brain: the ventral stream, which governs the recognition of objects; and the dorsal stream, which is responsible for comprehending their place in three-dimensional space.

The speed is part of the reason images tend to "hit us in the gut" quicker and more consistently than the written word, and why some images are more fascinating than others. There is a physiological reason that we laugh out loud more readily at a funny movie than at a comedic novel: it is because our visual pathways are tapped more directly into the inner, "reptilian" core of the brain that houses pleasure-reward centers and that governs our basic responses.

We trust our eyes in a way that we trust almost no other sense, even if we remain unaware of the reasons for this. There is extensive research showing this, from studies that demonstrate that people make almost irreversible decisions on whether a potential sexual partner is attractive within one-fifth of a second, to how "visual learners" will even convert words into pictures in their minds in order to master a subject.

To better understand how the science of the mind is going to play a critical role in the visual revolution, I spoke to some of the people who understand it best. And what I learned surprised me.

I started my journey into the brain by visiting one of the more senior members of the emerging fraternity of neuroscientists trying to understand visual processing.

Rafael Malach is a professor of brain research at the Weizmann Institute of Science in Rehovot, Israel. As he began to talk,

I watched him get more and more animated. He explained what he views as the most important first premise: that seeing is a subjective and creative act.

Vision is an example of exquisite specialization, with different sections of the brain simultaneously processing different aspects of an image and combining these data into one cohesive still image. This is done at an extraordinary speed, as we construct these images in our brains approximately every twenty-fourth of a second. This is the same speed as the typical projection of a movie at twenty-four frames per second, which is the not-coincidental reason that the illusion of motion works so well in the cinema. By viewing, we are actually clicking a picture of a still image into our minds and interpolating the data in between. We then experience the image as "moving."

This comparison between a projector and movie screen in the mind is not as far-fetched as you might think. We filter out the blackness when we blink, which occurs on average more than fourteen thousand times per waking day, yet the experience of this blackness rarely registers in our sense of vision.

Malach explains that we don't simply read, or see, an image—we take in a range of data, including shapes or patterns, colors, and motion across a series of sequential images. Instantaneously we compare these data to files we have been constructing since the first time we opened our eyes as babies. Each image we encounter is subject to interpretation and construction and is then deposited in a bank for us to withdraw from at a later time.

An example: on the street, we glimpse a large, red, rectangular shape riding atop a set of smaller black circles. Within a few twenty-fourth-of-a-second frames, we see that the image is shifting; we perceive that the circles are rotating rapidly and that the red rectangle is moving along on top of them. We reach into our database to "understand" that what we are seeing is a fire engine. In essence, we construct this image out of available data, both within our frame of vision and within our minds.

Learning to see begins with babies as a primary stage of development. Yet, until now, it has been difficult to study—as newborns aren't the most communicative of subjects. Dr. Pawan Sinha, an associate professor of vision and computational neuroscience at the Massachusetts Institute of Technology, has been studying a population of people in India who have been blind since birth but have had their blindness reversed through medical procedures. They can literally see things for the first time, even though they are well into adulthood. Project Prakash (Sanskrit for *light*) is not only providing people with sight, but is allowing the scientific team led by Sinha to study how sight develops.

Traditional thought in the scientific community was that such patients still wouldn't be able to see normally, as their brains' visual cortex would have been underdeveloped and stagnant. Sinha and his team found that this was true—at first. It took several days before patients could begin to process light and the most basic of images. During the first year of sight, they still had only rudimentary visual abilities: they were able to see two-dimensional objects such as squares and circles painted on a wall, but not three-dimensional objects, or even squares and circles if they were overlaid upon one another.

This slowly began to change over time, however, as the newly sighted populated their visual database in the brain. Images, in other words, must have something to relate to in order to be meaningful. Sinha talks about one particular patient—a man called "S.K." who was blind for the first twenty-nine years of his life. For the first year after surgery reversed his blindness, he had only the most basic visual skills. But by eighteen months, "he had begun to make sense of his world, building his visual vocabulary through experience and recognizing more complex objects with varying colors and brightness." He was learning to see, to construct images.

Motion in an image helps the process of recognition significantly—think of the fire engine racing down the street. When S.K. looked at a cow, for example, he could recognize only disconnected patches of black and white. But when the cow began to move, the image suddenly resolved into a cow for him.

Our brain consists of more than a hundred billion neurons, and 85 percent of the real estate in our brain that houses these neurons is involved in the visual processing system. As we see an image in the flash of a second, up to a million of these neurons are triggered in a combination that is totally unique to that image. If we think of each of those million neurons representing a note from a particular instrument, and then extrapolate this to a series of images, we can envision the most magnificent of orchestras playing the most spectacular of symphonic scores.

So, in theory, if we were able to isolate and stimulate each of these neurons in exactly the same combination, we would "create" that image for a person.

This can be seen in a 2004 experiment at the University of California–Los Angeles in which patients undergoing brain surgery (a difficult subject group to arrange) were fitted with electrodes and shown a series of photographs of things such as cats, furniture, famous faces, famous paintings, and other objects that are easily recognized. The patients were then asked to recall those images.

As the patients brought an image into their memory, the same neurons lit up as those activated when the image was first shown. The link between recalling a picture and actually seeing it was shown to be strong.

Malach pushed this theory forward a bit in his own experiment, in conjunction with Itzhak Fried, a professor of neurosurgery at both UCLA and Tel Aviv University. They showed patients sixty-four video clips, from sources ranging from *The Simpsons* to a Tom Cruise film, noted the neural response, and then asked them to say into a microphone what they had seen. You can probably guess the outcome. When speaking about the clip, they experienced the same burst of activity in the neurons as when the clip was shown.

Seeing is an extraordinary feat, highly complex and highly creative. But what does that say about the power of this process and why we are hardwired to respond to images so powerfully? It appears that we possess not only a visual "recognition" system but also a visual "action" system, and it is this latter mechanism that takes over when we see compelling images on a screen. The psychologist and philosopher William James, an investigator into the human experience of the spiritual, who also seems to be a spiritual grandfather for many neuroscientists, saw emotion as "preparation for action."

Malach believes that James's formulation is indeed true when it comes to images that produce an emotional response. When we see a picture of a frightened person, we feel the slight sensations of fear ourselves, and get ready to "fight" or "flee." When we see a scene of jubilation, or of a horse drowning and a young child watching with horror, we experience a twinge of those same emotions, and we get ready to spring into action.

We don't experience the sensation nearly as quickly (or at all) while reading a description of a battle or of a drowning or of jubilation. Images and visual processing are directly linked to natural behavior, while the language of words is more recently evolved, and necessitates an indirect path from reception to cognition. It keeps us further removed from its emotional core and leaves lots of room for us to fill in our own experiences. This is certainly one of the great pleasures of reading, but it is also a peek into why the less-mediated visual experience is so powerful.

There is an obvious example of this phenomenon at work, and it happens to be an immensely profitable one in our times. Pornography is now about a $15 billion business in the United States. It outpaces the sale of conventional movie tickets, and is said to be responsible for about 30 percent of the content of the entire Internet. Not for nothing is the business called "the Other Hollywood." These films aren't known for their captivating storylines. So why is the demand for pornography so huge? In 2006, researchers at the Christian-Albrechts University Medical School in Germany put forward an insightful theory.

They measured the brain activity of several volunteers who viewed pornography while lying in a functional magnetic resonance imaging machine, or fMRI—it doesn't sound like a lot of fun to me, but science must go forward. The volunteers were an equal mix of gay and straight, and the videos they were shown were a mix of gay porn, straight porn, and totally nonsexual images.

When the straight subjects were shown straight porn, and the gay subjects shown gay porn, an interesting thing happened in their brains, especially the ventral striatum and the ventral premotor cortex. This latter region is the home to a set of neurotransmitters called mirror neurons, which are responsible for imitative behavior in humans—as in when we watch a person eating an apple and we can taste a little of the apple in our own mouths. The conclusions of the German researchers was that when we watch people of our own preference having sex, it is not merely the suggestion of sex that arouses us. It is that the section of our own minds that provides the intense pleasure associated with having sex is tickled into believing that *we* are having sex in that moment.

Like the work of William James more than a century before, studying the gap between emotion and action is partly brain science, but also partly psychology. We are primed to experience unconsciously—or even, in a sense, to imitate—what we watch.

Marco Iacoboni has an easy and relaxed demeanor, and spending time with him is a pleasure. He is a friendly man with a square skull topped with professorial white hair, and he speaks with a courtly Italian accent. His jokes are quiet ones, and he asks intelligent questions that reveal an innate curiosity as well as good manners.

I met him in his office one summer day at the Transcranial Magnetic Stimulation Laboratory at UCLA. It was a few minutes into the discussion when I noticed he was smiling when I smiled and leaning forward at the same time as I was. His movements were subtly imitating mine.

What previous generations might have thought was social gracefulness now appears to be the result of something more deep-seated in the mind. Iacoboni happens to be an excellent personal case study in his own research specialty, which is the field of mirror neurons.

This is the portion of the brain that responds to the facial expressions and actions of another human being. When you observe someone picking up an ice-cream cone and licking it, your own mind imitates that action even though you are not actually performing it. When somebody smiles at us, the neurons that govern the action light up in our minds as if we were actually smiling. This is the part of the brain, says Iacoboni, that allows us to feel empathy, friendship, and even shared suffering for other people.

Another amazing thing about the mirror neurons is that they will activate even if we are witnessing actions performed not in real life but on the computer or television screen. The new science of mirror neurons is therefore critical for understanding the implications of the power of the moving image.

Let me unpack the science just a bit. A neuron is a brain cell that responds to chemical and electrical charges. Neurons are the basic building blocks of the mind. Memories are stored in them in complex networks. When we smile, laugh, cry, wave, sing, play, write, or kiss, the action is preceded by the firing of millions of neurons behaving in concert.

In the late 1980s, researchers at the University of Parma in Northern Italy experimented with macaque monkeys by hooking up their brains to electrodes and then making them perform simple tasks with their hands and eyes, such as raising a banana up to their mouths. They found a surprise: the same neurons that lit up during these actions also lit up when the monkeys were watching another monkey, or even a person, performing the same task. These neurons are located in the inferior frontal cortex and the superior parietal lobe of the brain, and the activity inside them has been monitored with the help of an fMRI.

You may have been in an MRI at one time, for various medical tests. It's a big, loud machine with an aperture shaped like a donut. The MRI uses a powerful magnet briefly to align the protons inside the trillions of atoms of water inside the body. This provides a clear multidimensional snapshot of what the inside of the body looks like. The fMRI, for its part, is specially designed for the brain, and can measure heightened activity in certain regions by charting an effect called "blood oxygen–dependent levels." When a section of the brain is activated, it calls for freshly oxygenated blood, which is an activity the fMRI detects in vivid detail, almost down to the level of individual neurons. This gives researchers a small clue as to how the person under scrutiny might actually be thinking or feeling in that moment.

This comes with an important caveat, though. Just because oxygenated blood is flowing to a particular region of the brain when an image is shown does not mean we can necessarily discern exactly *what* the person in the fMRI is thinking about that image or how it might affect his choices to act on the image. The columnist David Brooks put it well to Jeffrey Goldberg of *The Atlantic*: "My fear is that this is like flying over Los Angeles at night, looking at the lights in the houses and trying to guess what people are talking about at dinner," he said. Yet the effectiveness of fMRIs in studying brain activation is widely accepted.

In 1999, Iacoboni and his colleagues at UCLA recruited subjects for a simple experiment to gauge whether the effect noticed in the monkeys in Italy was analogous to what happened in humans. Subjects were given high-definition goggles and asked to watch and imitate hand movements shown on a screen. Sure enough, the researchers located two areas like those in the monkeys: one called P5, in the frontal lobe, and another called PF, in the parietal lobe. The former is a critical region for the development of language, which suggests a strong link between empathy and the means to communicate it. Iacoboni has also theorized that a damaging effect of autism is the "brokenness" of mirror neurons that allow a person to understand social dynamics.

This principle plays a key role in our understanding why visual means of communication are going to be the dominant media form in the new century. As I've said, film has a gut-level power to influence areas of the mind that writing simply does not. This is also the hidden science behind the emotions we feel tugged when we watch a particular piece of video. Our mirror neurons fire just as easily when we watch an action on the screen as when we see it in real life. William Hutchison of the University of Toronto found that the cingulate cortex of a subject had at least one cell within it that responded to the sight of a researcher being pricked with a pin.

This leads us to an old question—an answer to which would instantly bring riches to any Hollywood director smart enough to deploy it in a film. What *kind* of image makes the biggest impression on the emotions and stirs the deepest feelings?

Science has no answers yet, Iacoboni told me, though there are most definitely certain phenomena that elicit a strong neural firing.

"Big, bright colors, fast and sudden movements," he told me. "The attention is captured instantly. It makes sense, because all these factors are things that could be dangerous." This brain activity is likely an adaptive response. But there is no evidence of a correlation between that immediate seizing of attention and a deep emotional impact that will motivate the person to behave in a certain way that doesn't involve ducking or weaving.

On Super Bowl Sunday of 2006, Iacoboni and his colleagues tried a novel (and press-friendly) experiment. They gathered five subjects and showed them the big, splashy Super Bowl Sunday commercials that are designed to grab attention. One ad, for Federal Express, showed a dinosaur crushing a caveman. Not surprisingly, the patients who viewed it showed a leap in activity in the amygdala, the walnut-size region that responds to fear and danger. Another ad, for Disney World, which played on the famous "I'm going to Disney World!" line after a victory, showed a response in the orbito-cortex and ventral striatum, which are two areas that process perceived rewards, such as tasty food or sex.

When the participants were asked afterward which ads they preferred, there was almost no link between what people said they liked and the level of brain activity happening while they watched the ads. Iacoboni concluded that what people say they enjoy and what they actually respond to on a neurological level may be two different things—which is why the tendency of film-makers to pour all kinds of stimulation on the screen might not be the best strategy.

"If you look at commercials now, it's like a race to grab the attention," Iacoboni told me. "This may be self-defeating. We just filter them out."

What seems to work much better is a piece of video with a co-herent narrative, which elicits an empathetic response. Another UCLA experiment throws light on this idea.

In that experiment, Iacoboni showed pictures of happy cus-tomers shopping in a department store to two groups of people—those who had a particular brand of credit card and those who didn't. Those who had the card showed high activity in the mirror neurons when the card's easily recognizable logo was shown in the lower left-hand corner of the screen. No such level of activity was found in those who were non-cardholders.

"It is as if," Iacoboni has written, "these cardholding subjects, while watching the pictures with 'their' logo, were thinking, 'Those people are like me.'"

The neurologist Dr. Michael Smith of the company Neuro-focus in Berkeley, California, agrees that slick images are ulti-mately useless if they are not attached to an engaging story. "While it might be fun to process video with really fast cuts, the world doesn't like that," he said. "Fast cuts will attract attention but they won't stick in the memory or keep you emotionally engaged. We're hardwired to want to learn about the world in the form of stories. Storytelling was key for us to learn the accumulated base of wisdom. Those people who can take compelling imagery and combine it with a powerful story are going to be so much more effective. Your visual system is not wired for abrupt changes in the environment."

The ideal character in a video would be one who projected a high level of empathy—a sense that they would understand and relate to us.

"Politicians are an example," said Iacoboni. "We make a decision about whether we like them immediately. When it comes to faces, processing them has been so important to our survival. It is built deeply. We have many ways of saying things that are rooted in the voice and body. The person who is effective is really focused on getting across what they want to say."

The empathetic person also needs to be at the center of a story, even a brief story. This is because of the brain's automatic tendency to filter out extraneous material like so much white noise and focus on one central subject, which is where learning and cognition take place.

Advertisers who specialize in product placement, for example, have known for years that the way to really make a brand name stick in the customer's mind is not merely to place it in a scene where it can be viewed. The Pepsi can on the desk is not going to be effective unless Matt Damon doesn't just drink it but makes it a part of an ongoing plot.

The absolute gold standard was set in 1982, in the movie *E.T.*, in which the lead character, Elliott, uses Reese's Pieces to make a trail for the little alien to follow. The candy was tied up in the plot, not merely seen, which forced the viewer to have a different level of cognitive experience. Sales of Reese's Pieces climbed 65 percent in the weeks following the movie's release, and it is not a wild leap to think that part of this was the result of mirror neurons in the audience helplessly firing in empathy as they watched the candy being eaten by a preadolescent and a visitor from another planet. For many of them, whether they wanted to or not, they were eating that candy themselves.

"When people watch a movie they love, they're truly living the things taking place on the screen through their mirror neurons," Iacoboni told Jeffrey Goldberg.

This emerging field of science was called "neurocinematics" by the Princeton University psychology professor Uri Hasson. He is investigating some of the same phenomena as Iacoboni, though Hasson's work is focused more on a "whole brain" response to what's on the screen. For him, storytelling is not just a nice intellectual concept, but a hardwired physiological truth.

I went to talk to him one spring day on Princeton's leafy campus. Hasson is a tall, soft-spoken guy. That day, he wore a black T-shirt, jeans, and Nike sneakers. His eyes were set off with square black square-frame glasses. He was clearly of the Steve Jobs school of fashion.

Hasson contends that a skillful director doesn't just trigger pleasurable or fearful sensations. The director has, in a sense, actually entered the viewer's mind and made it feel what he wants it to feel. "Now we have scientific proof that some filmmakers actually take over a viewer's brain," he told me.

What helped convince him of this startling conclusion was a study he conducted in 2004. Five subjects were placed in an fMRI and shown the first half hour of the classic spaghetti Western *The Good, the Bad, and the Ugly*, a masterpiece of story and setting by the Italian director Sergio Leone. Hasson compared the spikes in subjects' brain activity to the time line of the movie and found that roughly 35 percent of the brain reacted the same way to the same dramatic moments.

What seemed to create the highest levels of oxygenated blood movements were those moments when a new character's face appeared on the screen. It was as if the brain had made an instantaneous recognition of a "new person" and was struggling to integrate him or her into the pattern of the larger story. Furthermore, when the eye movements were tracked during a showing of film, results showed that the center of vision in multiple viewers tended to follow the locus of the action on the screen, even when it wasn't in the geographic center of the screen. Participants' eyes tracked Clint Eastwood's eyes, the entrance of another character into the room, the movement of Lee Van Cleef's gun. Leone, in other words, was deliberately leading not just the eyes but the mind.

A closer look at one of Hasson's favorite directors, Alfred Hitchcock, throws further light on this sweet science of manipulation. Hitchcock was one of the greatest directors of twentieth-century cinema and also a deeply complex man. He was unapologetic about his desire to torture an audience with unbearable suspense, spasms of violence, and emotional cruelty that bordered on the sadistic. Some have accused him of being more interested in doling out pain than pleasure to his audiences.

Born in London in 1899 to stern Irish parents, Hitchcock was given a good education but often felt lonely and miserable. Once, his father sent him to the police station and asked that he be locked up in a criminal's cell for ten minutes because he had misbehaved. His classmates teased him about his weight. Hitchcock grew up with a streak of latent anger. As a young man, he wrote short stories that hinged on themes of obsession, mistaken identity, and jealousy, and after he got a job in the title card department of the company that would soon be Paramount Pictures, he found his medium. His early films, such as *The Man Who Knew Too Much* and *The 39 Steps*, took viewers through shadowy landscapes in which the shape of reality could not be fully trusted. He developed a knack for scenes in which his characters were led unaware into danger—while the viewer was given enough information to understand more than the character—and then held over the precipice of disaster for an unbearably long time.

Think of Jimmy Stewart's hapless detective in *Vertigo*, not knowing just how badly he is being played by Kim Novak. Or Janet Leigh happily staying at the Bates Motel. We know something doesn't add up, but she doesn't. "Indeed, it is a rule of Hitchcock's cautionary tales that no pleasure can be wholly harmless—the more needling the harm, the more pointedly the pleasure will be pricked into a thrill," wrote the film critic Anthony Lane.

Hitchcock was not a neurologist, but it turns out that a lot of his success might have come from being able to play so uniformly with the amygdala, the part of the brain that governs fear and anxiety. When Hasson showed his subjects a segment of Hitchcock's 1961 "Bang! You're Dead," an episode of the television serial *Alfred Hitchcock Presents*, he found that 65 percent of the brain activity in the viewers was exactly the same. In other words, Hitchcock's images and stories were affecting the viewers in their frontal cortexes just as consistently and predictably as if each one had had his flesh seared with a poker.

An episode of *Curb Your Enthusiasm*, by contrast, showed a level of engagement that was significantly lower—only 18 percent. The lowest engagement of all, 5 percent, was shown for a one-minute clip of random people wandering around Washington Square Park, a bit of what the researchers called "unstructured reality."

This doesn't necessarily prove that Hitchcock is a superior director, says Hasson. It means that whatever he was doing on the screen was more consistently engaging to the hidden neurologies of a wider group of people, and thus was able to touch a more diverse span of moviegoers.

The implications for directors are obvious. Imagine a test screening of a movie in which you aren't asked to fill out a survey before leaving the theater, but instead are hooked up to a giant magnet so that your brain can reveal just how engaged you actually are with the material. Once again, it wouldn't necessarily be an indication of what constitutes art. There is abundant room for error. Bright noises and flashes are going to light up the mind more than a conversation between two people, and I think most people can agree that *Kramer vs. Kramer* is a more accomplished movie than *Jackass Number Two*. But as a crude divining rod, the fMRI scan has tremendous value.

One thing should be made clear about this new science. Images *must* be accompanied by a narrative if they are to have any value. Some of Hasson's most important work shows that this is not just a picturesque idea, but one that is built into the very architecture of the brain.

He once hooked up several subjects and showed them a ten-second clip from the classic silent movie *City Lights*, showing Charlie Chaplin pushing a hapless companion into a swimming pool. That's what the complete clip showed, anyway. Some subjects were shown just 150 milliseconds of the film—enough to show only a brief splash of water. Others got 1,000 milliseconds and were exposed to the push and the splash. The final group got to see 7,000 milliseconds, which made the push part of a comic routine.

You probably have already guessed where this is going. Brain activity was the highest in the group that could understand the event in the context of a larger story. Other groups were shown the same film run backward, and a final group was shown the frames of the film in a scrambled fashion. Their activity was predictably flat. Yet every group was shown the exact same pictures. Only those who were able automatically to understand that a story was unfolding showed a neurological reaction. "The brain does not respond to gibberish," commented Hasson. But when you connect images in a fashion that creates a narrative story in a literate way, you elicit powerful responses.

There's an old saying in Hollywood: "Nobody knows anything."

Nobody knows what kind of storytelling formula is going to capture a big audience, and nobody knows whether what looks like a surefire hit is actually going to be a massive flop. For every *Avatar*, there is an *Ishtar*. In both cases, studios, directors, and everyone else involved set out to make what they thought would be a critical and commercial success.

For more than a hundred years, filmmakers have been feeling their way around, making guesses at what audiences might like, and hoping for the best. The only real predictor for the future is what's happened in the past, and this is a big reason why sequels are so prevalent. Studio executives figured that if you liked *Cars*, you'd probably also put down money for *Cars 2*. Whether society really benefited from having *Rocky IV* in the universe is a debatable matter, but I understood perfectly why it got made.

Thanks to neurocinematics, the next shoe to drop will likely be the specific tailoring of a story to fit the hidden mental hungers of the audience. There are a few companies working in this extremely speculative field, and one of them is located in a bland low-rise industrial park close to the Miramar Marine Corps Air Station, outside San Diego. The company's front door faces a horse barn across a chain-link fence.

On a recent winter day, I was buzzed into the office and met by one of the partners of MindSign, twenty-eight-year-old Philip Carlsen, who has an easy smile and a surfer's tan. His first question was whether I had a pacemaker, which he says can be affected by the fMRI machine they keep in the back. I assured him that there was no metal on me but the keys in my pocket.

As he reached for the door to the fMRI room, he mentioned that I should keep my cell phone and credit cards outside, because the massive magnets are always on and they will erase information from magnetic strips. I thought of all the zeros and ones embedded in my phone that would be compelled to leap from my cell phone's data chip and into the ravenous magnetic monster.

Carlsen explained that the Siemens fMRI machine is a $2 million piece of equipment and that MindSign is the "only privately owned fMRI research center in the United States." The big contraption looked like any other MRI that I had visited as a patient over the years, with one exception: there was a box of multiple mirrors, about four by six inches, attached to a plastic structure above where the patient's head would lie. Sitting on a shelf in the wall at the far end of the tube was a projector that threw images onto a plastic screen in the back of the tube. The images would fall onto the mirror apparatus above the patient's head for him to view, while the magnet would record the response deep within his brain.

MindSign was founded in 2008 by Carlsen, along with neurologist Dr. David Hubbard and his son Devin Hubbard. Medical expertise was not a criterion for employment. Before starting MindSign, Carlsen attended the Brooks Institute of Photography and struggled as a novice filmmaker, finding low-level work with producer Lawrence Bender, and then at DreamWorks, in its TV department.

The only partner with medical experience, Devin's father, went to Yale Law School, dropped out in 1969, and found himself at Berkeley and then Stanford, receiving his medical degree from the University of Connecticut. He made most of his wealth through a drug he designed (and patented) to treat muscle tension in the back. Hubbard Sr. is also a meditator, and a few years ago he decided to buy his own fMRI machine to be able to study the impact of meditation on the brain.

With this expensive toy sitting around idle for most of the time, Hubbard invited his son and Carlsen to play with it, and they all decided to look at how brains respond to different movie trailers. Carlsen wanted to get into the marketing department of DreamWorks at the time, and he asked someone in the department to share with him the kinds of questions DreamWorks has test audiences answer. Why not, he reasoned, take pictures of the brain while the subjects watched trailers for upcoming movies?

They placed a subject (often themselves) in the fMRI tube and then showed a commercial or trailer, followed by several seconds of black screen (to establish a baseline and response pattern). They monitored the two primary areas of the brain that clocked activation to visual stimuli: the ventromedial prefrontal cortex and what is called "Brodmann area 25," which is responsible for developing a sense of self.

This basic methodology formed the foundation for several amateur studies. MindSign once looked at twenty commercials for fast-food companies to determine which ones were most effective at activating the hunger area of the brain. It seems a Jack in the Box ad was the most activating commercial. I wondered if one could correlate the broadcast of that commercial to people flooding into Jack in the Box for a burger and fries.

Most of MindSign's subjects are literally off the street, recruited through ads on Craigslist, which offer thirty dollars to anyone willing to be scanned. Carlsen told me they'd love to have my brain in their database, and offered to scan me while I watched clips from a few movies.

I couldn't resist this offer, and returned a few months later. Carlsen instructed me to change into hospital scrubs, and then led me into the room with the futuristic donut of the fMRI. He had me lie on the table, secured my head in a stabilizing device, and then fitted me with a kind of helmet with a screen near the eyes.

As anyone who's been through one of these scans can tell you, it's a bit claustrophobic, and I had been instructed to lie perfectly still. As the machine rumbled to life, I tried to drown out the noise and just watch the movie clips I'd brought along.

"All right, Steve," came a tinny voice through the speaker. It was Carlsen, speaking through the glass partition. "I'm looking at your brain right now."

"Anything inside?" I asked.

"The hamster's still on the wheel," he said dryly.

Several inches above my nose, a black crosshair test pattern sat squarely in the middle of the screen. I watched it intently, waiting for the study to begin. For the next forty minutes, I would watch four different clips, each from one to three minutes in length. They were set up in random order and viewed twice, with about twenty seconds of the crosshair pattern separating them, sort of like a scoop of sorbet to cleanse the palate between courses at a fancy dinner.

The first short film was an early version of a trailer for a big-budget movie called *War Horse*, directed by Steven Spielberg, which tells the story of a young man who travels to France during World War I to save the horse he'd grown up with on his farm in England. I had seen the play, and when I heard that Spielberg had optioned the rights to make it into a movie, it made complete sense. I was excited to see his take on the story. As I watched the trailer, I felt moved by the spectacular horse running through a war-torn landscape as cannons boomed and munitions exploded around him.

The next clip was significantly creepier: a disturbing scene from the 1973 science-fiction drama *Soylent Green*, set in an overpopulated earth where excess people are encouraged to commit suicide and then are consumed as food. This was a movie that had left a profound mark on me as an adolescent, and while I hadn't seen it in years, one particular scene had continued to haunt me. The scene in question features Charlton Heston as he bursts into a euthanasia "processing center" to try to save his older friend, played by Edward G. Robinson, who is laid out on a clinical table (not unlike, I realized, the fMRI machine from whose mouth I was now protruding like a popsicle stick).

I then watched a second version of a *War Horse* trailer. While it differed in construction from the first, it felt essentially similar, and familiar, and I couldn't discern a sense of being more or less stimulated by it than by the first. Presumably the rotating magnets in the tube could reveal something more.

The last clip was a short scene from *Ana*, a documentary done a few years ago by two of our students at the Media Arts Lab, Riley Ziesig and Jessica Kingdon. In the sequence, we meet a Chilean American social worker who is working with a community of Latino domestic workers and is talking passionately about her love of her home country. She sheds a tear as she talks about how she wants for her country as much as we want for ours.

I watched all these a second time, in a different order, with as clear a mind as I could manage, trying to scrub my thoughts clean like a blackboard and let the movies "write" whatever impressions on my mind they would.

A few weeks later, a set of pictures arrived in my e-mail. They were of my brain. It is awfully strange to see the biological seat of your personality and memories sliced open like a walnut, with different regions highlighted in bright colors. This was a map to the flow of blood and electrical activity that took place in my mind while I viewed those film clips and (crudely enough) a hint as to how I might have been reacting on a subconscious level to what I was seeing.

I got on the phone with Carlsen, and he explained what kind of conclusions he could draw from the blood flow within my brain, precisely measured by the fMRI. The findings had also been reviewed by Dr. Hubbard.

"There's not a lot of general claims we can make off one subject," Carlsen cautioned before he started. "We can make better claims off sixty subjects," but he explained that we can see the level of my brain activity while watching each piece of media.

He drew my attention to a scan taken during the showing of the *Ana* clip, and explained how the heightened activity in the prefrontal cortex, highlighted in bright yellow, pointed to the stimulation of "executive functions," meaning intellectual engagement with the topic. But here is where the science gives way to guesswork.

This activity could have happened because the film was exceptionally well made, said Carlsen. Or it could merely have taken place because I happened to connect with the issues being touched on by the sequence—that the images triggered other neural connections within my brain beyond the context of the actual story on-screen.

The next video I had watched was significantly more unsettling— the *Soylent Green* voluntary suicide sequence—but oddly enough, it showed no activation around the amygdala, which govern the mind's fear response, the famous fight-or-flight reaction zone. Instead, most of my mind's buzz seemed to be in the temple area. Carlsen explained that this probably meant I was unconsciously more affected by the music than the images.

In this case, it was a medley of Beethoven's Sixth Symphony, Tchaikovsky's Sixth Symphony, and the *Peer Gynt* suite by Edvard Grieg. These are quite beautiful snippets of music, but in the context of a man laid out on a table and "coming home" via euthanasia, they are incredibly eerie. Still, I wondered why that clip didn't seem to have made me afraid. Was I tougher than I thought? Or was there a more banal answer? "If you've seen this scene before," Phil explained, "it'll lessen the activation. But we can say that almost none of the language of this scene engaged with you. It was all in the music."

Perhaps in seeing *Soylent Green* this time, as an adult, decades removed from the child who first encountered it, I was less susceptible to Heston's overemoting, or perhaps I was predisposed to see instead the gun-loving Charlton Heston I knew through the Michael Moore documentary *Waiting for Columbine.*

The biggest surprise of all came with the *War Horse* trailer that was filled with the shouts and alarms of combat. Amazingly enough, my cortex was no more mentally engaged while I watched this polished promotion for a multimillion-dollar Hollywood movie than when I was watching the static black symbol that came between the clips. Again, Carlsen explained that this limp response didn't speak directly to the quality of the presentation.

"I wouldn't say that this trailer is better or worse," he said. "It could be there were things weighing on the mind that were beyond what was in the trailer. Basically you were not as mentally engaged. It washed over you. You cared less. You might have been thinking about other things. Or you might have been so over it that you were disengaged altogether."

He elaborated in another conversation: "How the brain works is that when it uses that area of the brain, it will call more blood into that area, and our magnet just tracks the iron in that blood so we can see where the blood is going. It doesn't absolutely mean that this trailer is better, but more engagement is what we think is obviously better. A trailer with no engagement is comparable to a crosshair. Even if you absolutely hate it, that's better than no engagement at all."

Perhaps this also helps explain why trailers increasingly seem to "give it all away," telling the complete narrative of a film in order to get us to want to buy a ticket.

As Hasson showed in his Chaplin studies, the more a series of images is part of a narrative story, the more we respond. These attempts at conveying a 146-minute, sweeping epic film in a minute-or-so-long trailer weren't working for me, as I couldn't find the narrative to respond to.

There are two interesting codas to this particular story. Steven Spielberg and the DreamWorks team didn't need an fMRI reading to know that the early trailers needed work. As it turned out, Spielberg found a solution to this at the Jacob Burns Film Center. Spielberg was being honored at the center as part of our Tenth Anniversary Celebration. When he saw the short film that one of our staff members, Todd Sandler, had put together, he was blown away. He congratulated Todd for his work and told him that in all the years of these kinds of "tribute films," not one had moved him the way this one had. As Todd turned away in tears, I knew that something special would happen. Two days later the phone call came. Todd was hired to take a shot at cutting some *War Horse* trailers for television.

When I had a chance to see his work, I thought it was terrific. He had built more of a narrative structure for the trailer, which gave me a fuller sense of the story. The *War Horse* team must have agreed, as they not only used Todd's spots on television, but they also had him recut the theatrical trailer, and ultimately replaced the earlier versions that had been sent out to movie theaters around the country with his. I was left wondering what the fMRI would have revealed while I watched Todd's new trailer, relative to the first two I saw.

Whether the new trailer brought in a bigger audience for the movie than the previous ones would have, we'll never know. When I had an opportunity to see the actual movie, I found myself very engaged—and immersed in an epic story told by one of the consummate filmmakers in a way that no one-minute-long trailer could have provoked. I was sure that my brain was well activated, even if this would escape detection by a whirling magnetic donut.

Still, this experience got me thinking. What did it say about the future of the moving image if one short clip about a Chilean social worker—made by a few students with equipment that cost a few hundred dollars—could engage me more on a neurological level than a trailer for a state-of-the-art production that cost hundreds of millions of dollars, plus a human army of technicians, actors, sound operators, executives, marketers, theater operators, and thousands of others? It told me that the possibilities for a more democratic form of expression were dazzling. This helped explain why Freddie Wong and his DIY approach was phenomenally successful. It also explained why simple visual ads often worked better than slick multimillion-dollar extravaganzas.

The prospect of this type of prescriptive testing of media to create the perfect stimulus for our "Buy button" is both seductive and repulsive.

Carlsen has worked extensively with self-proclaimed marketing expert Martin Lindstrom—author of *Buyology* and chairman of a consulting company with the same name. Named one of *Forbes*'s "Most Promising Companies" in 2011, Buyology says that it "utilizes its global neuroscience database to develop rigorous tools that bridge science and business so as to provide a provocative and proprietary understanding of consumer decision-making."

This global neuroscience database is in part constructed through fMRI scans of people viewing corporate logos, products, and advertisements. Lindstrom is a small but growing player in the almost $60 billion market for television advertising, which is supplemented by the close to $30 billion in additional money allocated to online advertising.

I asked Carlsen about my greatest fear as it relates to video: manipulative politics. He told me that MindSign had compiled the two-minute opening statements from the first Republican debate in New Hampshire and was preparing to bring in sixteen registered Republicans to study their brains upon viewing the statements in the hope of determining which candidate had the most effective opening. He predicted that within ten years, consumer product companies would be able prescriptively to create ads that drove purchases most effectively. Political candidates would have this power as well.

Not only is the sheer volume of images, in news and politics, and in advertising increasing at a staggering pace, but their effectiveness is increasing as well. Makers of these images are becoming more and more proficient at manipulating us. There is one clear path in response. We must develop the skills and proficiency with the grammar and tools of visual media to be better consumers— and to produce our own images.

■ THE EVOLUTION OF THE AUDIENCE

In making a speech one must study three points: first, the means of producing persuasion; second, the language; third, the proper arrangement of the various parts of the speech.

—ARISTOTLE

On March 5, 2012, a San Diego–based charity uploaded a thirty-minute video created by its founder and "grand storyteller and dreamer," a handsome and charismatic evangelical Christian named Jason Russell. The video was the latest in a string of media that began with the production of a 2003 documentary by Russell and two of his classmates, Bobby Bailey and Laren Poole, that bore the name of the nonprofit it ultimately brought to life: *Invisible Children.*

That film was first screened for family and friends at a San Diego community center, but then quickly found traction with the high school and college set. Shot on a small video camera, it followed three young white filmmakers as they traveled through Uganda exploring the plight of child soldiers and the scourge of the rebel leader of the Lord's Resistance Army, Joseph Kony.

The film, subtitled *Rough Cut*, was indeed rough, not at all slickly produced, yet it is just this kind of edgy quality that attracted its youthful audience; its immediacy and authenticity resonated.

Over the past eight years, the documentary has been seen by more than five million people at thousands of high schools, colleges, and places of worship and has spawned an organization that continues to focus on this issue. Still, nobody was prepared for the reaction to a short follow-up called *Kony 2012*.

This somewhat self-indulgent video began with the birth of Russell's son, Gavin, which became his motivation and audience for explaining the history of Joseph Kony and the need for the world to find him, so that children just like Gavin across the globe in Uganda could be safe. Russell encouraged viewers to demand U.S. military intervention to catch the Ugandan warlord by the end of 2012. "Make him famous," the video urged its viewers.

And this it did. The reaction was immediate—in its first week, the video had more than one hundred million views (forty million in just the first three days), and Kony suddenly became the most famous war criminal in the world since Pol Pot. In one stroke, the filmmakers had done what years of international diplomacy and UN reports had failed to accomplish.

What was also remarkable was the strength of the negative pushback against the video and its makers. Invisible Children was accused of trying to build donations (it sold thirty-dollar "action kits" containing wristbands and brochures) through exaggerating the scale and brutality of Kony's Lord's Resistance Army. There was little evidence that the LRA had been operating inside Uganda for the past six years, and informed observers speculated that Kony himself might be dead. When the film was screened in Uganda, audience members booed and threw objects at the screen in response to what they perceived as a patronizing and inaccurate film. The awareness of the film's deficiencies spread on blogs, tweets, and counter-videos nearly as fast as the film. A group called Uganda Speaks put together its own video to respond to the negative image and "American story" it said had been promulgated by Invisible Children. The pressure was apparently enough to drive Russell into an emotional crisis; San Diego police detained him the following month after he was spotted half-naked and yelling at passing cars in an episode of what his family called "extreme exhaustion."

But the video indisputably put Kony on the consciousness map not only of young people but also of U.S. policy makers. Six U.S. senators produced their own video in response, pledging their support. Chris Coons, the Delaware senator and chair of the Senate Foreign Relations Subcommittee on African Affairs, said, "The level of engagement we've seen from Americans—especially young Americans—because of the Kony 2012 movement has been truly extraordinary." He explained, "We had two goals in mind for this video: reiterating the Senate's deep bipartisan support for stopping Joseph Kony, and embracing and encouraging this once-in-a-generation interest in a humanitarian cause abroad. Because so many Americans first learned about Kony and the Lord's Resistance Army online, and because that's where people are talking to each other about it, we wanted to engage with interested Americans there, too."

Russell and Invisible Children answered their critics with the release of *Kony 2012: Part 2: Beyond Famous*. While this video has received far less attention or views than the original, its construction is significant. It begins with a rapid sequence of nineteen different clips from the mainstream international media first touting and then denouncing the earlier video. These images begin in a smaller frame nested within the screen and proceed to grow in size as the criticism mounts, until we hear a British broadcaster declare, "They haven't a clue what they are talking about." We then cut to a talking head, identified as Norbert Mao, former presidential candidate of Uganda, who attests that "this one grabs you by your gut and shakes you until you are forced to pay attention. That is the essence of awareness. People are now paying attention."

Russell and his associates were polarizing, but nobody can argue with their masterstroke of galvanizing interest through a compelling piece of visual media that could be distributed instantly with a click.

The seeds for this remarkable event, however, lay not only in the power of YouTube. They were sown further back in the history of the technological revolution—in the notion that the exercise of power lies mostly in what people *see* of their leaders and their enemies, and that the power to make people see things outside the official narrative, and to persuade them otherwise, has been slipping from the hands of the elite for at least a generation. Technology only accelerates this effect.

Though the realities of government are often tedious and hard to follow, we tend to make political decisions based on gut-level instincts and emotional impressions that come through our visual processing apparatus. It is no accident that the dawn of the electronic moving image should be so drenched in political content. Then again, the relentless gaze of the camera is a viewpoint with which we already have some comfort and literacy.

Think of the famous film of the last helicopter leaving the roof of the U.S. embassy in Saigon in 1975. Or even the 1963 Zapruder film, shot by a Dallas clothing manufacturer named Abraham Zapruder, an immigrant from Russia who went down to the edge of a presidential motorcade with an 8 mm Bell & Howell of the

Zoomatic Director Series, Model 414 PD—a top-of-the-line camera, the Flip of its day. He stood on the edge of a concrete plinth and asked his secretary, Marilyn Sitzman, to hold him steady while he waited for the president's limousine to roll past him in Dealey Plaza.

A common observation about the Zapruder film is that it was "accidental," and in one sense this is correct. Abraham Zapruder certainly did not leave his office in the Dal-Tex building with the intention of filming the murder of an American president. But in another sense, it was not accidental at all. Zapruder set out to capture the parade of a president, the meeting of the governor with the governed in a street theater of flaunted power that went back at least as far as Queen Elizabeth I. Zapruder may have intended his home movie to be shown only in his living room, to his family and a few bored friends, but for him it was supposed to be something special, the magic presence of the chief executive—a constructed political image. It has since entered the cultural vernacular, existing as a constructed image of a different sort.

Spontaneous violence and the random cameraman have become a well-known trope in American political discourse. Even before the era of pocket cell phones, it was a tool of the citizen against the abuses of the state. The violence itself is often a sharp distillation of a long and painful experience—existing not so much for its own power to outrage but for the lengthy narrative of outrage for which it serves as a touchstone.

This was the potency behind a grainy video shot by an unemployed plumber from Argentina named George Holliday, who stepped out onto the balcony of his cheap apartment off the freeway in the San Fernando Valley on March 3, 1991, and happened to see four Los Angeles police officers using a Taser on a man they had pulled over for drunk driving. Holliday's instinct was to reach for his camcorder and hit Record. In the video, we can see Rodney

King rise to his feet and start to move toward Officer Laurence Powell, who swats him with a baton. King falls and is set upon by other officers, who club him as he lies stationary on the ground.

Holliday called the LAPD the next morning and offered to show them what he considered to be a problem of excessive force that should be handled internally. He got the runaround and then decided the police weren't interested. So he took the footage to the KTLA television station, which broadcast the whole tape and turned it into a focal point for years of frustration between the African Americans of Los Angeles and what they considered the routinely heavy-handed tactics of the police. When the four officers were acquitted of assault three years later, portions of the city erupted in violence, as the community could not reconcile the verdict with the images they had seen in Holliday's video.

Multiple realities of modern America were revealed in the Rodney King episode, but none more so than the power of the average citizen to trigger momentous events simply through the use of a technology that was becoming democratically available.

Think what would have happened if George Holliday had gone to the LAPD with a verbal complaint about watching a drunk driver beaten up by the cops? They of course would have told him to get lost, but what if Holliday had then gone to the studios of KTLA and offered to tell his story on the air? They almost certainly would have told him to get lost. The power to shock was not in the verbal description, which is notoriously subject to interpretation and unreliability. Not even King's bruises would have been enough. To be "real" enough to be taken seriously, the event had to be *seen*. We had to *see* Officer Powell's baton striking the hapless King, to *see* those vicious baton blows being administered to a fallen man—and unless you are on a Los Angeles–area jury, those images are hard to deny.

What happened with Rodney King—as well as with Joseph

Kony—was a clash between old and new methods of literacy. In both cases, the underlying injustices had been written about and documented for years. Those who were paying attention knew all about the abuses of the LAPD in the African American community, and of Kony's slaughter in the Ugandan countryside. Reams of reports and data on each were available. But it took a video to galvanize the public at large, bringing a visceral emotional capstone to a mountain of written material. The video made it all "real." Make no mistake: the printed material provided the fuel for the outrage and put it in a proper and accurate context. But the moving images were the spark that lit the fire.

The ideology did not drive the message. *Technology* drove the message. And the widespread technology of the portable video camera and the security camera created the "language" of the grainy and eerie peek into what the authorities didn't want us to see.

As the media critic Dan Gilmor noted, "By 1991, home video gear was becoming common, heading toward today's near-ubiquity. When people saw that video, they realized a number of things, not least of which was the possibility that average citizens could hold powerful people—the police in this instance—somewhat more accountable for wrongdoing they committed in public places. Witnessing was being transformed into action, we all understood."

In May of 2006, the drugstore CVS became the first chain store to stock a very inexpensive disposable video camera, which was soon thereafter renamed the Flip. This product had two things going for it. First, it was as easy to use as a point-and-shoot. Second, it had its own Web-based software system for editing and distribution. Two million of these cameras were on the streets within two years, and in March 2009 the company was purchased by Cisco Systems for $590 million.

The Flip camera was poised for great commercial success when, just two years later, Cisco announced that it would be closing down all Flip operations and discontinuing the camera. This was not a result of the loss of interest in consumer-shot video. In fact, exactly the opposite. The Flip had found a market that then exploded on it. The camcorder that had preceded it required a lot more technical savvy to edit movies into new creations, but the Flip made this easy on a laptop. Then cell phone cameras began to do the same trick, and the release of the iPhone in 2009 helped seal the Flip's fate.

With more than a hundred million smartphones sold in just one quarter of 2011, it will not be long before most of us are walking around with devices in our pockets that not only make phone calls, but can capture and distribute video images worldwide at the push of a button. This is the pocket telegraph of our time. And a startling portion of the content being zinged around the globe by ordinary individuals is overtly political in its content. In short, the era of the Flip is flipping political discourse.

The 2008 U.S. presidential campaign was the first to feature a significant amount of video pamphleteering that didn't air on television but on computers. What was striking about the new wave of campaign videos was that the really popular ones were not created by political consultants with their stacks of money and reams of polling data. For example, the musician will.i.am created the enormously popular "Yes We Can" video lauding Barack Obama, which was seen more than fifteen million times.

Image making is no longer solely in the hands of the candidate or his opponent, because it no longer takes significant time or resources to create these pieces or to disseminate them. This will continue to change politics at both the national and the local levels. It is also changing the very nature of the role of the political journalist.

A gruesome but important example took place on the night of December 30, 2006, when a Shiite guard in a prison in the Baghdad suburb of Kaizmain surreptitiously captured footage of the crude and chaotic hanging of Saddam Hussein. Within moments of the act, anyone with access to the Internet, regardless of where he lived on this planet, could watch this historic execution (carried out in amateurish and thuggish fashion) and intuitively understand the event in a way that written reports would struggle to communicate with equal intensity. This chronicle was not done by a reporter, but by an extremely biased individual taking pleasure in the execution. Even George W. Bush had to concede that the proceedings "looked like a revenge killing," and they brought embarrassment to the new government of Nouri al-Maliki. This was no constructed piece of documentary reporting, but rather a "home movie" that happened to be a snuff film, one that was shared with millions of people in an instant, a raw slice of an event with no embellishment or interpretation. Scholars would call it a "primary source"—the genuine article—that also symbolically stood for the closing of an era. This may seem like a new development in the visual literacy of politics, but it was actually the culmination of a force that has been building a long time in international politics, à la JFK, Saigon, and Rodney King.

Quite often, as in the examples just given, the most compelling of politicized images involves violence. In 2000, international furor erupted after a gunfight in the Palestinian Territories in which a boy named Muhammad al-Durrah was killed in a hail of bullets. Incidents like this are far too common in war zones around the world, and their casualties rendered as statistics in the news columns, but what set this incident apart was that it was captured on video by a freelance cameraman for the French 2 news station. The video shows the heartbreaking and pathetic image of Muhammad's father trying futilely to shield his son from the onslaught.

Controversy has swirled ever since as to who actually fired the shots—the Israel Defense Forces insist it wasn't they, and argue that their position didn't allow for bullets to reach the boy and his father, who were crouched behind a concrete barrel. Still, the video was disseminated far and wide, supported with commentary by newscasters in studios explaining that we were seeing the boy and his father die as victims of IDF soldiers, and it was widely seen as a diorama of Israeli heartlessness. The pose of the father and son ended up on posters and postage stamps. In *The Atlantic Monthly*, James Fallows writes, "The image of a boy shot dead in his helpless father's arms during an Israeli confrontation with Palestinians has become the Pietà of the Arab world."

But to this day, there are more questions than answers around what actually happened that day. France 2 has refused to make public the section of the video that purportedly shows the boy's death agonies, although others argue that this footage might actually exonerate the IDF. More important, the video does not show the positions of the combatants firing bullets at the father and son, and it is left unclear whether they were hit by bullets from Israeli or Palestinian forces. Visual symbolism is enormously powerful when it comes to moving images, and careful viewers must also be aware of what is *not* seen in the frame, and is only implied.

What actually happened to Muhammad al-Durrah might forever remain a mystery, but one thing that all sides can agree on is the way a video, even a questionable one, put the incident into an exalted position. In his *Atlantic* article, Fallows concludes: "The images intensify the self-righteous determination of each side. If anything, modern technology has aggravated the problem of mutually exclusive realities. With the Internet and TV, each culture now has a more elaborate apparatus for 'proving,' dramatizing, and disseminating its particular truth."

Recognizing this, human rights organizations within Israel

such as Witness, B'Tselem, and Videre have given away video cameras to local individuals and trained them to document and publicize acts of violence. Documentary filmmaker Yoav Gross of B'Tselem explains that his group "spent more than twenty years writing reports and issuing press releases" that were largely ignored; yet when they began to use video to capture images of routine abuse, not only were these stories picked up by the media and broadcast on national networks, but they also inspired strong reaction and debate within Israeli society.

More recently, we watched electronically as unrest and revolution arose in the Arab Spring. Masses of people convened to protest against their autocratic governments in places such as Tunisia, Egypt, Libya, and Syria. Hosni Mubarak did not have controls to block images from being broadcast from Cairo's Tahir Square, and these were captured and shared both on stations such as Al Jazeera and across the Web twenty-four hours a day. Facebook posts and Twitter text messages were credited with being the tech channels for the revolution. But this is only partly true. The oxygen that fueled international pressure and support for the demonstrators were the provocative video images being shared with the world in perhaps the most heavily documented uprising in world history, complete with video of soldiers on horseback charging the square.

In the years ahead, there will be many more of these moments shot and shared—news that would never have been considered "news" before—as we become the most documented society that has ever existed, powered like never before by bystanders who "just happened to be there." Cameras are becoming almost ubiquitous, and the channels of distribution are easily accessible. Mainstream media outlets such as the BBC, CNN, and Fox News are relying more and more on images provided by citizen journalists not connected with any news-gathering operation—and usually not compensated for their footage.

Still, as viewers of these images, we have many questions to ask. What happened before or after the camera was recording, and how might that footage change the story? What is outside the frame that might help tell a different story? Who is shooting the footage, and who is distributing it, and what agendas might they have?

Those last three questions were of paramount concern in the September 2012 riots in Libya, which provided cover for a terrorist operation that claimed the lives of three Americans, including the ambassador, J. Christopher Stevens. Angry crowds had stormed the embassy in a protest over a meretricious piece of video that emanated from California—a badly shot promotional trailer advertising a D-grade propaganda movie called *Innocence of Muslims*, which depicted the prophet Muhammad in an unflattering light. That it depicted him at all was already an offense to Muslims, who believe that such images deify the Prophet and steal glory away from God.

The crowds were led to believe from Egyptian media reports that the video—uploaded to YouTube, of course, where it could be seen by millions—was a product of Hollywood, produced and directed by a transplanted Israeli, and therefore represented the beliefs of the United States at large as well as the Jews. But the maker, as it turns out, was Nakata Bassely Nakata, a fringe character, an Egyptian Coptic Christian living in Cerritos, California, who had been in prison for bank fraud. He shot part of the trailer in his own house using actors who had been misled into thinking they were shooting an adventure movie called *Desert Warriors*. The offensive dialogue was dubbed in later.

Here we have a case of an ordinary person in obscurity being able to move world events with a camera and a computer. But the example is a dismal one. There is a comparison to be made here with the Nazi filmmaker Leni Riefenstahl, whose film *Triumph of the Will* helped cement racial stereotypes and create villains of innocents in the 1930s. The comparison is only partial, though, because Riefenstahl had access to the best equipment and crews that the Reich had to offer. She was also a talented filmmaker. The makers of *Innocence of Muslims* were neither well-equipped nor talented. But their race-baiting was impeccable. They were "visually literate" in the way only a bully could be.

There is another point to the Libyan riots that went almost unmentioned in the days afterward. The filmmaker knew that the "sore spot" of Muhammad's image was a very sensitive one, and they pounded it with a hammer. Yet it would have had a diluted effect—or no effect at all—if the targeted audience were visually literate enough themselves to ask critical questions about the material. Who was producing it? Why was this message being sent? What is the intended effect? Demagogues cease to have any power when we can see beyond their lies and deceptions. But such questions were not asked by that mob.

Addressing the United Nations General Assembly, President Obama addressed the "crude and disgusting video [that] sparked outrage throughout the Muslim world."* He felt compelled to reiterate that the United States government was in no way involved in the video's production or dissemination, yet also defended the values of freedom of speech—and video. He continued: "I know that not all countries in this body share this particular understanding of the protection of free speech . . . But in 2012, at a time when anyone with a cell phone can spread offensive views around the world with the click of a button, the notion that we can control the flow of information is obsolete. The question, then, is how do we respond?" I believe that the only way to control response is to

---

*While President Obama's initial focus on the video-inspired protests rather than the terrorist actions became a major election issue and resulted in a shift of momentum, there is little doubt about the Libyans' deep offense at the video.

prepare people around the world with the literacy tools to question and critically consume the extraordinary volume of media they will be exposed to.

This movie was a fiction, but similar questions of "framing" are central to factual material as well. What is being left out of the shot? With filmmakers who have an axe to grind, there is a temptation to cut corners and simplify things to the point where the camera is *not* telling the whole story. Everything that you might consider in framing and shooting a documentary or narrative film in a more controlled setting can inform the shots you get surreptitiously and can help make that footage more effective.

We must also consider the ethics around privacy and the distribution of certain images in these circumstances, as they can have an impact both in ways you imagined and intended, and in ways unimaginable and unintended. Once images are in the public's view, they in essence have a life of their own—again, Rodney King and JFK—divorced from the creator, and subject to interpretation as their own reality.

And when these are grafted onto another image, a whole new conception of reality can take hold—for better or for worse.

The political power of the heroic image was well known to people of antiquity, who cast statues of their leaders in order to inspire respect, awe, and a sense of "that's just how things are" between the people and those who governed them.

Power, wrote the classic scholar Jas' Elsner, "is as much a matter of impression, of theatre, of persuading those over whom authority is wielded to collude in their subjugation. Insofar as power is a matter of presentation, its cultural currency in antiquity (and still today) was the creation, manipulation, and display of images."

The Romans understood that their leaders had to be seen as

elevated personages, almost demigods, in order to command subjects who would never know them personally and perhaps never
see them in the flesh. Statues were routinely commissioned to
portray figures such as Augustus, Trajan, and Pompey in heroic
garb, wearing garlands and holding spears. These served as remind-
ers of a ruler's majesty and benevolence, and perhaps as vague
threats, deterrents to revolt. Their effect, however, was necessarily
local. The statues could not travel across distances or have projec-
tive effects, unless the citizens or slaves traveled to them. When
they did, the statues' craftsmanship spoke loudly. Here is somebody who was able to pay or intimidate some of the best artists in
the known world to shape their faces out of stone or bronze. Such a
man—even if in image—is worthy of obedience. Coins with royal
heads stamped upon them later performed the same function.

A fundamental shift in the nature of political image making
occurred in Gutenberg's era, when it became possible for the first
time to create mass-produced images through mechanical means
that didn't involve foundries or minting coins. As such, these
images were not individually crafted by an artist but rapidly
produced by a journeyman. The process only accelerated with photography.

In his classic 1936 essay "The Work of Art in the Age of
Mechanical Reproduction," Walter Benjamin said that the process
of sending an image around the world strips it of a certain authenticity and immediacy, which he called "the aura" that surrounds an
original production. There is a difference between in seeing a print
of Pierre-Auguste Renoir's *Luncheon of the Boating Party* on a dorm
room wall and seeing the original work hanging in the Phillips
Collection in Washington, D.C. "One might generalize by saying:
the technique of reproduction detaches the reproduced object from
the domain of tradition," writes Benjamin. "By making many re-
productions it substitutes a plurality of copies for a unique exis-

tence." What is gained by distribution, in other words, is offset by the loss of immediate experience.

He elaborates: "An ancient statue of Venus, for example, stood in a different traditional context with the Greeks, who made it an object of veneration, than with the clerics of the Middle Ages, who viewed it as an ominous idol. Both of them, however, were equally confronted with its uniqueness, that is, its aura."

With traditional images of political power, that immediate experience of aura was sucked into the eyes in an all-at-once understanding of where authority lay. The live display of royal pomp was an important element of the "theater of power" used by British sovereigns to impress and intimidate their subjects. Queen Elizabeth I was a mistress of the procession, which featured parades through London led by a platoon of nobles dressed in their finery, followed by court flunkies bearing the scepter and the sword of state, and then the queen herself, the train of her gown being carried by a female courtier. To observers from the street, the effect was said to be transfixing. The vision of the exalted personage was enough to call forth strong feelings of loyalty and patriotism.

This was nothing that needed to be "read"—it had to be swallowed whole by the eye, and has been replicated time and time again, recently in the storybook wedding of Britain's Prince William and his bride, Kate Middleton, which was broadcast live to more than a hundred million viewers on television and to even more than this number of viewers watching a live stream on the Internet.

Political images are much less logical than they let on—in fact, they rely on the image makers' ability to tap into primitive emotional centers that govern adaptive urges such as fear, comfort, and love.

This is why the constructed images of modern American political ads so often rely on tones and "feelings" rather than hard data about the candidates. This was on vivid display in what many historians consider to be the first widely circulated negative television ad in a presidential campaign: the "daisy" ad used by Lyndon Johnson against Barry Goldwater in 1964.

A young girl is plucking petals off a daisy in a meadow and counting up to ten. When she reaches that number, a harsh male military voice that seems as if it would be right at home at Strategic Air Command takes over and begins counting down from ten, as the camera zooms to a still shot of the girl's terrified eye. Then a nuclear mushroom cloud envelops the screen, and a voice-over of Johnson's voice can be heard, echoing a poem by W. H. Auden. "These are the stakes," he says. "To make a world in which all of God's children can live, or to go into the dark. We must either love each other, or we must die." An announcer then implores, "Vote for President Johnson on November 3. The stakes are too high for you to stay home."

The visuals were chilling: few things can tug at the emotions like a child at risk, and the nuclear blast at the end was made for the viewer to understand as a worldwide burning of all children. The voice of LBJ comes across as fatherly and soothing, in a time of increased rancor with the Soviet Union and the belligerent rhetoric of Goldwater, which Johnson's team was trying to cast as a temptation to war.

The ad aired only once. Johnson's team pulled it after a flood of criticism, but it still got wide attention because television reporters seized on it as a story, and its images received repeated free airplay for weeks. This enshrined a method in the minds of political consultants henceforth. Your imagery and your message could be outrageous, but as long as they were emotionally affecting, they stood a chance of being talked about in the news with far more impact than if you had had to pay for them every time they aired. The campaign could back away from the extreme message and still reap the benefits from the visuals.

In this dismal art form, one name stands out from the rest: Willie Horton. His name wasn't even Willie—it was William—but Willie sounded "blacker" to Lee Atwater, a consultant for George H. W. Bush in the 1988 presidential campaign. Horton had been on furlough from a Massachusetts prison when he raped a woman in Maryland. Atwater seized on the incident as evidence that the Democratic candidate, Massachusetts governor Mike Dukakis, was "soft on crime." A cheap ad featuring a police mug shot of Horton ran just a few times on local cable stations, but it was enough to elevate the incident into a turning point in the election. The ad received hundreds of hours of news coverage.

"The mug shot of Horton was obviously the most emotionally powerful image in the ad, playing on every white person's fears of the dangerous, lawless, violent dark black male," wrote the Emory University neuroscientist Drew Westen. "Research shows that even subliminal presentation of black faces activates the amygdala in whites, and implicit racial appeals are far more effective than explicit ones because they don't raise people's conscious attitudes toward racism." Willie Horton became a household name, as Atwater predicted, not because of the hazy facts of the case—the furlough law had been signed by a Republican governor—but because the menacing face got such intense news coverage.

Few in American political life were better at riding free news coverage on pure visuals than our first actor-president, Ronald Reagan, whose advisers learned during his first term that the handsome, wrinkly president looked best when surrounded by flags and red-white-and-blue bunting, and they took pains to wrap him in such at every public appearance. Television coverage, even when negative or cynical, usually framed the president in those images, and those were what the viewers tended to remember.

When providing commentary at the 1984 Republican convention to renominate Reagan, the NBC anchor Tom Brokaw noted just what a contrivance the proceedings would be. "This will be an evening of scripted, colorful pageantry, kind of like an old-fashioned MGM musical, in which thousands of people and bands and balloons and confetti will move right on cue directed by an unseen hand," said Brokaw. "And at the climactic moment, Ronald Reagan, just like his good friend Fred Astaire, will glide into view." But Brokaw's comments made no difference. The spectacle of the Gipper as the American nonpareil was what went straight up the ventral stream of the viewing audience.

In her memoir, *Reporting Live*, the CBS reporter Lesley Stahl remembered doing a critical story about Reagan cutting funding for public health and opposing the expansion of programs to help children with disabilities. The segment was five minutes long, extremely verbose for network TV news, and was illustrated with footage of the president speaking to residents of a nursing home. She wondered what kind of a reaction she'd get from the president's team, and sure enough, adviser Richard Darman called her that night.

"Way to go, kiddo," he told her. "What a great piece. We loved it."

"Didn't you hear what I said?" Stahl replied, wondering if they had bothered to listen to her critical reporting of Reagan.

"Nobody heard what you said."

"Come again?" she asked.

"You guys in Televisionland haven't figured it out, have you?" said Darman. "When the pictures are powerful and emotional, they override if not completely drown out the sound. I mean it, Lesley. Nobody heard you."

This is a sad reality of political discourse in the visual age, which the makers of *Kony 2012* well understood. Facts matter much less than images. The 1992 presidential campaign between Bill Clinton and George H. W. Bush included an ad whose production values could have come from a zombie movie. The ad, called "Arkansas," depicted Governor Clinton as doubling the state's debt, doubling spending, and signing the largest tax increase in the state's history, yet ignored the record of prosperity and job creation that the then-governor had also left behind. It featured ominous black-and-white shots of a country road in twilight, blowing grass, forked lightning, and gathering clouds, complete with a whistling that sounded like the moaning of damned souls. "Now Bill Clinton wants to do for America what he did for Arkansas," summed up an urgent female voice, the voice of a scolding mother. Bad lighting can be used to create a sinister image around even Billy Graham, and this is the most common negative technique used in hundreds of congressional races across the nation every two years. The grammar in these ads is as plain as that in Dick and Jane primers.

These kinds of ads feature the "good guy" (your candidate) surrounded by positive images such as children and veterans, with the camera shooting the candidate from slightly below and in crisp focus, but with soft lighting to make him look powerful but compassionate. The bad guy (the opponent), meanwhile, is shot with bad production values, grainy like those from a security camera, often out of focus, and shot from either way below or way above to make him look, respectively, either sinister or weak and out of touch. Ominous music lends the further impression that the opponent is a greedy troll. And if you're lucky, the local TV news will do a story on your opponent denouncing your outrageous and misleading ad, thereby handing lots of free coverage your way. Even a "fact check" of the ad results in a replaying of those images.

After analyzing the way negative ads get a lot more steam from free media, Kathleen Hall Jamieson at the University of Pennsylvania proposed a different kind of "visual grammar" for covering negative television ads. She suggested framing them inside a graphic of a television set and then using a rubber stamp–like graphic to brand them as either "accurate" or "misleading." To cover the ad by playing it in the full screen runs the risk of giving it an unintended free ride, as the audience might not even listen to what the fact check has concluded.

We are slaves not to what we know, but to what we see, and this is how we elect our presidents.

There is hardly a book on the modern presidency that does not mention one particular turning point in the way Americans perceived their choice of commander in chief: the television debates between John F. Kennedy and Richard Nixon. These four encounters helped decide the election and have been a classic parable of image-based politics ever since.

In the first debate, held on September 26, 1960, in the studios of WBBM in Chicago, Nixon appeared tired and edgy, even a bit desperate, as he spoke into the unforgiving vacancy of the cameras. He wore a charcoal suit that bunched at the waist. The physical awkwardness of Nixon was on display, even as his actual spoken performance was on target. Kennedy came across as relaxed and confident, the picture of American hopefulness, sleek as a jaguar in a dark suit and shiny shoes. He spoke about developing the full potential of the United States, and the charisma oozed from him.

What viewers didn't know was that Kennedy had spent most of the day getting a suntan on top of a hotel roof and had taken a nap just an hour before the event. Nixon had been recovering from a hospital stay for a knee injury and had banged the injured knee on the car door on the way into the studios. His aides had applied a product called Lazy Shave to his cheeks, to blunt the image of a dark-whiskered menace, but his nerve-induced flop sweat began to melt this product as he spoke.

Nixon was arguably better briefed on the issues than his challenger—and a small and unscientific poll of radio listeners in Philadelphia showed a listener preference for Nixon—but none of that mattered to the TV-viewing audience. The polls took a turn after the debates, and Kennedy squeaked out an upset victory. Just as the secret intentions of the author can be communicated only on the contents of the page, the motives and contradictions of a political figure are both revealed and concealed in the wordless visual image he projects—the accoutrements of a simple human face.

It is part of the accepted folklore of the debates that Kennedy was the master of the image and understood that the power of television could reach into a voter's mind and transform her thinking about which candidate to choose or which political platform to support. After the election, Kennedy himself is supposed to have said, "It was TV more than anything else that turned the tide." Nixon drew the same lesson: "I spent too much time in the last campaign on substance and too little time on appearance," he said, in a candid moment. "One bad camera angle on television can have far more effect on the election outcome than a major mistake in writing a speech." Nixon used television images with alacrity in his next presidential campaign, in 1968, which was noteworthy for its scripted precision and its carefully cultivated portrayal of a "New Nixon." The author Joe McGinness wrote a precise and devastating account of the television-friendly campaign in his book *The Selling of the President*, which further elevated the mythology of the 1960 debates.

But Kennedy was hardly the first to discover the principle of the refracted human face or to manipulate it. He had tapped into a lever in the psyche more primal than mere facts, yet one that has been pulled by leaders long before him. The bearing and aspect of a man is important in person, yet that handicap can be overcome with a disassociated image sent out widely, one that stands in for the man himself.

The first presidential candidate to use film in a campaign was William McKinley, who was facing off in 1896 against the Nebraska populist William Jennings Bryan, perhaps one of the most energetic orators the nation has ever produced. Bryan made spellbinding appeals to the decency of the common man and the rapacity of big-money interests back east, for whom McKinley had sympathy. A debate between the two of them would have ended in disaster for McKinley and the Republicans. Mark Hanna, McKinley's campaign manager, recognized the possibility of a "virtual campaign" and simply invited reporters to come interview the candidate on his front porch in Canton, Ohio. Among the guests was the founder of American Mutoscope, W.K.L. Dickson, who worked up a hokey reenactment of McKinley "receiving the news" that he had been nominated at the convention. Pure theater, but the little loop played in nickelodeons across the country and gave McKinley a stateliness that he arguably had not earned. He had become the first American presidential candidate to appear on film, and the "presidential looks" of a contender would soon become more important than his ideas.

That election and its lessons were still reverberating when a fateful meeting took place. When the political boss Harry Daugherty first spotted Warren G. Harding outside the Globe Hotel in Richwood, Ohio, he developed an instant man-crush. Here was a man, Daugherty realized, whose visual charm could win an election. The historian Mark Sullivan reimagined the moment:

Harding was worth looking at. He was at the time about 35 years old. His head, features, shoulders and torso had a size that attracted attention . . . an effect which in any male at any place would justify more than the term handsome—in later years, when he came to be known beyond his local world, the word 'Roman' was occasionally used in descriptions of him . . . His suppleness, combined with his bigness of frame, and his large, wide-set rather glowing eyes, heavy black hair, and markedly bronze complexion gave him some of the handsomeness of an Indian.

Daugherty went on to mastermind Harding's campaign for the U.S. Senate and his Republican nomination for president in 1920. The image makers that surrounded Harding promoted a "front-porch campaign" very much like McKinley's, an exercise in media manipulation in which Harding supposedly campaigned for the office only from the porch of his home in Marion, Ohio. Mass-circulated images and films of the kindly and handsome small-town senator serving iced lemonade to his neighbors and jawing about current events were charming and reassuring to a public increasingly relying upon newsreels to aid their sense of who the candidates were purporting to be. Harding's easy good looks also helped him with female voters, who had just been given the right of universal suffrage. Harding would become a dismal figure as chief executive, overseeing a scandal-plagued administration and complaining privately that he'd never been up to the job. He died mysteriously in San Francisco after eating a plate of spoiled crabmeat.

He was, of course, not the first man to enter the White House based on a certain "look" the voters craved. Abraham Lincoln was born with a voice pitched higher than normal, and it worked against him in his spoken performances, but he had a striking face, the visage of a frontier Cicero, which reinforced his nonvisual persona as an honest lawyer from the countryside. His campaign for the presidency in 1860 featured photographs of him sent out to political meetings all over the nation. An aide to Lincoln thanked the photographer Mathew Brady after the election, just as Kennedy credited television. "I am coming to believe," said the aide, "that likenesses broad cast, are excellent means of electioneering."

The reverse was also true. Brady photographed the New York City mayor William Magear Tweed and made him look equally commanding and honest. But as the scholar Kiku Adatto has pointed out, the truly revealing images of "Boss Tweed" were the merciless political cartoons being drawn by Thomas Nast in *Harper's Weekly* that depicted the mayor as the fat king of patronage and bribes. "Stop those damn pictures," Tweed is supposed to have demanded of his flunkies at City Hall. "I don't care so much what the papers write about me. My constituents can't read. But damn it, they can see pictures."

Before the era of mass-produced photography, those engraved images that Nast used to such effect were an important tool of American political communication. Images of the war hero George Washington were widely distributed throughout the new colonies in a way that made him out to be like a Roman conqueror. "Not a king in Europe but would look like a valet de chambre by his side," said the London *Morning Post*, not without a hint of sarcasm. When Gilbert Stuart was hired to come paint Washington's official portrait, he found "features in his face totally different from what I had observed in any other human being. The sockets of the eyes, for instance, were larger than what I had ever met before, and the upper part of the nose broader. All his features were indicative of the strongest passions, yet, like Socrates, his judgment and self-command made him appear of a different cast in the eyes of the world." Stuart said that if Washington had been born among a savage tribe in the wilderness, he would have become their chief by default.

What has changed in the electronic visual age is the way the studio of political imagery is open to anyone. Instead of coming from a candidate or party or a political action committee, images are emerging from the initiative of voters who are discovering the ease of use of cameras and editing software.

A tawdry episode from 2010 shows the fuzzy line between the spontaneous and the constructed. A U.S. Department of Agriculture employee named Shirley Sherrod was giving a talk at an NAACP Freedom Fund dinner when she described how she came to help a white farmer secure some assistance. She did so reluctantly, she says, explaining, "What he didn't know, while he was taking all that time trying to show me he was superior to me, was I was trying to decide just how much help I was going to give him. I was struggling with the fact that so many black people had lost their farmland. And here I was faced with having to help a white person save their land. So, I didn't give him the full force of what I could do." Later on in the speech, she explained that she had come to realize that his skin color did not matter, and that her government service was about helping all people in need. But the video was leaked to conservative blogger Andrew Breitbart, who chose not to tell the whole story, but rather manipulated the experience for viewers by posting only the first section, which, taken out of context, is damning, as Sherrod appears to be saying the white man's skin color had worked against him. Fox News commentator Bill O'Reilly broadcast the video on his program the same day Sherrod was forced to resign by nervous White House officials.

The quality of the video itself added to the content of what was actually said. Sherrod, a heavyset, middle-aged African American woman, is wearing a professional suit and rimless glasses, and is standing behind a lectern. The camera is positioned about twenty feet away from her. She sways back and forth gently as she speaks, and her bearing is confident. Her face is expressive, and she rolls her eyes as she talks about believing that the white farmer was trying to assert his superiority. She is surrounded by a small crescent of black faces, both old and young.

How the viewers perceived Sherrod had a lot to do with their preexisting bias (much like, I might add, the preexisting bias Sherrod recognized and corrected in herself, which was the very point of the talk). You could see a practical, accomplished professional woman speaking from a perspective of wise authority. Or you could see an oppressive and even aggressive representative of an overreaching government trying to exact some petty revenge for the racial injustices of the previous century. That America was in the first term of its first black president only added to the racial dimensions of this kerfuffle, which touched an old nerve in American public life.

There was another element: the video had an uncontrived look to it. The picture is a bit grainy and unprofessional, the coloring fuzzy. The lighting was "off." It looked like it had been created by an amateur, which it had. This only heightened the sense that what Sherrod was saying was a moment ripped from obscurity, a shocking admission that "people were not supposed to hear," a kind of unguarded moment taken out of its private context and displayed to the public as an exposé, posing the question in viewers' minds: *If we caught her saying this when she thought only a few people could hear her, what else is she saying when the camera is not around to catch her?*

The effect would have been quite different if the video had been professionally produced and lit, and the whole speech made immediately available to the public. Sherrod's statements would undoubtedly have seemed more acceptable—and less vulnerable to manipulation by citizen journalists such as Breitbart, who played on his readers' lack of visual literacy.

That was the whole irony of the video. To watch the full forty-three-minute speech was to see an encouraging example of a woman who had refused to allow her beliefs to be manipulated by the pressures of history or of her own first impulses. It was a sophisticated take on race, somewhat similar to President Obama's famous speech in Philadelphia that acknowledged the lack of easy answers in this question that has haunted the United States ever since the first shipload of slaves arrived at Jamestown.

The iconography of race, class, and politics is one of the most powerful tools a filmmaker can use, and this brings us to a film called *9500 Liberty*, which tells the story of an immigration law passed in Prince William County, Virginia, in 2007. Anticipating Arizona's harsh documentation law by several years, this local ordinance required police chiefs to inquire into the immigration status of anyone they stopped who showed "probable cause" for not holding a U.S. passport or other correct documents. The roots of the crisis were economic: the county had thrived in the nineties, and there were a lot of construction jobs available for unskilled laborers. Many of these laborers had come up from Mexico or other Central American nations. This annoyed and frightened a number of locals, including a blogger named Greg Letiecq, who publicly fretted about the proliferation of Spanish signs and the possible influx of gang members and drugs. His blog had previously been concerned about Islamic terrorism and was filled with images of training camps in Afghanistan. When he switched to illegal immigration as a top concern, he started creating videos for his website, using images of shadowy figures jumping fences in Arizona—stock footage that television reporters are also fond of when illustrating stories about illegal immigration. The times changed, said one observer, but the ancient question remained the same: *Who among us is one of them?*

Letiecq started a pressure group called Help Save Manassas,

and persuaded the county board chairman to back the resolution cracking down on illegal workers and their families, who by that point constituted about 20 percent of the population.

Two people sat up and took notice: Eric Byler, a Chinese American from a nearby county in Virginia, and Annabel Park, a Korean American who'd grown up in Texas. They heard of the confrontation brewing and showed up with a camera to document what was happening.

Their film, *9500 Liberty*, took its title from the address of a vacant lot where a man named Guadencio Fernandez had erected a giant sign: "Prince William Co. Stop Your Racism to Hispanics," it read. "We Do the Jobs That Nobody Else Wants to Do." Passersby added their own notes to the sign, either for or against. Eventually somebody tried to burn the sign down. It became a symbol for the nasty little "civil war," as one man termed it, that had erupted in the county over questions of lawbreaking, American identity, and overreaching government.

Byler and Park recorded footage of residents arguing with one another and shots of the defaced sign in the lot at 9500 Liberty, and realized they were in the middle of something very important. Rather than simply observe and document with their cameras until the story had completely played out (and they had a feature-length documentary), and realizing that the power and immediacy of these images lay not just in their documenting a story, they decided to influence the story while it was unfolding. They posted some of their unfinished video to YouTube. This drew wide attention to the controversy.

"We gradually came to realize that the footage we were capturing was vital to the public," Byler told me. "It was our duty as citizens to share it."

With editing and postproduction, the spontaneous images were molded into a constructed whole. A remarkable aspect of the film is the video shot inside the meetings of the county board. Government meetings are not usually regarded as arenas for high drama, but some of the film's finest moments come when members of the public were invited to approach the microphone and state their support or opposition to the law. At one point, Robert Duecaster, a cofounder of Help Save Manassas, says, "It's about an invasion of this county. This county is being invaded no less as if a horde of armed people came across it borders. This invasion is not armed, but it's got weapons. The weapons they use are its anchor babies . . . Mark these words, we are going to repel this invasion."

9500 Liberty is an unusual piece of political imagery that straddles the border between constructed and spontaneous. Park and Byler captured a litany of spontaneous moments that stand as expressions of the deep divide that had emerged in Prince William County. In an opening scene, an agitated man in a baseball cap and glasses comes up to a group of Latinos near the sign and berates them for not knowing English. Park herself starts to argue with the man. The camera cuts to a young girl, who appears to be eight years old, who says, almost to herself, "The Indians were here first."

You can see the dawning consciousness of herself as both native and immigrant, in the midst of one of the oldest disputes known to mankind: Who belongs here?

The scenes from the Prince William County board meetings themselves were iconic in that they captured local government at work, the building blocks of what we consider American self-government. They were full of passion and even occasionally nasty, but wholly representative of the "public meetings" of our old New England roots.

In a self-conscious piece of scene setting, the filmmakers took some opening shots of the nearby Civil War battlefield of Manassas. That battle was the first big armed confrontation of the clash between North and South, fought in July of 1861, a conflict that surprised both sides with its heavy casualties and particular viciousness, a foretaste of the nearly four-year conflict that was to follow. Like most Civil War battlefields across the mid-Atlantic region, Manassas is regarded as "hallowed ground," and its soil protected from development by the National Park Service. Byler and Park make visual use of the silent cannons and grassy expanses in an opening establishing shot, pointing out without using words that America has fought over questions of racial identity and economic justice before. One man is interviewed in front of a ceremonial cannon near an old railroad depot that was a target of the Union Army during the battle; it happened to be right across the street from Fernandez's polarizing sign.

The filmmakers looked for ways in which they could relate their story in images as opposed to words. The camera captures a meeting of Help Save Manassas, the group pushing for the anti-immigrant legislation. All of the attendees are white, and nearly all are over fifty years old. "We didn't have to say it," said Park. "We could just pan the room."

Another pan shot that has wordless emotional effect: the parking lot of a grocery store called Giant Food, which is deserted except for a taxi driver taking a break. Weeds grow in the asphalt cracks. The shot is contrasted with an interview with the economist Stephen Fuller, who explains how the climate of fear surrounding the ordinance has drained away a good portion of Prince William County's customer base, leaving struggling retail stores and empty homes in the breach. Park and Byler also captured a pathetic image of a lone child on a bicycle riding through a landscape of For Sale signs. The message: he has lost all his friends in the economic disaster. One sign, which might describe the boy or Prince William County itself, reads HOME FOR SALE, OWNER DESPERATE!

9500 Liberty is a wordy, talky film—which is not surprising, as it is in essence about a community dialogue, about the power of words in a community—but the power of the film, its emotional core, is found in its images.

You don't need to be a professional filmmaker to command the language of visual expression to make change occur. Ordinary people now have tremendous power to do just that.

Here is one story out of many that could be told:

The parents of Danny Chen certainly had an insatiable thirst to make a difference. Their son enlisted as a private in the U.S. Army and was deployed to Afghanistan. On October 3, 2011, Chen was found dead, in what the military termed "an apparent self-inflicted gun wound" in his guard tower somewhere in the Kandahar province of Afghanistan. He was nineteen years old.

Chen's parents were distraught by the news of their only child's death, and felt in their bones that there was more to the story than just suicide. In letters to his family, their son had been detailing instances of abuse and humiliation around race by his peers and platoon leaders. The Chens wanted to know the truth of the circumstances surrounding their son's death. Concerned that the military would pass this off as just another suicide and not investigate further, they turned for help to the New York chapter of the Organization of Chinese Americans (OCA-NY), who got Chen's story in *The New York Times* and other media outlets. But it didn't seem to move anything at the Pentagon.

Liz OuYang at OCA-NY knew that they needed to find a better way to convince people that they should care about the Chen case, and to pressure the military to do something. The family wanted to convey their loss, tell a story about their suspicions around the case, and get others to ask these questions and demand an investigation. The group understood that as important as print media could be, "visual media would have a bigger impact." Together with the Chen family, a New York University graduate named ManSee Kong decided to create a video asking, "What Happened to Danny Chen?" shot with a cheap video camera.

They shot everything in one day, and OuYang and Kong spent just a few days more sitting in front of Kong's six-year-old Apple laptop computer editing the piece. The video begins with several people talking about what they are most looking forward to during the holidays. Each of the subjects is nicely framed—placed comfortably to the side of the screen—and speaks easily and happily. Several people into this sequence, Lily Woo, identified as the principal of P.S. 130 in Chinatown, says that she is happy that each holiday season "so many of our graduates come home to visit us." Holiday piano music has been playing softly, but the music fades and Woo says, "But Danny won't be one of them."

The film cuts to a group of Danny's friends asking, "What happened to Danny?" They are shot in a diagonal line cutting across the frame, which helps suggest that many more with them are asking the same question. The next shot adds even more intensity and weight to the piece, as we have the first directly centered shot of someone, an older Chinese American man, identified in text as Tom Lee. He is wearing a hat that identifies him as a Vietnam veteran, and he talks about being happy that he is alive, but he proclaims that Danny Chen will not be coming home and asks, "What happened to Danny?" Danny's cousin next appears, telling us that Danny died on October 3 in Afghanistan, but that "he did not die in combat." Over images of Danny's dog tags and a picture of him in uniform, we begin to hear from his friends and family about what a great young man he was—full of life and promise until "he was beaten by his superiors."

A series of recurring shots of people asking "What happened to Danny?" is capped by a shot of his clearly distressed father asking the same question, and then a cut to his cousins standing around his parents, with his mother holding all she has left of Danny: a framed picture of him. The video had tremendous emotional impact. Mainstream media covered the YouTube piece as a respectable ten thousand viewers eventually watched it, and within days the online petition grew by several thousand more signatures. The pressure ticked upward to the military, and it started to become more forthcoming with its information to the Chen family.

Less than four weeks later, the military disclosed the truth. Chen's fellow unit members had dragged him out of bed and forced him to crawl across the floor as they threw rocks at him, to punish him for forgetting to turn off the hot water heater when he went to bed before his shift. There had been a long history of racial humiliation and taunting of Private Chen during his service in the unit. Eight members of his unit, including his commanders, were charged with a variety of crimes that the investigators contend led to Chen's suicide.

The military says it would have conducted this investigation with or without public outcry or pressure from the family, and this may be the case. But there is little doubt that the family's and OCA-NY's efforts to publicize the case, and their emotional visual plea for public support in demanding an answer to the question "What happened to Danny Chen?" helped achieve this goal. Chen's is a horribly sad story, but it is a good example of how, when told with the new paint of the electronic moving image, by quite ordinary people, a story can make change happen; it can affect the world in a small but meaningful way.

Being able to meld text with images is a key skill and part of the new way we define literacy. But being a literate communicator does not mean having to invent a whole new language for yourself. It means mastering a language that already exists.

■ THE BIG BUSINESS OF IMAGES

Well over a hundred million viewers tune in to the Super Bowl each January or February, and many of them aren't there for the football or bean dip. They are there for the unveiling of the year's best television commercials. Advertisers have long flocked to this Sunday afternoon spectacle in pursuit of these viewers, who have been conditioned not to leave the room when there is a break in the action on the field, because that is when the real moneymaking competition airs: that of the dark arts of the televised commercial.

If you wanted to advertise during the first Super Bowl in 1967, you had to fork over $42,000. In 2012, corporations paid $3.5 million for a thirty-second spot. Corporate livelihoods can hang in the balance with these ads, as can individual careers. The ads have become Hollywood-scale productions as they vie for viewers' attention and compete for a place in viewers' minds.

Super Bowl XLVI, as in past years, was fiercely competitive for the best ad talent in the world, yet the big winner was an advertisement that cost twenty dollars to make—and was written, produced, and directed not by a professional advertising agency or filmmaker, but by a young graphic designer who stole the show (as well as a $1 million prize as the highest-rated ad as voted on by a *USA Today* poll of consumers).

Jonathan Friedman was one of 6,100 entrants to submit a thirty-second ad in the Doritos "Crash the Super Bowl" campaign. His concept was simple, as was the execution of the piece. A dog wanted to cover his tracks over a missing cat and offered his owner some hush money in the form of a Doritos bag with a note attached to it reading, "You Didn't See Nuthin!" The twenty-dollar budget included a few bags of Doritos and some pet toys.

Needless to say, Jonathan Friedman can afford a few more bags of Doritos today. He had a clever idea, and had fun making the ad. He used a camera he already owned, borrowed a neighbor's dog, and cast a friend in the role of the witness to the crime. The ad is neither exceptionally cinematic nor made with high production values, but it is a good story well told—and it is literate.

In a less family-friendly spot, on May 25, 2008, Giovanny Gutierrez surreptitiously* shot his panty-clad girlfriend gyrating her very attractive posterior to the beat of a Wii Fit video. Within the frame we see the Wii Fit character gyrating on the television screen while the girlfriend keeps pace. After about a minute of this, the boyfriend swings the camera around to capture his own face, complete with tongue hanging out. The video was uploaded to YouTube with the title "Why Every Guy Should Buy Their Girlfriend Wii Fit." The video caught on like wildfire, and to date has been viewed more than twelve million times. Whether planned by Nintendo or not, it undoubtedly led to increased purchases of Nintendo Wii consoles by young men.

---

* Many people have speculated that this was not a candid moment, but rather a scripted video along the lines of "Bride Has Massive Hair Wig Out," to sell Wii Fit products. Nintendo, Giovanny Gutierrez, and Gutierrez's girlfriend, Lauren Bernat, deny this.

Over the past few years, these ultra-low-budget spots—costing from twenty to a few thousand dollars, broadcast on television and the Internet—have routinely been among the most popular spots with viewers, competing and beating out ads that cost millions more. What matters is not the flashy graphics or the high-paid directors but the quality of the story, an arena where anyone with a cell phone and an idea can be a player. This is the ultimate media meritocracy.

The world of advertising—and, for that matter, all corporate communications—is a library of cinema experimentation, as television ads are tightly constructed stories meant to persuade, to connote meaning and value, to entertain, to inform, and to meet a multitude of other objectives, all within a ten- to sixty-second period. If you want to see effective media making, just watch the most successful advertising campaigns. And today, those campaigns are not the domain only of high-powered, slick Madison Avenue advertising firms, but also of individuals like you and me.

Many corporations are increasingly focused on building equity in their brands by reaching their customer base not only with advertising messages, but also "knowledge content." They have developed internal teams that bring together brand managers, product developers, and others in a collaborative effort focused on creating this kind of visual content.

Procter & Gamble has long been one of this country's premier marketing corporations. It gave birth to the "soap opera," in an effort to create an audience that would watch its commercials (and hopefully buy its soap); it was the marketing force and sole sponsor behind the People's Choice Awards, introduced in 1975; it has worked with the top advertising agencies to create impactful promotional spots; yet it has turned to an internal team to create digital media content that will have a long shelf life around its brands for YouTube and its own websites.

One of P&G's subsidiaries is Gillette, which has introduced a series of Web videos. If you search "how to shave" on YouTube, two of the first three videos that come up are from Gillette. The company's animated video "How to Shave Your Groin" is particularly popular, with more than five million hits. This off-color (but literate) content, unlike that of a televised commercial, isn't about just brand promotion, but offers knowledge to the consumer, and thus has more chance of sticking in the memory and having a longer shelf life. It becomes an asset for Gillette rather than an advertising expense. And along the way it might help persuade you to use that corporation's product in, um, new ways, extending its reach and brand equity.

American Express created OPEN Forum as a way to bring additional value and a sense of connection to small business customers. OPEN Forum's in-house production team produces videos on entrepreneurship and best practices at a current pace of almost fifty per month. And those small businesses are also harnessing the power of visual media to connect with their customers. If you want to know how to do anything, ranging from fixing a running toilet to decorating a cupcake, it is likely you can find a video, courtesy of a small business in Anywhere U.S.A.

And then there is Andrew Grantham, a young man from Halifax, Nova Scotia, in Canada, who has created a series of talking animal videos that recall the old television series *Mister Ed*. You may not know his name, but if you have spent any time on the Internet or around the coffee machine at the office, you've probably heard of his work. He essentially captures his dog moving its mouth in such a way that it seems as if it were forming words, and he lays down an audio track of a "canine voice-over" and a human voice-over that makes it look as if the animal were in conversation with him. Never underestimate the power of cute animals on the Internet. One of Grantham's videos, known by viewers as

"Ultimate Dog Tease," drew more than seventy million viewers in its first six months, part of an entire Talking Animals Channel that Grantham created on YouTube, which features a store where you can buy all kinds of Talking Animals paraphernalia. (Lest you think Grantham is profiting at the expense of the animals who are teased, proceeds from the sale of products go to support the Nova Scotia SPCA—although he does keep the advertising revenue created by the channel's success.)

Unlike its source material, *Mister Ed*, which could be seen on only one channel in the same half-hour time slot each week, Grantham's work can be watched anytime, and shared across the world. Even as traditional a broadcaster as CBS has jumped on the bandwagon, hosting the video on the CBS News website The Feed. This is not just because it thinks the video is worthwhile news, but also because it wants the advertising revenue. (The page is surrounded by advertisements as well as other content.) Grantham's video represents free content that drives advertising dollars.

The power of visuals extends to the smallest building blocks of corporate identity. Visual media can be distilled into its simplest of forms in a logo. A picture or even the insignia of a corporation or a brand can bring instant recall to an advertisement we were exposed to decades earlier, along with a flood of emotional associations—comfort, excitement, reliability, sex—built around that product. Entire campaigns are oriented around the single image of a "brand" being driven into a customer's mind like a railroad spike into a soft wooden tie. How is this done? More than any other factors, it seems, the magic of persuasion comes from the seductive quality of a pleasing image.

Dr. Clotaire Rapaille, a neurological consultant who helped Chrysler design the enormously successful PT Cruiser, operates on the theory that visual conclusions, formed in an instant, are a direct pathway to what Rapaille calls the "reptilian mind." This lies at the core of the spine and is responsible for our most basic functions: breathing, hunger, defense, and reproduction. What influences the reptilian mind most, he says, are visual messages that have no words.

"How can I decode this kind of behavior which is not a word?" Rapaille told an interviewer. "My theory is very simple: The reptilian always wins. I don't care what you're going to tell me intellectually. I don't care. Give me the reptilian. Why? Because the reptilian always wins."

There is hardly an American alive who cannot visualize the famous logo for McDonald's, seen on tens of thousands of plastic marquees all over national roadsides. That giant friendly yellow *M* against a red background was going to be discarded and updated in the early 1960s, but a consultant named Louis Cheskin persuaded executives to hold on to what had been an enormously successful image for the company. Why? According to Cheskin, the big curvy *M* subconsciously reminded customers of a big pair of "nourishing breasts," as he put it—which inspired a sort of infantile confidence in the brand.

How can "behavior that is not a word" be harnessed for the purposes of persuasion in the business world? This skill is more important than ever in the age of digital media, and it pays to examine some of the historic examples of corporate visual rhetoric. Remember the lesson of Doritos and bear in mind that a company does not have to be a behemoth to create effective visual media. Most of this stuff could have been done in a garage, or a single employee's cubicle. The techniques are simple, and the tools for creating and distributing these images have never been more accessible to small business.

The television producer Matthew Weiner has turned the advertising men of the early 1960s into satiric fodder for his award-winning series *Mad Men*, in which talented rakes spin nifty images around products that audiences were told they needed. Today's advertising is based on the same premise: condition an audience to associate your product with the kinds of positive values that will make them want to get off the couch and buy it, looking for those positive values to wash off on them and hopefully make their lives better.

Philip Morris was one of the sponsors of *I Love Lucy*, and its executives insisted that the show's opening feature a scene in which Lucy and Desi light up. Years later, on April 1, 1970, President Richard Nixon signed the Public Health Cigarette Smoking Act into law, banning cigarette advertising from U.S. airwaves and sending the Marlboro Man out to pasture. In an effort to appease the tobacco lobby, the act didn't take effect until January 2, 1971, so that advertisers could have one last shot of marketing to young football fans during the New Year's Day college football bowl games. They used every moment of airtime they could, as the last tobacco advertisement was broadcast on Johnny Carson's *Tonight Show* just before midnight, pitching Virginia Slims cigarettes to the show's women customers.

Virginia Slims cigarettes were designed and marketed exclusively for women, and the advertisements used images of suffragettes. One television ad placed a frumpily dressed early feminist in an oversize birdcage as a folksy male singer sang, "You were only a bird in a gilded cage, a beautiful sight to view." Over images of the woman sweating as she irons, scrubs, and washes, while still encaged, the song continues "so dainty and delicate you seemed, no rights would they give to you." As the woman peeks around to make sure no one is looking, and lights up a cigarette, the singer croons, "When you said you should vote and you said you should smoke, the men were in a rage."

The music is overcome by drums, and a series of rapidly repeating images flashes on the screen, alternating between a shot of the birdcage and that of a young, sexy woman strutting toward the camera as a hip female voice starts singing the new Virginia Slims theme, "You've Come a Long Way, Baby!" All this in less than a minute. The lesson here is that you can prove you're a sexually liberated woman by sucking polluted air into your lungs. The slenderness of the cigarette is meant to evoke the lynxlike contours of the body the woman wishes she had; the oral fixation on the object evokes an eroticism that is never explicitly acknowledged, yet is indisputably present.

Television ads depicting cigarettes are now relegated to the archives of YouTube, but images remain one of the primary tools that corporations can use effectively to make up stories and, in a sense, lie to consumers. We are regularly told that certain drugs, beers, or even automobiles can make us look prettier, more attractive to the opposite sex, more fulfilled and healthier. It is surprising that even with the knowledge we have of media distortions, the United States stands alone with New Zealand as the only developed country to allow direct-to-consumer pharmaceutical advertising. Pharmaceutical companies today spend far more in advertising than they do on research and development.

Beer companies recognize that even if they are not allowed to show someone drinking a beer in their commercials—have you ever noticed that no one in all the beer commercials we consume actually puts a bottle to his lips and drinks?—they can still take advantage of our visual processing to sell their wares. It turns out that seeing someone holding a bottle of whatever brand beer while being chatted up by a hot girl who is "way out of his league," or while having some great football viewing experience in his "man cave," does the trick. We the viewer can construct the rest of the story, and the work of the image is done.

The use of images in advertising has not been wholly for pecuniary purposes, even though a night spent flipping through the channels might make us think so. One of the most powerful commercials ever broadcast hit the air just as tobacco ads were forced to leave.

Keep America Beautiful is a community improvement organization funded by corporations—notably those who use a lot of packaging—with a stated mission of "bringing the public and private sectors together to develop and promote a national cleanliness ethic." The organization created its first public service announcement in 1956, but it was in 1971 that Keep America Beautiful found its moment in the sun.

The spot begins with images of a Native American paddling along a creek in his canoe in a rustic setting. After several cuts implying the passage of time, we see a closer shot of his paddle hitting the water with some trash floating nearby. As he turns a corner, we cut to a wider shot of him paddling into a part of the creek that finds him surrounded by factories billowing smoke. As he beaches the canoe and steps onto the shore, he finds the ground littered with refuse. We see him in a medium shot as he climbs a hill, and we hear a narrator's voice for the first time, saying, "Some people have a deep, abiding respect for the natural beauty that was once this country." We cut to a shot of the Native American reaching the top of the hill and standing next to a highway as the narrator continues: "And some people don't." Just at that moment, a bag is thrown from a passing car and hits the ground at the Native American's feet, with fast-food trash covering his moccasins. As the narrator says, "People start pollution, people can stop it," the actor turns his head and we see a single tear falling down his cheek.

The "crying Indian" ad landed in a period of post-Vietnam guilt and national uncertainty over environmental despoilment. It was a brilliant tug on the emotions of viewers who felt as though America had become too fat, self-indulgent, and careless. As a piece of literate media, it fulfilled the requirements of building on what came before it and of containing an open text. There is hardly an American alive who does not understand the myth of the peaceful aboriginal past of the North American continent. The tear down the Indian's cheek also left the inference that the noble soul of the continent was weeping over its occupiers—a powerful visual cue to the viewer.

The ad spawned multiple parodies, and helped put the moral problem of litter onto the heads of consumers instead of, arguably, where it belonged: onto the manufacturers of consumer goods and packaging who were wrapping their products in excessive amounts of Styrofoam and plastic and creating the underlying structure for the waste. These remain powerful images, even if the chemical and petroleum companies were doing far more to foul the land than my paper cup on the side of the road ever was.* Still, the guilty images are seared into our brains, creating a lifelong sense of responsibility and shame (as we also self-identified with those white marauders in the speeding car), one that certainly precludes me from throwing anything from the window of a car and spoiling the land we "acquired" from this Native American.

Image plus image equals something greater than its parts—

---

* A final irony: the crying Indian wasn't even an Indian. Though the actor's stage name was "Iron Eyes Cody," his birth name was Espera Oscar de Corti, and he was the son of immigrants from Sicily who had moved to Louisiana. He was about as Native American as Christopher Columbus. But viewers didn't know that. They knew only that they were making the sad, wise Indian cry when they tossed fast-food wrappers out of car windows.

much, much greater. This is a critical understanding for those who want to thrive in today's corporate world.

But if we focus only on advertising, we miss the larger point: visual communication skills are critical to virtually anyone hoping to succeed in the competitive global marketplace, regardless of profession. It is not just about creating commercials that sell product. Over the past decade, visual storytelling has become one of the new important communication tools for those who want to succeed in business. This is no surprise. The core skill we need almost regardless of profession is communication. It is how we learn, how we share information, and how we build professional relationships and communities. As screens multiply around us and permeate our environments, it is reflected in how we do business.

The use of visual communication in the corporate world can be traced back to the earliest use of overhead projectors, but the real sea change occurred in 1987, when a team of Microsoft engineers, headed up by Robert Gaskins, introduced PowerPoint 1.0 to the world.*

Gaskins had experience in the world of corporate presentations, and was aware of a 1981 study conducted by the Wharton Applied Research Center at the University of Pennsylvania—"A

---

* Gaskins had earlier left a PhD program at UC Berkeley a dissertation short of graduating, with a desire to go into business. He found himself at Bell-Northern Research, the Canadian equivalent of Bell Labs. Bell-Northern, like many other corporations, relied on projected overhead transparencies for both internal and external presentations. Gaskins was part of a team trying to envision and deliver the "office of the future," and it is from here that some of the early ideas for PowerPoint came. He later joined Forethought, a start-up software company that was developing Presenter, which would be renamed PowerPoint when it was purchased by Microsoft.

Study of the Effects of the Use of Overhead Transparencies on Business Meetings"—which concluded that presenters who used visuals were "perceived as significantly better prepared, more professional, more persuasive, more highly credible, and more interesting" than their nonvisual presenting compatriots. They elicited support for and approval of their projects at twice the rate of the others. Yet Gaskin saw that only one meeting in forty incorporated visuals of any kind. Herein lay the opportunity that Bill Gates and others at Microsoft understood. PowerPoint 1.0 allowed the user to present only black-and-white slides that were primarily graphs or bullet point outlines; 2.0, which came out in 1988, added a few additional features, such as the capability to use color slides processed by a third party; but the critical shift was the introduction of PowerPoint 3.0 in 1992, when the software really began to access the power of visual media, allowing the user to incorporate live video, color slide shows, transitions, animations, and even synchronized sound and video clips into a presentation.*

In just the first year of PowerPoint 3.0, more than a million copies were sold, and only a decade later the visual presentation software was in use on more than five hundred million computers, with more than thirty million presentations being made each day. Use of the software would double again within the decade. Virtually no student can graduate from middle or high school today without having used PowerPoint or another visual software program in a classroom presentation, and it is highly likely that you've used it, too. Several competing software packages have sprung

---

* In its earliest days, video presentations for large groups required bulky projectors that cost in the area of $100,000, as well as the time of a dedicated technician. Today you can buy projectors that fit in your briefcase that are even more powerful, are simple to use, and cost less than $1,000. The ability to share or "distribute" these presentations is an essential element in the explosion of video-based PowerPoint presentations.

up, but they all do essentially the same thing: allow the user to create and deliver a talk that incorporates text, graphs, animations, still images, and video. If you are an Apple computer user, you might be using Keynote, Apple's version of presentation software, but PowerPoint has become the generic name for this kind of visual presentation software in the same way that Kleenex stands for tissues and Coke for cola.

Perhaps the most well-known and certainly the most celebrated PowerPoint-type presentation was delivered by former vice president Al Gore, in *An Inconvenient Truth*. Documentary filmmaker Davis Guggenheim turned a straightforward, well-produced visual presentation—essentially a slide show constructed and presented on Keynote that Gore had given hundreds of times—into an Academy Award–winning documentary that grossed close to $50 million at the box office and, more impressively, reshaped the international dialogue about climate change; in the process, it also helped Al Gore win a Nobel Prize. One blogger titled his review of *An Inconvenient Truth* "Eco-Apocalypse and the PowerPoint Film."

Gore did have one benefit that most of us shouldn't anticipate in making our presentations: a mechanical lift that allowed him to rise and drop along with his graphs being presented on a big screen; but it wasn't the theatrical aspects of the presentation that moved people, it was the images of glacial ice crashing into the ocean, the animations of a tragic polar bear being relegated to a smaller and smaller landmass, and the visual simulations of water levels rising around Manhattan island and other shorelines that drove the point home. No words could have accomplished this with such force and resonance.

The TED Conference, founded in 1984 as an "idea" conference, has mastered the use of oral presentations bolstered by visual elements in the form of eighteen-minute talks on a wide variety of subjects. In 2006, TED decided to film those presentations and make them available online. Chances are you've seen one of the more than one thousand presentations that have been viewed well over half a billion times around the world.

Visual presentation software took a leap forward in many ways with the 2009 introduction of Prezi, developed by the Hungarian architect and visual artist Adam Somlai-Fischer. Prezi offers many of the functions of other presentation software, yet also lets you pan, zoom, and navigate through a seemingly endless canvas on which your presentation sits. All these programs will continue to evolve as a result of our drive to make our communication more visually effective and even cinematic.

It is virtually impossible to go to a professional meeting or conference in any industry and not find oneself in the audience at a PowerPoint presentation. And with the rise of the tools of video production and editing, such presentations continue to grow in sophistication and in the use of moving images. Bullet points and clever graphs will no longer be enough in a world of moving images. The bar has been raised, and those who respond will succeed.

PowerPoint itself is not the answer, however; it is merely the structure on which one can deliver a presentation. It is neutral in terms of its impact—and can deliver dud presentations as readily as superb ones. Visual literacy is the key to using this powerful software in the most effective way possible.

While PowerPoint is still king of the boardroom, some professions are increasingly relying on the Internet to carry a visual message. Biologists no longer need to rely solely on print journals or conference presentations of research methods. They can now turn to the online *Journal of Visualized Experiments*, or JoVE, to understand and see life science experiments in action. This is only one of many sites offering the distribution of video-driven papers and live examples of research methodologies. Those scientists who acquire a facility with this mode of presentation will undoubtedly have a leg up in competing for attention and for the resources of funders and others in the field. This translates into value for their company, laboratory, or academic institution, and this is playing out from industry to industry.

A profession that relies heavily on persuasion is that of trial law, and increasingly a lawyer's facility with visual media can make a tremendous difference in the outcome of a case.

A profitable side business in the law has long been the production of big eye-catching placards known as "boards," which diagram a complicated story to a jury. The boards often contain photographs of evidence, and smart lawyers know to make them simple, straightforward, and persuasive—never too busy or confusing. Lawyers use boards as a college professor would, "teaching" the judge and the jury their client's point of view in a case. But a new generation of lawyers is now learning the value of using moving digital exhibits to make points and win cases.

Few have evangelized more for this new frontier of legal argument than Neal Feigenson, a professor of law at Quinnipiac University and an associate researcher at the Yale Department of Psychology. Along with Christina Spiesel, Feigenson wrote a 2009 book called *Law on Display: The Digital Transformation of Legal Persuasion and Judgment*, which explores the promise and pitfalls of using short media in court.

"Most lawyers are not used to couching their arguments in visual terms," Feigenson said. "They tend to be helpless with visual displays presented by the opposition."

But there is no reason for this, as the visual displays can be more eloquent and visceral than anything even Atticus Finch could say. They rely on realms of knowledge that no words could express. There is a reason criminal defense attorneys object when prosecutors want to circulate autopsy or crime scene photos in murder trials. The grisly images are generally shocking and sobering, and bring home to a jury the brutality of the crime and the humanity of the victim. They set the table for vengeance.

There are two types of visual media that lawyers deal with in court, says Feigenson. There is the actual evidence—the crime scene photos, surveillance video, and the like—which must be presented in its pristine condition, unaltered by the attorneys or the police. And then there is the visual media created for rhetorical purposes: videos that present a theory of the case, for example, or a PowerPoint presentation that lays out a complicated set of facts and makes it more digestible.

A landmark for this type of courtroom rhetoric was the tabloid-ready case involving Kennedy cousin Michael Skakel, who was accused of the beating death of his fifteen-year-old neighbor Martha Moxley. He was arrested almost a quarter century after the crime. The case was cold, and the facts were flimsy, but prosecutors were determined to win the high-profile case against the now-doughy middle-aged father, and they hired a computer consultant to create a digitized CD-ROM that contained virtually the entire array of visual evidence, including crime scene photographs, which could be viewed on a screen in the courtroom. The presentation was as slick as a video game, and projected a sense of confidence that the state indeed had its man. Witnesses used laser pointers to highlight their testimony, and in a closing argument rebuttal, the lead prosecutor walked the jury through a re-creation of what Skakel had done the morning after the crime, mixing an audiotape of Skakel's own voice with photographs of the smiling Moxley and then her corpse. Particularly devastating was the juxtaposition of a gruesome crime scene photograph and Skakel acknowledging that he had "a feeling of panic" when Martha's mother asked him where her daughter could be found. It was hardly a confession, but the link between the sound and the image created a strong sensibility with the jury that Skakel was indeed the killer. Why? Because the jurors had been raised on televised court dramas and movies, where such dramatic "confessions" and webs of evidence are longtime conventions, even though life does not always furnish such tied-in-a-bow climaxes.

"The multimedia display thus enabled the prosecution to merge its version of historical truth with narrative truth, providing jurors with the satisfying impression that the factually true account of events, verified by the component pieces of admitted evidence, was also a coherent, compelling story and vice versa," say Feigenson and Spiesel. The outcome of the Skakel trial caused lawyers all around the country to sit up and take notice of multimedia rhetoric, which is even more prevalent today among lawyers who like telling visual stories.

For reasons we have already explored about the lizard-brained power of images, this may have been more effective than any verbal closing argument. Visuals create a sense of inference that allows lawyers to "sell" a theory of a case in much the same way Budweiser sells beer or Doritos sells chips. Drinking that beer is not necessarily going to get you into bed with the model, but the seed of the idea has been planted nonetheless, and we construct ways to justify our choice with whatever facts we can marshal. As Feigenson puts it, "You can make an implicit argument without saying it. You can say it, but it will be so much more powerful if the audience figures it out on their own." This is the manipulative effect that filmmakers have known about for generations, and that lawyers are only now learning to master, especially now that computer animations have been ruled admissible by some judges.

"Animations re-create reality in abstracted and thus simulated form, clarifying case-relevant information and omitting whatever might obscure it," write Feigenson and Spiesel. The sine qua non for a lawyer is being able to make a coherent argument about the evidence, and visual literacy becomes especially useful when a computer animation can help a jury of average education make sense of the intricacies of a tax statute or a DNA model.

There is no forum in which the authenticity of an image is more important than court—millions of dollars or a person's freedom may hang in the balance, and the penalties for altering a text are not merely public embarrassment but possible jail time. So where do you draw the line between "truth enhancement" and actual evidence tampering? This is not always clear, says Feigenson, and lawyers have to take care to keep digital evidence pristine while still advocating vigorously on behalf of their clients: one more high-level skill necessary in an age of digital text.

An important precedent was set in 2001 when a man named Alfred Swinton was found guilty of a murder in Connecticut. The victim's body had been found in a snowbank, and one of the only pieces of physical evidence was a pattern of bite marks on her chest. Police took a mold of Swinton's teeth—which, for some reason, he allowed them to do—and discovered that they were a match for the pattern on the corpse. When Swinton went to trial, the prosecutors created a blowup computer enhancement showing how his teeth matched up with the bite marks on the victim's body. The program they used was similar to Photoshop, in that it exaggerated and amplified the image to make the evidence plain to the jury. Some might have called it a smart way to use narrative images to tell a story. The defense called it distortion, and demanded an appeal.

The state got an expert witness to demonstrate to a judge in open court how the computer program had magnified the images but had not altered the essential reality of the bite mark pattern. You could say the defense of the image in court was yet another image-based argument.

While visual media are transforming most professions, this is no more apparent than in journalism. We have had a long-standing relationship at the Jacob Burns Center with the local Gannett affiliate *The Journal News*, as it has covered not only our programs in the schools, but also the college and adult courses we offer. Along with many other regional papers, *The Journal News* has been racing to stay relevant and afloat in this changing landscape for news. Over the past several years, it has felt that its future as a news-gathering organization was dependent on getting readers to click on videos as well as text, and it believed that it was in a race to develop an online, image-based presence before the newsprint version of the paper disappeared. In an act of seeming desperation, it went so far as not even publicly to reference the connection of its website to its printed paper, instead calling the online creation *lohud.com*.

In early 2010, we were approached by *Journal News* senior management with a simple request: to retrain its reporters and columnists to tell their stories not only in words, but through the camera. The print journalists had been told that the key to maintaining the paper's ability to continue to operate, and for them to stay employed, was to acquire these skills. No longer would reporters be out in the field with only a small notebook and a pen; they would also have a video camera slung over their shoulders.

Over the next year, we worked with these reporters to help them acquire shooting, editing, and visual storytelling skills. Some were curmudgeonly old print guys who, you could tell, were not long for this new world that required multiple communication skills, but many of them took to it readily and began to feel as if these newly developing storytelling skills were helping them grow as print journalists. One young woman explained how her focus on the visuals had allowed her to find more nuance in a story. She felt that her writing reflected this closer look, and she was excited to see the transference of skills.

One of the guys who understood the importance of visuals but who needed to move from stills to video was Rory Glaeseman. Glaeseman had started as a staff photojournalist at *The Journal News* in 2003. In the last eight years, he had seen a shift in emphasis in the paper's journalistic efforts, and was part of the first group of print and photojournalists trained to shoot and report through video as well. He says, "We don't write in words and distribute newspapers because it's cool—it's because that's how the audience communicated. This is changing rapidly." He believes that journalists, at their core, are driven to communicate, and that video has certain advantages over print. "Audiences need to commit more sensory inputs to consuming video," he said, "which necessitates that they dive more into the story than if it is just in words."

Make no mistake, Gannett was making this shift not out of any deep journalistic commitment, but rather after seeing a staggering drop in readership and the resulting stampede of exiting advertising dollars. It had to try something new, and today *The Journal News* looks different as a result. Whether it ultimately survives or goes the way of so many other regional papers in the wake of this new media age remains to be seen.

At the beginning of 2012, Glaeseman left the Gannett regional to join *Newsday* as the senior digital photo and video editor and is focused on its new mobile news applications. He says that all reporters will be trained to shoot video, and that the first person on the scene of a story needs to be thinking about the visuals at the same time he is taking out his pen and notepad.

"A decade ago, when I first started, visuals were a distant second place in this business, but that has forever changed. Now editors will stress that the visuals drive the story," he said.

The Journal News and *Newsday* are just two examples of a sea change as the world of print publications converges with not only online print but also visual storytelling. Pick up any of the newspapers or magazines you currently read and you will find an online version, and that version will undoubtedly offer a rich array of video content. The journalists who survive will be those who adapt to this powerful storytelling medium.

A brief personal digression. When my son was in seventh grade, he expressed a strong dislike for his Language Arts class by essentially refusing to write. We were called in to a parent-teacher conference. Faced with the situation, our son calmly and earnestly explained (as we seethed) that he really didn't need to learn to write, as he had determined that he was going to be a musician. After a few deep breaths, I explained to him that we were thrilled with his choice of careers, but worried about how he would navigate the world of music—with contracts, marketing, management, and even songwriting—without putting pen to paper. I am not sure he heard my words or could even see beyond his adolescent need to communicate with anyone but adults, but thankfully he later outgrew this rather limiting philosophy.

Communication remains at the heart of most social and corporate enterprises, and those people who communicate effectively are the ones who rise to the top. Anyone just starting out or trying to bolster skills for a current or future employer, or to maximize his opportunities for success, must think about communication, and today that means not only listening and speaking, reading and writing, but also the visual communication skills of critical viewing and the production of media. It is hard to imagine trying to enter the workforce today without at least some facility with e-mail and basic Web skills. These are essential requirements for success in the workplace. These core skills will soon include visual communication. It is not inconceivable that résumés will soon feature hyperlinks to visual media. Visual communication can represent an area of relative weakness or a competitive edge, and the basic skills are readily available to anyone willing to begin to think in this language.

■ GRAMMAR, RHYTHM, AND RHYME IN THE AGE OF THE IMAGE

Perceptually, films are illusions, not reality; cognitively, they are not the blooming, buzzing confusion of life but rather simplified ensembles of elements, designed to be understood.
—DAVID BORDWELL, *Film Historian and Theorist*

Who hasn't seen a television show, film, or YouTube video and thought, *I could have done that?* You can. But it takes some practice and some understanding of film grammar and technique. The reason it all seems so easy is a combination of the seductive nature of images and the way the majority of what we watch has been composed and constructed.

Since the advent of Hollywood editing, back in the earliest days of cinema, the goal of filmmakers has been for us to feel the movement of the camera but not to be aware of it, to look past the construction of the media, to ignore the seams in the material. Just as an Olympic diver smiles and hides the effort as she catapults skyward and manages to pull off multiple flips while seemingly twisting in both directions, good storytelling—whether oral, in print, or visual—typically hides the construction and the hard work that go into making it. Both the medal-winning dives and the best stories are more intricate than they appear.

We are not starting from scratch, however. All the times in our lives we've spent feeding at the trough of television, movies, the Internet, and other assorted screens, consuming supersize amounts of visual media—all that time was not wasted, not one minute of it. We have reaped the side benefit (albeit unintended) of building sophisticated databases of visual information and language that we now must learn how to access. Each movie, sitcom, news broadcast, or Internet video we have seen has been internalized and has helped our understanding of visual language evolve and deepen.

Just as the writer has tools and structures to use in his craft, so, too, does the visual storyteller. Concepts of written texts (exposition, plot, metaphor) and principles of composition and grammar have their equivalent ideas in visual media, which is "written" with a different set of tools. It is important to begin to develop a facility with each of these tools, and to understand the essential principles of composition. Strunk and White's *The Elements of Style*, published in 1914, lays out essential rules for written composition. While the book is still relevant, no one would argue that each of its rules must be followed religiously. Plenty of great literature and written text violates one or all of Strunk and White's rules. Still, there is a need first to understand these rules of composition before you decide to break them. This is true also for visual media.

This chapter is intended to function as a basic primer for visual storytelling, rooted as it is in some of the timeless rules of film vocabulary that have been proven effective since the very first days of Hollywood. It is not a technical manual—those are readily available elsewhere, and the truth is, the tools of creation are all pretty intuitive and accessible. It is also not merely a guide to acquiring these skills in the service of making visual media. The truth is that every day, we are more and more inundated with constructed images. Just as knowing grammar and appreciating the construction of a sentence, paragraph, or story make you a stronger, more sophisticated reader, acquiring a facility with visual storytelling skills will make you a stronger, more sophisticated viewer. You will be able to see what the "writer" of images is doing, understand her rhetorical devices, and even know when and how you are being manipulated. You will then be in control—at each moment deciding whether to study the construction of the narrative, be attentive to the manipulation of the piece, or simply sit back and allow the images to flow over you like a dream. In any case, you will be making a choice rather than having the choice made for you. In this case the ancient maxim "Knowledge is power" is true, but one could add to it: "and is readily available."

Two important notes: Filmmaking is, usually, a highly collaborative process. Sit through the credits of any film and you realize how many specialized functions there are. Screenwriters might be the ones to take the first steps in bringing a particular story to life, but many others will join in before the story is finished. For our purposes, we'll focus on the perspective of the director, who is ultimately responsible for what ends up on the screen. When we hear the term *director*, we think about the artistic soul in the canvas folding chair yelling "Action!" or directing actors within a scene. These images are true, but the real essence of the job is the "chief storyteller," or the person who "directs" the audience—at each moment directing our focus; showing us what to see, what to hear, what to understand, and what to feel. We'll use that orientation in its broadest sense in order to touch on the critical aspects of creating visual media.

Also, there can be substantive differences between fiction and nonfiction filmmaking, between narratives and documentaries.

For our purposes, we will move between both these worlds, since the core issues of storytelling are similar in both.

The Tools

While the writer has pen and paper (or keyboard and printer), the visual storyteller has a camera, microphones (or other ways to source sound), and editing systems that allow for the construction of story. All your power as a filmmaker can essentially be placed into three large buckets: frame, sound, and editing.

- **Frame**. Everything we can see: the images on the screen, the faces of the actors or subjects, the motions they make, the lighting, the background, the props, and even the text.
- **Sound**. Everything we can hear: from voice-over narration to dialogue to sound effects, music, or ambient sound.
- **Editing**. Everything that constructs a story: the movement from scene to scene that guides us through a story; how images are placed next to other images to create new or deeper meanings; how sounds are mixed and laid over images to drive emotion or narrative.

Now imagine the contents of each of these buckets being poured into one larger bucket that holds everything together. That larger bucket would be called *story*, the heart of the entire enterprise.

Some of the steps for creating literate stories, whether written or visual, are quite similar and even commonsensical, but the choices you make and the language you use vary greatly. All involve a working dynamic of frame, sound, and editing.

There is no foolproof formula for excellence, no tricks that work across *all* kinds of stories, but there are some clear steps to making a piece of literate visual media.

So you are ready to grab a camera and microphone and head out to begin shooting. My first piece of advice: put them down. Visually driven media is powerful because it can be multilayered, rich in sensory information, and complex in the choices that are made in its construction. Writers have the advantage of an eraser or a Delete button, and they can craft their story and introduce new elements as often or as late in the process as they would like. Filmmaking, however, requires us to commit to the story and essential elements well *before* we begin the construction or editing process. It can be difficult (and at times expensive) to bring all the essential people and locations together to shoot new scenes, and in the case of documentary filmmaking, the moments we'd like to capture might never be replicable.

Before we get into the basics of frame, sound, and editing, let's first address intention and planning. Preproduction can spell the difference between a literate or an illiterate visual text, and the most effective directors typically address four basic elements of this process up front.

Preproduction: Intention and Planning

1. Know Your Goal

Just as with any form of communication, you have to start by knowing what you are trying to achieve. Are you advocating for a political cause, attempting to change minds, motivate action, inform, amuse, entertain, or outrage (to name just a few potential goals)?

The answer to this question will begin to shape many of the choices you make in constructing your story—from the form and length, to the way you shoot it, work in sound elements, and edit with a particular mood in mind. All the choices we encounter in the making of a moving image can be framed by one overriding question: What are we trying to accomplish at each moment and in the larger piece?

The goals you might envision are limitless, but the clearer you can be about this question, the greater your chances for success. Whatever the goal or goals, the effort is captured within what we see, hear, and feel. And we are led there by the powerful and intoxicating combination of frame, sound, and editing, the choices of which are going to be (or *should* be) influenced by your primary goal. So first, you must know that goal and be able to describe it to yourself in one sentence.*

2. Know Your Audience

For whom are you making this? You might be trying to communicate something to a handful of people who already have basic knowledge of what you are talking about, or you might be trying to reach a mass audience not at all familiar with the subject. In either case, recognition of who your intended audience is will help you shape a literate piece. If you are generating a short advocacy piece that plays on collective cultural knowledge, you can use images as metaphors, or even choose the type of construction to use to tap into this.

---

* A question that relates to this: How do you know if you're succeeding? With film studios, success is purely related to box office results, but for many other filmmakers it is about critical reception. Your video might be expressing a point of view in a local or national debate. Or it might be about delighting a family member with something that celebrates him or her during a family occasion. Considering your metrics of success up front is helpful for refining your goal and shaping the piece.

When Hillary Clinton set out to make a campaign commercial back in 2007, she enlisted the help of her very recognizable husband and a small film crew and headed to a local diner to create a parody of the last episode of *The Sopranos*, a show that months earlier had been watched by close to twelve million viewers on its premier broadcast and millions more in the succeeding few months. She was banking on the fact that almost everyone watching her video had some previous knowledge of this series and episode.

If you were to show Hillary's video to anyone who has not seen *The Sopranos*, even down to each individual shot and edit, it would seem amateur and campy, or might not even make sense. This is why the campaign chose not to buy airtime on television, but rather to put the video out on the Web and trust it to go viral among the vast community of *Sopranos* fans (and potential Clinton voters), who they hoped would share it with one another. They would get the references without need for explanation— understanding the message and humor, while hopefully achieving the campaign's goals of connecting their candidate with the national mood and giving her a more playful, hip image.

Your piece does not exist outside the context of all the other media your audience has consumed, but in fact is in a dialogue of sorts with it. The more you know your audience, the more you can tap into this database of cultural and visual references.

3. Choose the Appropriate Format

What is the best method for telling your story? The experience of the piece will be conveyed through not only the linear narrative, but also the essence of the structure. Your answers to the two questions just posed—goals and audience—will help drive this decision, and this decision will then drive everything else.

The genre of the film makes a big difference. There are certain accepted structures or tropes within each genre that allow us to anticipate the range of what we will see next, allowing for us to process the information more quickly.

An easy example: we know in a romantic comedy that the formula is essentially "boy meets girl" and they fall in love, boy loses girl, boy and girl find each other again and overcome all obstacles to live happily ever after. With Shakespearean roots in plays such as *A Midsummer Night's Dream*, or more modern fare such as *When Harry Met Sally* or one of my youngest daughter Maayan's favorites, *The Notebook*, literally thousands of films follow this formula. We as an audience count on a predictable structure in these stories, and are disappointed and surprised when they fail to materialize.

Of course, we can also play on this when we purposely subvert expectations. That's when the stories can get really interesting. For all the romantic comedies that follow a conventional structure, there is an *Annie Hall* or *500 Days of Summer*, where boy meets girl, boy loses girl, and girl stays lost forever, as it often is in life. Other genres include gangster movies, detective stories, coming-of-age dramas, film noir, documentaries, and horror movies (just to name a few), and each has its own conventions.

Just as with narratives, audiences immediately begin to sense what kind of structure a filmmaker is employing, and the more consistent you are, the better chance of keeping the audience with you. If this is your first time thinking about how to create a visual story, it is not likely that you'll be jumping into a ninety-minute narrative or documentary film. Rather, you might be making a film to celebrate your parents or your child, or to tout a local candidate, or to support (or rally against) a particular issue. While these might be only three- to five-minute films, they are stories—and should be well told if you want them to work.

And speaking of length, remember where your story will be

viewed. If it is meant for the Internet and will be watched on a computer screen or iPad or cell phone, keep it short, and you'll have a better chance of its being seen.

4. Plan, Plan, and Plan Some More . . . and Then Show Up

Most visual stories actually start in print. A screenplay, or script, lays out all the dialogue, action, and even camera movement that will later be shot. It allows you to plan how the story will evolve, what the characters will say, and even how the camera will move in order to help tell the story. There are specific conventions to screenplays, and some very good books that can teach you how to structure yours. You might want to consider a software program, such as Final Draft, that can assist you in formatting your screenplay properly. Also, there are some good tutorials embedded in this software.

If you are working on a documentary, you likely don't have a screenplay or script to work from, but your planning should still begin with paper and pen. Try to describe what story you are hoping to tell, who your characters are, in what style you will be shooting, and where the conflict might be. By doing this, you will begin to orient your mind and your eyes for when you are ready to pick up the camera. The more you approach the project with intent and forethought, the easier it will be to know and feel where the camera should be and whom you should be following as your documentary story unfolds.

The next part of the plan is to imagine each of the scenes—what you want to show. An easy way to do this is to write a story-board, which is like a cartoon strip that represents what a series of shots looks like. Take a piece of ordinary paper and draw a series of rectangular boxes that represent the screen. Then use crude stick figures and lines to indicate what images will be in each sequential shot. This is a visual map for how your film will progress. It isn't necessary to draw up a storyboard when you're shooting raw, unrehearsed video of, say, a city council meeting or a baseball game or a birthday party, although it can be extremely helpful to imagine what it might look like in order to anticipate the shots you'll need in the editing room later. For a narrative film, this stage is especially important. When you're ready to use your editing software to chop up that video into sequential shots that tell a coherent story, you'll find the storyboard invaluable.

At the Media Arts Lab, we use storyboarding with third-graders to help them visualize their written stories before they actually begin putting words to paper. They are always shocked to find out that this storyboard process is exactly what is done with the blockbuster films they see in the theater. The storyboarding process has been used throughout Hollywood history and can be one of your most important planning tools. Don't worry if you don't know the right way to format a screenplay, or can't draw to save your life, let alone draw a storyboard. Free or relatively inexpensive software packages are available to help you with these processes, including sophisticated storyboard applications for the iPad and other devices. It is helpful to play with these applications, as getting comfortable with the storyboard process can help immensely as you visualize your stories. There is also a slew of books that can provide more details if you want to go deeper. Check the notes on sources for some more specific suggestions. But the basics are as simple as we've just laid out here, and you can begin today.

Your screenplay and storyboard can then be broken down into a shot list. While your audience will be forced to watch your film in the order in which you construct it, it isn't necessarily shot sequentially. Think about a dialogue between two characters that involves the camera alternating between them. The camera isn't shifted each time you see a cut. Instead, all one character's lines are

A BASIC STORYBOARD SEQUENCE

① EXT PLAYground, Day
Foreground Boy watches
Kids play.

② cut to:
Med. C.U. on Boy,
he wants to join them

③ cut to:
Med shot on kids,
they wave him over
(Boy's P.O.V.)

④ cut to:
C.U. Boy, he reacts

⑤ cut to:
Boy runs over,
CAM push in with him

⑥ cut to:
Med. shot, kids invite
Boy into game.

shot first, and then the other's, and then the footage is chopped up and put back together in a different order. This is true of entire scenes. So a critical step in the narrative filmmaking process is to create a "shot list," which is essentially a list of each time the camera is turned on and off and what will be in its frame.

Frame: Show Your Story—Don't Tell It

Cinema is a matter of what's in the frame and what's out.
—MARTIN SCORSESE

Frame is everything we can see. The images on the screen, the faces of the actors or subjects, the motions they make, the lighting, the background, the props, the text. The choices within the frame are determined by what you want the viewer to see. This involves focusing the camera just as an eye focuses on what's in the field of vision.

1. Selecting the Right Frame

Unlike the painting or photograph hanging on your wall, which was first created and then fitted with a frame, in filmmaking you first have to choose the dimensions of the frame you will be filling. The size of the frame is also referred to as the "aspect ratio." This means the relationship between the width of an image and its height. If you have purchased a television anytime in the last twenty years, you know that the dimensions of TV screens have changed. The traditional formula for TV screens, and the shows broadcast to them, was that the screen was 1.33 times as wide as it was tall. This was set up to mimic the dimensions of early films, and in fact, in the classic movies of the 1930s and '40s, that's what you'll see. The recent silent film *The Artist* used this ratio to great effect.

After World War II, studios began to shoot their films in new wide formats and "Cinemascope," which has an aspect ratio of 2.35:1. The horizontal dimension of the screen kept stretching out into a broad canvas. (For those of us under the age of sixty, this is simply the proper dimension of a movie.) This shape promised a distinguished and majestic product, and it gave each film that feel, even when the movie itself left something to be desired. There has been an increasing convergence between cinema and television in recent years, however, and the aspect ratio for the new generations of television monitors and the programs broadcast on them (and most computer displays) is typically 1.78:1 (also referred to as 16:9).

Most cameras today give us the choice as to what aspect ratio we'd like to have for our film, and this setting can be found on the console of your camera. The aspect ratio is the first important piece of emotion we can communicate to our viewers. If we are looking for something to have an "old-television feel" or a grainy, hard-scrabble look, we might opt for 1.33:1. If we'd like it to have a more dramatic, bijou cinematic feel, we'd likely go with 16:9, 1.85:1, or another wide aspect ratio. Aspect ratio is one of the most basic elements of film language. (Note: Using the same aspect ratio you will be shooting in as your frame in your storyboard will make visualizing your film easier.)

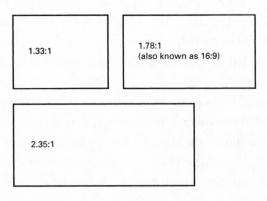

2. Filling the Frame: Shot-by-Shot Composition

Now that you have your frame, you have to decide how to fill it. It helps to think not of a movie but of a still picture. Remember that a film or video is really not moving but is an optical illusion with anywhere from fifteen to thirty still images cycled and projected each second. When we take a camera and focus it on something, we are creating a universe that exists *only* within the frame. When we watch a piece of visual media, we in essence contract with the filmmaker that we will lend him our eyes, in the form of his camera, and he will take over and direct our eyes to see just what we need to see at any moment.

The basic element of the frame is the composition of your shot, which has roots firmly planted in the long history of painting and other visual art. The artist gets to decide what will be in the picture, where the various things in the picture will be placed relative to one another, what will be in focus or out of focus, what will be lit or not lit for emphasis.

If you have ever picked up a camera (or a cell phone) to take a picture and positioned the subjects to make for a better shot; or zoomed the camera in or moved closer in order to have your subjects more fully fill the frame—which likely means all of us—you already understand the basics of composition.

When you create motion pictures, you shoot many of these individual frames, which will be combined in various ways to tell a larger story, but it is helpful to think of each frame as a small story nested within the larger one.

What is within the frame inhabits a three-dimensional space. If everything were on the same plane, as in a two-dimensional world, we would need to talk about only left and right and up and down, which are represented by the x axis and the y axis. But in a three-dimensional world, we introduce depth, which is captured

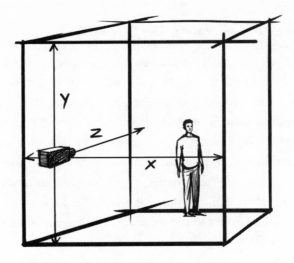

by the z axis, which extends into infinity behind the screen. While visual media have been viewed largely in two dimensions, they are shot and experienced by the viewer as a three-dimensional world.

There is often more than one object in a frame, and the film-maker must decide how the different elements of a scene (or what is captured in the frame) relate to one another. Is one above the others, or placed farther away from the camera or more in the background? Is someone or something pushed to the extreme side of the frame, away from the main action? These are questions of composition.

A classic example of this kind of use of composition within a frame comes from *Citizen Kane*, which is considered by many to be one of the greatest films ever made. Directed by twenty-six-year-old Orson Welles, the movie is an encyclopedia for visual storytelling. One particular scene highlights this idea of composition on different planes within a frame. When Charles Foster Kane is a little boy, we are inside his house, with his mother sitting at a table with the lawyer. Both are on the right side of the frame, in the foreground, about to sign papers. His father appears farther back, on the left side of the frame. Between these two groups we see a glass window, and through the window we see the young Charles Foster Kane playing in the snow, unaware of what is happening inside the house. Welles keeps each of these planes in focus, so we see three different pictures telling a larger story to great effect: a young boy in the hands of distant forces of which he is unaware.

On an even more basic level, almost any movie you see will contain a wide variety of shots where the things in the frame (either characters or objects or landscapes) appear in different sizes, and we'll get different information and have a different experience of each of these different-size items as a viewer.

If we are attempting to bring the viewer "into a world," or a new place within that world, we might locate our camera at a distance from the subject and create a series of *extreme long shots*, or *long shots*, each one getting progressively closer to where the story or that sequence of the story will take place. These kinds of shots can function as *establishing shots* to help us locate our story. They might be extreme long shots that show an entire landscape in which the story will take place, or they might focus on a smaller landscape. An exterior scene of a house might precede a shot of an interior, telling the audience that this is where the scene is taking place: not just in a random room or set, but in this particular building.

In fact, most of these kinds of exterior/interior shots are quite often "cheats." The interior is shot either on a set or in a completely different location than the exterior, establishing shot, but the filmmaker colludes with the audience to tie these two shots together and create meaning. D. W. Griffith pioneered the use of establishing shots and interior shots, and today very few things you watch don't utilize this visual grammar. In fact, many shows or movies start with this convention. Everything from *All in the*

Family to *Family Guy* begins each episode this way. Establishing and interior shots can also be used in reverse, as we exit a world and leave the film to return to our own realities. This simple technique can help make your stories more understandable and more literate.

By choosing different kinds of shots, you can also force the viewer to engage with a character or an object more deeply and more intimately, or see something more closely. A *full-figure shot*, or *full shot*, allows us to see an entire subject or object within the frame without moving too close. This is like a play where we can see the entire subject as well as the context of where he is or what he is doing.

Full shot

A *medium shot* brings us closer along the z-axis to an actor or object. This is often shot from the waist up, and is close enough for us to see facial expressions and feel a sense of connection, while also being able to see body language and the context of the environment.

Medium shot

The *close-up* typically frames a person from the shoulders up, and allows us to continue to see some contextual information from the rest of the environment, although the shot is firmly focused on the speaker or one smaller aspect of a subject. The close-up can create emotional intimacy with a character, as we are brought into his private space. This technique is also used in documentaries that feature interviews of subjects, to establish them as important characters with something to say.

The *extreme close-up*, or *ECU*, creates the sense that we the viewer (as represented by the camera) are intimate with the subject. When the ECU is of a person's face, this kind of composition can allow us to crawl inside a character's head, especially when the shot is focused on her eyes. This can be contrasted to a *point-of-view* (or *POV*) shot, which allows us to crawl behind her eyes to see what she sees. The close-up or extreme close-up can also be used to highlight an important element, such as a gun or a clue that we will eventually need to solve a mystery, or help highlight what is at stake in your story. In this way, the shot forces us to assign priority to the information it provides. If the shot is used inappropriately, your viewers will start to lose trust in you, so use it judiciously.

Close-up

Extreme close-up

You will likely be mixing a variety of these kinds of shots in order to tell your story. While in many ways film acting has its roots in theater, and documentaries have their roots in lectures and oral presentations, the camera creates a substantial difference. There is an intimacy with the camera as it is moved and as shots are framed that bring the audience closer to the subject. These moments in many ways become smaller and more real, and the actors need not emote as in plays. This contributes to our experience of the film or visual story as being more authentic. Using each of these different shots can help bring your story to life in amazing ways.

Here's an example of how they might be used together.

In Hitchcock's thriller *Notorious*, Ingrid Bergman's character's identity as an American agent has been uncovered by her German husband (played by Claude Rains) and his mother. The two decide they must poison her slowly so as not to arouse suspicion. In one scene, they are all sitting around the coffee table in the morning. The camera fixes on Claude Rains as he uses a draw poker, a syringe-like instrument, to poke a hole in his cigar. The camera then pans (or swings) over to a coffee cup at Ingrid Bergman's lips. Without a word being said, we in the audience understand that poison has been "injected" into the coffee. Later in the film, as the poisoning progresses, Hitchcock draws on this knowledge as the characters are again sitting having coffee. We understand what is going on, and Hitchcock uses several extreme close-ups of a coffee cup to heighten the tension and to ultimately convey the moment that Ingrid Bergman understands she is being poisoned when he connects an image of her eyes and an image of the cup.

In choosing what to put in each frame, it is important to think about what is going to help the viewer stay within, and deepen his involvement in, your story—where the camera or the viewer's eyes need to be focused at each moment. So, for us, if we are shooting a scene of a boy trying to explain to his teacher why he was late once again and the boy keeps making up bigger and bigger excuses, as an audience, we might learn more about what is actually happening here by focusing on the amused and nonbelieving teacher while we listen to the boy.

Or we might be hearing from a boxer about the toll of a life in the ring. We could be focused on the boxer telling his story, or we could find ourselves staring at two hands twisted in arthritic pain, with bulging knuckles that belie the quiet, aging voice of someone who long ago left the ring. Either of these shots could be right, depending on the larger context of the piece, but they are important choices we make in constructing a literate story.*

Sometimes it is about not what is in the frame, but what is outside the frame. There is probably no one better at this than Hitchcock, who didn't put the moments of true violence on the screen, but left them to our imaginations, which is often more terrifying if set up well. In the famous shower scene of *Psycho*, we do see a victim and a perpetrator. We see a knife in the air and we hear screams, and the unmistakable phallic symbol of the knife held

---

* Sometimes the image that conveys the most meaning is found in the characters' eyes or the hands, or some other aspect of their physicality, and sometimes it is found elsewhere, such as in their environment. One of the Maysles brothers' classic films, *Grey Gardens*, chronicles the life of then-eighty-year-old former socialite Edith Bouvier Beale and her daughter, Edie, who at the time were living as near recluses in an old, decaying mansion in tony East Hampton, New York, notwithstanding their familial connections to former First Lady Jacqueline Bouvier Kennedy Onassis. The film is full of amazing shots of the two women vamping and playing to the Maysleses' camera, yet some of the most powerful images in the film are not of the mother and daughter, but rather a recurring series of images throughout the film of an old wall in the house that is slowly being eaten away by a family of raccoons living inside it. It is literally being eaten away from the inside, and time and decay are measured by the raccoons' slow destruction.

close to Janet Leigh's abdomen, but we never see the actual act of stabbing. Anyone who has had the terrifying pleasure of watching this film can understand how one can use a series of images (in this case fifty different shots combined to create the three-minute sequence) to tell a story.

Composition of the frame is a question of what we are capturing not just with the camera, but from what perspective.

3. Placement of the Camera: From Where Is the Viewer Looking?

Just as we allow the filmmaker to hijack our eyes through composition, we also agree to sit wherever he would like, allowing him to have us view a scene from any place that suits his fancy. That's the contract.

But we're now the filmmaker, so the first question for us is: Where is the camera (and ultimately our viewer) sitting? If the camera is placed on the sidewalk and directed straight ahead, level and low, we might see only feet walking along the path ahead. Or the camera might be at waist height, capturing only midsections.

You might choose to place the camera low and tilt it upward, in what is called a *low-angle shot*. This gives us the sense that we are looking up at the character or shot, and is often used to make the subject more important or powerful. Think of how any political campaign ad shoots its candidate from slightly below in order to impress upon the viewer the candidate's stature. When taken to an extreme, the low-angle shot can also be used to make someone appear menacing—so be careful here.

The reverse of this would be to place the camera higher than the subject it is shooting and to shoot down at it—a *high-angle shot*. This technique can put the character into a weaker or powerless position. These two techniques might be used together in a two-person dialogue scene where the camera angles are exaggerated to

Low-angle shot

emphasize one person's power over the other. This technique is often used to contrast the relative size of two subjects within the frame in political or advocacy pieces, with the candidate that is being touted shot from below and displayed larger in the frame, and the opponent shot from above and displayed smaller in the frame.

High-angle shot

Another technique that filmmakers use to change the viewer's perspective is to shift the camera from its usual position of being essentially parallel, or level, with the ground and creating what is called a *Dutch angle*, or *canted shot*. This technique creates a sense of unease and discomfort within the viewer, as the world he is watching is quite literally "askew."

Dutch angle shot

We might also have the camera be positioned in the line of sight of a character in order to create the sensation that we are seeing the scene directly from his perspective or point of view (hence the term *point of view* or *POV shot*). A character is pictured gazing at something we can't see. The next shot is of that thing, and we, the audience, suddenly inhabit the eyes of the character. "It is natural to suppose that the camera is an extension of the eye," says the philosopher Stanley Cavell. Then it ought to follow that if you place the camera at the physical point of view of the character, it will objectively reveal what the character is viewing. But the fact is, if we have been given the idea that the camera is placed so that what we see is what the character sees *as he sees it,* then what is shown to us is not just something seen but also a specific mood in which it is seen.

If you've watched any television at all, you're familiar with the *over-the-shoulder shot,* typically used in a conversation between actors or, in a documentary, between interviewer and interviewee. The camera is placed behind one of the characters and captures the back of the person's shoulder and head on one side of the frame, while looking at the front of the other person. The image would be typically reversed within the scene to capture the complementary shot from behind the other person in a series of *reverse shots.* This puts the viewer in the room with the two people, but clearly "outside" the dialogue.

Again, you will likely use many of these kinds of shots even within the same piece. The more comfort you have with the effect of each of them, the more facile and effective a visual storyteller you will be.

4. A Few More Grammatical Ideas on Composition

The filmmaker can choose to focus the viewer's eye not just through what is in the frame, but literally what is in focus in the frame. We might place a subject in the foreground of a shot, and while we see the background—perhaps the landscape she is standing in, or even another character—this other element could be out of focus, not making the subject compete for our attention in the frame. The focus might also change within a shot, shifting our focus. Or we might be in a POV shot and the character who is "seeing" with the camera is focused on a nearby object. Everything beyond this is out of focus. Then the focus resolves to a new object. This is called *rack focus,* and it effectively shifts our gaze and attention from one place in the frame to another. We also might choose to have the shot deliberately out of focus, if it is a POV shot from someone who is drunk or otherwise visually impaired, or we might show his view of the world through a Dutch angle, to convey his state of mind. Again, the camera is the viewer's eye.

When it comes to composition, there are no universal rights or wrongs—it all depends on what you are trying to achieve at any particular frame of your story. There are, however, a few general rules that can help you create more engaging visual images.

One of those rules can be traced back to the field of painting and is referred to as the *rule of thirds*.

John Thomas Smith, in *Remarks on Rural Scenery*, published in 1797, quotes the eighteenth-century painter Sir Joshua Reynolds:

> Two distinct, equal lights, should never appear in the same picture: One should be principal, and the rest sub-ordinate, both in dimension and degree: Unequal parts and gradations lead the attention easily from part to part, while parts of equal appearance hold it awkwardly suspended, as if unable to determine which of those parts is considered as the subordinate. And to give the utmost force and solidity to your work, some part of the picture should be as light, and some as dark as possible.

White, meet black. So far, so good. But then Smith adds a caveat:

> Analogous to this "rule of thirds," I have presumed to think that, in connecting or breaking the various lines of a picture, it would likewise be a good rule to do it in general, by a scheme of proportion; for example in a design of landscape, to determine the sky at about two-thirds; or else at about one-third, so that the material objects might occupy the other two: Again, two thirds of one element (as of water) to one third of another element (as of land).

This has been an artistic and photographic standard for many generations, and we ought to make use of it. Think of the person or thing you'll be shooting. Then draw a line breaking the y-axis of a frame into three equal pieces; then do the same for the x-axis. You'll end up with a tic-tac-toe-like box of nine squares imposed on the frame. There are four points of intersection within the frame.

The rule of thirds says that your eyes will be naturally drawn to each of those intersecting points and that the lines are natural points of division within the frame. You can take advantage of the audience's natural inclinations by working within this framework. Try placing the main focus of the frame at one of these points of intersection instead of dead center. In addition to this, a lesser but interesting object might be placed at an opposite point of intersection, effectively to balance the frame.

In the example below, we notice the composition that places both the protagonist's eyes and the object of his attention, the diamond ring, at key coordinates of the grid.

The rule of thirds, like other rules, is ripe for being broken—

Rule of thirds

and of course there are many wonderful cinematic shots that place a character squarely in the center of the frame. The knowledge from the eighteenth century remains true: the rule of thirds works by creating more pleasing, effective visual messages. Of course, visual storytelling is not just about creating pleasing visual images; it is at its core about story—so don't take this rule too literally. Play with different compositions and see what each of them does for your particular story.

You'll find, even when you place your character or object directly in the center of the frame, that the eye line (or the subject's mouth, or some other central characteristic you'd like your audience to focus upon) will find itself on one of the lines of division suggested by this rule. You should also use this rule as a way of guiding the composition of your shots in regard to environment.

As an example, imagine you are shooting a landscape that has a horizon line between land and sky. If you want the viewer to be focused on the land, you might have the horizon line two-thirds of the way up in the frame. Or, alternatively, you might switch this if you want the viewer to be focused on the sky. If you were to split the frame in half and place equal amounts of sky and land in the frame, your viewer would be less directed, and hence more unsettled.

Another rule that needs to be considered while you are composing your frames is the *180-degree rule*. Visual language allows us to combine a variety of individual shots to create a larger story. This story exists within a world that we ask the viewer to inhabit, and as it turns out, while the viewer is able to make certain, almost intuitive connections with these images, there are parameters that disconnect the viewer from that world. The 180-degree rule refers to one of those situations. Imagine a scene with two people in it. One is on the left side of the screen looking right, and the second is on the right side of the screen looking left, perhaps looking at the other character if the two are in dialogue. The camera can be placed in different places to capture different shots that will be combined to create the scene, but if it strays too far—more than 180 degrees, or more than halfway around the circumference of the scene—the characters will end up on opposite sides of the screen. This is unconventional and can wreak havoc on an audience (and the literacy of your visual story).

A few more hints. Don't crowd your human subject unless the story's intent is to leave him or her with no metaphorical space to breathe. Leave some head space or air between the frame and your subject. Or you might choose to move the frame in on the forehead, but you usually don't want to cut off the frame in the middle of the head.

Similarly, if your human subject is facing in one direction, you don't want to place him just on that side of the frame. By giving him space to move or gaze in a certain direction, you invite the viewer to do the same. Also, don't cut your characters or subjects off at the joints (e.g., the knees), as this is uncomfortable to the viewer. It turns out that we have no problem "filling in the blanks" and seeing the off-screen parts of a character if he is cropped *between* joints, but have a hard time visualizing anything more than a character with no feet or shins if he is cropped *at* the joints.

With every rule, we could of course find many examples of films that have broken it—sometimes with dismal failure, and sometimes to great effect, but it is often the case that the times that rule-breaking works is in films meant for very sophisticated cinephile audiences who can appreciate and understand the dialogue between that particular visual story and the conventions of film grammar.

As we would say to a young student who wants to be an improvisational jazz musician, first learn the notes, chords, and conventions. Then go out and break the rules. Unless your project is intended to be a candidate for the Palme d'Or at the Cannes Film Festival and you are determined to create your own cinematic language, the closer you stick to these rules, the more literate your efforts will be.

5. Moving Stories: Creating Motion

Up until this point, we have been talking about a still image that captures a singular moment in time. But there is a point where cinema and moving images divert from the world of painting and photography. Our images will be moving—or at least sequentially projected and shuffled in a way that expresses movement, one of the first grand illusions of cinema.

Movement can come from two different elements, whether in isolation or in combination. We can experience the movement of things within a frame (e.g., a person moving or a ball flying through the air), or we can experience the camera moving either through direct movement (e.g., the cameraman walking forward into a scene) or the movement of a lens (e.g., zooming in or out).

Each of these has a different visual effect. When the body of the camera is still and either things move in front of it or the lens shifts, with the camera as our eyes, we experience the movement the way we would in real life if we were standing still and adjusting our gaze. When the camera moves, it is as if we the viewers move, which is a whole different sensation.

The situation where the only things moving are the objects in front of the camera is in some ways the easiest to understand, but it takes some thought to control. We talked earlier about the positioning of people and things within a frame. But when we talk about movement of these things within a sequence of frames, we are talking about *blocking*, a term and a concept directly borrowed from live theater.

Blocking is how you keep the action neatly inside the frame. You can accomplish this either by making the frame large enough to accommodate all the movement, or by ensuring that everyone rehearses his movements in order to be in the right place at the right time and to stay within the frame. This is where the term *hitting your mark* comes from.

Of course, it's not just the things in front of the camera that can create motion, but also the camera itself. When we begin working with new students, we use the most basic camera—and in fact, even your cell phone can do the trick. If you wanted to get closer to a subject than in the previous shot, the simplest thing to do would be to use the zoom feature on the camera. The lens is moving, and not the camera. The eyes of the audience are adjusting their frame of vision, but the body is still not moving.

If we were to keep our bodies still but swiveled our heads, we could be looking up or down, left or right, reframing what we saw. This would equate to a camera on a tripod being swiveled up or down, left or right. The vertical movement is referred to as a *tilt*, and the horizontal movement is referred to as a *pan*.

Imagine yourself sitting on a park bench reading the newspaper. All you see are the pages in front of you and the small bit of sidewalk at the bottom of your gaze. Two shoes walk into your line of sight beneath the bottom of the paper; the rest of the body is blocked by your newspaper. You might look down and focus on the feet as you put the paper aside. You then slowly begin to move up the legs, and your gaze continues to rise until you reach the top of a very large character staring down at you. This would be an example of a *tilt*. If you began to turn your head down the pathway to see who might be approaching from your side, this would be an example of a *pan*.

Another option is physical movement of the camera. This

entails walking the camera forward, or allowing it to slide on some sort of track, which is where the name *tracking shot* originates. This can also be called a *dolly shot*, as in some cases the camera is moved not on tracks, but on wheels. Tracking shots are smoother and can move in any direction, toward or away from something, from side to side, up or down, diagonally—virtually any direction you can imagine, each creating the sense of movement in the audience. The smoother the movement, the more the viewer will sense she is almost floating, as opposed to the kind of movement our bodies typically experience. We experience this subtle difference as a viewer, but nonetheless suspend our awareness and allow the camera to take us for the ride.

Walking the camera creates a unique sensation for the viewer, as we physically feel the movement of the camera in a way that is more connected to our body. It gives the resulting film a raw, unofficial feel, used to great effect in films such as *Saving Private Ryan* or *Battle of Algiers*, and even in the television comedy *The Office*. The walking camera is called a *hand-held shot*. Roger Ebert calls it a "queasicam." The viewer experiences it in relation to the still, fluid, beautifully composed cinematography of Hollywood and feels it to have a certain sense of authenticity. It can feel more "alive" and unmediated—or it can make your story unwatchable, or the viewer sick, if it shakes enough.

One of the most profound examples of the distinction between zoom and a tracking shot comes from the epic film *Shoah*, a documentary about the Holocaust made in 1985 by French director Claude Lanzmann. He brilliantly uses movement of the camera along the tracks of a railroad, footage that is intercut with other scenes within the film but recalled at several moments.

As we first approach a concentration camp, the shot begins at a distance, moving toward a large prison-like compound. As the camera nears, we recognize the compound's gates as those of Auschwitz, and place ourselves on the outside of a concentration camp. We experience the physical movement of the camera, as if we, too, were literally traveling those train tracks, being taken into a camp. Just as we get to the entrance of the camp, the camera halts like a boxcar that has stopped in its tracks. Yet our gaze is being taken inside the camp through the lens of the camera, which begins zooming in. We experience these moments completely differently, more as voyeur than visitor.

Through this simple camera technique, we understand that Lanzmann is saying that he (and we) can move only so close to the experience and gaze in, but we can't inhabit that world in any real way outside of what the camera can impart to us through testimonies of survivors.

Undoubtedly your camera has some sort of zooming capability, and you have substantial experience with this function. Other features might seem a bit more intimidating, and you might also think of them as prohibitively expensive. They don't have to be. You can find inexpensive tripods that allow you to tilt and pan, and there are many sites on the Internet that can help you improvise the kinds of expensive tools that Hollywood studios have access to. There are plenty of creative ways to mimic equipment like tracks and dollies and Handycam equipment that allows for fluid camera movement. My son found a design for a Handycam system in one of his (and my) favorite magazines, *What Works*. The design used an old dumbbell lying around in our basement and a few dollars of supplies from the hardware store. My son jumped on it, and within an hour he was out in the street, camera and homemade five-dollar Steadicam in hand, running alongside a friend who was skateboarding. He even enlisted me to run all around the neighborhood and up and down stairs through the house as he chased me with his video camera. The footage was remarkably stable.

Your pans and tilts might be unsteady and not very fluid at first, but this will change quickly with a little practice. Getting comfortable with camera movement can help make your visual stories more deeply engaging and can better allow you to take full advantage of the language and grammar of filmmaking.

6. A Self-Contained World: Everything in the Frame Is Story

Mise-en-scène, French for "stage setting," refers to all the visual aspects of the film. While it can incorporate composition and even camera movement, for our purposes it refers to all the physical elements represented in the frame. This includes the set design, props, costumes, lighting, and even the acting.

It is good practice to keep the frame filled only with things that are relevant to and consistent with the story being told. Sets shouldn't be cluttered with stuff that distracts the viewer, unless that is your objective (or the character's environment is meant to be messy and confusing). Mise-en-scène, as with the other aspects of visual storytelling, is all about choices, and there can be a lot of them.

An important thing to keep in mind is that the camera captures everything it is pointed at, from the movement of things within the set or environment you are shooting to the set or environment itself. Everything lying on a table next to an interview subject or actor becomes part of the story, and the viewer can either find meaning in it (at best) or be thrown out of your story if that item is in conflict with the rest of the film (at worst).* Everything in your frame should have a purpose in advancing the story.

Lighting can be used to help focus the viewer on particular images within the frame, and can also lend an overall sense of professionalism to your project. There are whole crews that focus on lighting in a studio film, but it is ultimately the responsibility of the cinematographer.

The good news is that not only has the technology of digital cameras made visual storytelling more accessible and less expensive, but also digital video cameras are designed to deal with light conditions much more effectively than film cameras.

Depending on what you are shooting, you may want to use only natural light, as it is often easy for a viewer to sense the use of artificial light in a frame, which can send a message as to the authenticity of the image that may conflict with your story.

You can often take advantage of natural light coming in a window or, if you are outside, near where you've placed your subject. If you have ever taken a family photo outside, you know that by positioning the subjects so that the sun is behind the camera, you will get your clearest picture. You can use this natural light by bouncing it off something light-colored (try white poster board) and directing it exactly where you want it to shine. If you are inside, experiment with other sources of light. Lamps and even candles can be used to great effect.

If you're working on a project that includes subject interviews, whether in a documentary, public service announcement, or cam-

---

* Some people even make sport of this. You might have heard about the wristwatch on Charlton Heston in the famous chariot race of *Ben Hur*. This is a myth, but it is true that one of the characters in the Civil War film *Glory* can be seen to be sporting a digital watch. As a visual storyteller, you are a world builder, and that world must make intrinsic sense lest your viewers find their way out of it.

paign commercial, and you want to add an element of professionalism to it, you'll likely want to use the most typical lighting setup, which is called *three-point lighting*. Essentially you have one light pointed at your subject from an angle, illuminating his face (called a *key light*); one less-bright light from the other side (called a *fill light*), which balances the key light while softening some of the shadows the key light creates; and a third light (called a *back light*) placed behind your subject, most typically on the side. This light helps create a separation between the subject and the background of the shot and adds dimension to your images.

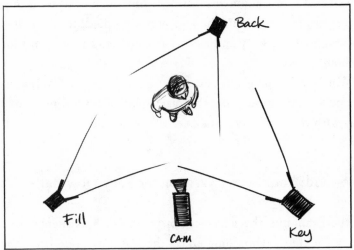

Three-point lighting

Plenty of filmmakers, especially documentary filmmakers, purposely don't use any artificial lighting and just move around the lights already available wherever they are shooting, to create more pleasing shots. Their films still manage to look pretty good. So don't feel too intimidated by lighting. Your knowledge (and comfort) will naturally grow the more you shoot. If you'd like to delve deeper into this topic, there are some excellent books and guides, which I have listed in the notes on sources.

Often one of the last things that comes into the frame is text, added after you've finished shooting. These could be *title cards*— the words that appear on the screen to orient viewers as to a location or period, identify a speaker, or provide some other bit of background that cannot be expressed through the images themselves.

There is one guiding principle in using text: it should always support and have integrity with the rest of your story. Think about the scrolling text in the opening minute of *Star Wars*, which disappears off into the universe. It not only provides us with important information, but in the way it is presented, it also helps set the stage for the story and alerts the viewer to the style of film he is about to see.

Your editing programs, even the simplest ones, will offer plenty of options and guides for the placement of text. The more you play with this, the more you'll see the possibilities.

Sound: Your Secret Weapon (or Your Downfall)

Notwithstanding the sentiment of people such as silent film star Mary Pickford, who complained that "adding sound to movies would be like putting lipstick on the Venus de Milo," sound is a crucial part of visual media today. Even though this book is about the age of the image and the importance of visual media, most moving images rely on sound in order to convey meaning.

Sound with filmic visuals evolved at roughly the same time as radio stations were blinking to life in the 1920s, and the two art forms complemented each other. Live theater could rely on visual cues to bring one into and advance a story, but radio had to rely solely on sound. Radio plays would include not only the actors' dialogue, but also voice-over narration, sound effects, and music or a soundtrack. From the familiar notes of the *William Tell Overture* as the narrator pronounces, "The Lone Ranger rides again!" to the sound of horses galloping, tumbleweed blowing, or townsfolk buzzing, sound is designed to create character and narrative and to take us from scene to scene.

Sound can spell the difference between an effective piece and one that flops. A piece can suffer from relatively poor visuals, but if you can't understand the dialogue or the sounds don't make sense in the context of the story, no image, no matter how high its quality, can save you.

We tend to think of sound as a single track, yet in reality it has several layers. If you were to look at the edit tracks of any feature film, you would actually find many more tracks devoted to sound than to image. Even if you are superimposing several images on top of one another, at any given moment you essentially have a minimal number of images on the screen at a time. Let's look at some of the layers that can help you construct your stories.

1. The Soundscape of Your World

The most primary sounds within a scene will invariably be all the *diegetic sounds*, which means the noises that might logically be found in the actual environment within which the scene is set. Such sound might be recorded at the time you are shooting, or added in later. The most common example of this is dialogue, but it could also include everything imaginable in the world portrayed in that scene: car doors closing, feet hitting the pavement, dogs barking.

The key here is that the sound must make sense in that world or it could distract from the image and throw the viewer out of the scene. For instance, if the camera places you squarely in a parked car sitting outside a restaurant, you shouldn't be able to hear a conversation in the restaurant (unless, of course, the table is bugged and the man in the car is a spy).

Diegetic sounds should work in support of the scene unfolding on the screen and should help give it depth and dimension. While shooting, focus on getting the sounds you absolutely need, such as dialogue, and avoid those sounds you absolutely don't want in your project. You might be able to eliminate some unwanted sounds later, unless they are captured at the same time you are recording someone speaking, or recording some other sound you hope to use later. There is a reason directors yell, "Quiet on the set!"

In fact, unless you are the only one present while you are shooting (in which case you have to focus on both sound and image), it is often helpful to have someone else with you who is thinking about only sound while you or someone else thinks about image. Both are separate components of storytelling that ultimately need to be as strong as possible to support the whole project.

Equipment can be minimal. Every video camera, or even cell phone with a video function, captures sound. If you are shooting with a video camera, you might invest in an inexpensive but up-graded microphone that sits on top of your camera, or you might consider a digital voice recorder that enables you to separate the sound from what the camera records and allow someone else on the crew to record sound.

You'll be able to supplement some of the natural, environmental, diegetic sounds later in the process either by re-creating them or by using sounds available from the many free sound libraries on the Internet. A number of my favorites are listed in the notes on sources.

One final hint here: consider room tone. Every environment, whether inside or outside, has an essential ambient sound. Try being quiet for a moment wherever you are. Even in the silence, there might be a baseline hissing of heat or air-conditioning, or other environmental sounds. When you go to edit your audio tracks, you will find that you are cutting up the audio in the same way you do the video, and you'll have large gaps of space in the silence. You will need these environmental sounds, or room tone, to keep the viewer within the world of your film. Whatever environment you are shooting in, quiet everyone down and record a few minutes of silence within that space. This simple technique will be invaluable later in the project, and can make for an effective piece of visual (and aural) media.

Sharpen your skills by paying close attention to the layers of sound that make up your environment. Stand on a street corner and take careful note of all the sounds you hear, from the buses rolling by, to the wind blowing the leaves in the trees, to the distant patter of children playing—whatever makes up that particular scene. You'll find it is like looking at stars: the more you stare up at the sky, the more stars you begin to see. So, too, with sounds in your environment.

2. Sound Beyond the World of Your Story

Once you have built this layer of diegetic sound, you can move on to *nondiegetic sound*, which refers to everything on your audio tracks that doesn't come from the immediate world depicted on the screen. Narration or sound effects that are added for emphasis are two examples of nondiegetic sound that can be used to construct a soundscape. Another nondiegetic sound is the music, which is often referred to by itself as the soundtrack (in actuality, it is typically *one* of the sound tracks).

If you were to stop and think about your favorite movies, chances are there would be a musical soundtrack beneath the images. Music works similarly to images in terms of evoking primal emotional responses in our brains, as it is prelingual. The sound editor David Zieff calls it "fairy dust." It can work *in concert with* images to elicit various emotions, or it can work *in contrast to* images to create different effects. Who could have imagined the choice of Beethoven's Ninth Symphony to accompany the stylized violence in the haunting scene from *A Clockwork Orange*, as young hooligans brutalize their victims? Yet that piece of music brought those images to a wholly different level.

I had the opportunity to sit in the editing room with Jonathan Demme while we were producing the documentary *I'm Carolyn Parker*. Demme is one of those directors who are keenly attuned to music, and he has an extraordinary library of songs on his iPod. We sat with a particular scene and played it over and over again, each time with a different song playing underneath it. With each song, whether upscale New Orleans jazz, a more bluesy song, or even a Middle Eastern percussive song, the images on the screen would morph in front of us and take on different meaning and emotion. The wrong music can risk turning a serious scene into campy overstatement or a comic scene into something unfunny, but it can be a powerful addition to the experience of the viewer.

Sound can also be an effective bridging tool in connecting disparate scenes. Just as you can *match on action* in a cut, you can also *match on sound*, seamlessly bringing the audience from one space to another. The sound of a door slamming might be matched up with the sound of a completely separate shot of a gavel being pounded by a judge in a courtroom. Just as with images, matching these kinds of sounds can take the viewer from one scene to another.

To tie scenes together, many editors like to make use of an *L-cut*, in which a character speaking in an oncoming scene has his voice overlaid onto the fading moments of the previous scene. This simple technique brings the viewer into the next scene through sound, and when the image follows after, we are already firmly entrenched in the scene and don't experience the cut between the two images as jarring. You'll start recognizing this technique in just about any movie you see today.

Sound can also be a crutch. Film is a visual medium, and if the images and filmic language don't carry the story and we over-rely on sound, chances are our work will not be as effective or as literate as it can be. Visual storytelling is about showing and not telling; it is often the case that the more minimal the amount of words, the better.

To become a storyteller in this medium of the twenty-first century is to become a keener observer of the world around you—in regard to both images and sounds. And once you have captured these elements, you are ready for construction.

Editing: Assembly Required

The essence of cinema is editing. It's the combination of what can be extraordinary images of people during emotional moments, or images in a general sense, put together in a kind of alchemy.
—FRANCIS FORD COPPOLA

This is the last stage of the storytelling process, but the one where it all comes together. Editing is often called *cutting*, because before the days of digital, someone picked up scissors, cut out the desired frames, and then spliced them together to create a coherent line. Alfred Hitchcock always argued that the better term would have been *assembling*, as it is the assembling of images and sequences that creates a visual narrative. We always shoot more than we use.

Visual stories work because of the compelling nature of images and because of how our brain is wired to receive them, but the true power of this medium resides in the magic that happens when images are put together to create a meaning that didn't exist until that moment. Think of individual shots as your words and sentences. In the editing process, they are spliced together to create sequences and scenes that are then combined to create narrative.

Walter Murch, editor of many great movies, including *The Conversation*, *The Godfather*, and *The English Patient*, is also a wonderful writer about the process of editing. "What is the audience going to be thinking at any particular moment?" he wonders in his book *In the Blink of an Eye*. "Where are they going to be looking? What do you want them to think about? What do they need to think about? And of course, what do you want them to feel? If you keep this in mind (and it's the preoccupation of every magician), then you are a kind of magician. Not in the supernatural sense, just an everyday, working magician."

1. Using Editing to Create Reality

As an editor, you are connecting images that are displaced or discontinuous from one another. This might involve subtle breaks, such as the shot of a person with a bag slung over his shoulder opening a door, to a later shot of him walking into the living room and putting the bag down on a chair. For purposes of moving the narrative along, the editor might choose not to show us a continual shot from the door to the living room, but we still understand these two to be connected.

The shots should be different enough so as to create a context in which the viewer can mentally "draw" what is not shown. If the shot after the cut is too close to where the last shot ended, we are jarred into seeing the obvious camera work and edit. This is referred to as a *jump cut*. An example of how language has evolved, it has also been used by many filmmakers to great effect. But don't do it unless you intend to—and you understand its effect.

Classical Hollywood cinema is based on the concept of *continuity editing*, in which the transitions of both sound and images are constructed in such a way that we do not feel the break, or the cut. These transitions allow, even seduce, the audience into experiencing the story as one piece of direct, personal, and immersive moment of reality. If a filmmaker is telling a story, just like a novelist, the narrative won't necessarily be linear or continuous. In fact, if there is more than one character, there will likely be multiple threads that are all relevant to the plot, but we ought to see it as one continuous moment. Harold and Carl Kress said it most simply: "We don't want the audience to know it's a film."

2. Using Editing to Tie Together Different Places and Characters

Editing enables the filmmaker to connect images happening within the same scene and to juxtapose images from different scenes happening in different physical places or even different times. This is called *cross-cutting*.

Think of a scene in which a woman is tied to a set of train tracks. We see a close-up of her struggling, and then we cut away to an image of a train racing along the tracks. We might flash between these two images, and as the shots of her struggling gain in intensity and the alternating shots of the train fill the frame more and more, we feel our hearts racing as we understand the implications suggested by the disparate images—which are no longer disparate in our minds. These images might have first found their way to the screen in the 1914 film serial *The Hazards of Helen*, but they have become a familiar trope—even being echoed by a woman saved by a duck in an Aflac commercial. Editing allows you not only to advance a scene along a faster time line, but also to connect completely disparate images to create new meanings and story.

3. Visual Metaphors: Written Through Editing

If you are trying to connect a moment with a particular emotion, you might look for visual metaphors that convey that emotion. You might also want simply to imply the passage of time or space. A series of images connected to one another, but not part of the narrative plot—think of the change in seasons and the falling of leaves from a tree—can do this in a way that is succinct and clear: through montage.

Think back to the original *Rocky*, in which we see images of Sylvester Stallone running through the streets of Philadelphia, passing under the elevated train tracks, hitting a speed bag, doing one-arm push-ups, using a side of beef hung from a hook as his heavy bag, back to the one-arm push-ups in the gym, out to a shot of him running through the streets by the waterfront, and ultimately up the stairs of the Philadelphia Museum of Art, where he dances and shadowboxes triumphantly. All this virtually without words, except for the theme song for the movie—"Gonna Fly Now," written by Bill Conti. Regardless of what you thought of the increasingly manipulative *Rocky* franchise of movies, seeing this montage will capture your imagination, even through the cheese.

4. Editing Can Hide the Blemishes

In the case of either a documentary or a fiction film, you might use editing to cover unwanted moments, such as camera movement in your footage. You will often be shooting with just one camera and without the ability to do more than one take—especially if you are trying to have your story feel less constructed and re-hearsed.

One choice, of course, is to show the camera movement. You might, however, also be manipulating the focus of the lens between the moments while continuously shooting, and this makes for a less-than-pleasing image. This is where *B-rolls* or *cutaways* come in. If you take time during the shoot to get some shots that capture the environment, or perhaps the object the character is talking about or holding, or anything that you think can help tell the story in place of the image of the person speaking, you'll be able to use these shots to cover the places in which you want to continue to use the audio track from your shoot but where the image itself isn't helpful. Thinking ahead about this can save you many gray hairs in the editing process.

5. Moving from Frame to Frame: Make Transitions Work for You

The language of editing is not just in the shot selection and assemblage, but also in the very transitions between frames. While a variety of techniques is available—and they all have their place (please, though, not the magic wand coming across the screen that always seems to crop up in wedding and bar mitzvah videos, with painful results)—let's focus on the three principal transitions you'll likely make use of.

A *cut* is when you make a sharp transition from the end of one shot to the beginning of another without hesitation. It might be used within a scene to tie together various camera angles; or between scenes, to emphasize the connection between images. In contrast to this, a *dissolve* essentially overlaps the final frames of one image and the first frames of the next, so that the viewer experiences the two clips literally morphing from one to the other. This creates a more fluid transition and can help tie the two scenes together, while also serving to denote the sequential passage of time or a change in physical space. A third option is the *fade-in* or *fade-out*, which utilizes the gradual softening of an image and then the intensification of the next—with the effect of coming out of one scene completely before we are taken into the next.

These techniques are almost used as punctuation in your visual stories, and when used well, they can lend a real sense of professionalism to your piece. And with today's editing software, the good news is that it is extremely easy to move effortlessly between each of these techniques to see what will work well at each transition.

When you are shooting, the tendency is to stop recording when you think you have your shot. But if you do this, you'll find yourself stuck later. Extra frames—both at the beginning and end of a clip—are critical to making transitions, so start your camera rolling several frames before you begin your scene or your interview and let it roll for several seconds afterward. Trust me on this: you'll be thankful you did. Otherwise, you might miss a telling facial expression. And the extra length makes it easier to eliminate the chaff.

6. *The Technical Stuff: What Do I Need?*

Even though the language of editing is still firmly rooted in film's early days, the actual physical process has changed significantly. While the first century of editing was done by literally splicing frames of film together, which necessitated a linear process, as each frame was joined together in sequential fashion, the advent of computers and digital technology introduced new opportunities and work flow. Editing software is readily available today for your PC or Mac, or even your tablet or cell phone. While the screens and technology might differ with each of the various software programs or applications, the digital process is basically the same. You will first log all your footage—breaking it up into individual shots or takes. These will be placed into individual bins, which you will label, to find them more easily later.

You will then take clips from each of these bins and place them in a time line, trimming them to where you want to come in and out and lining them up against other clips to form an assembly. You'll do this with both audio and video tracks in what could be a multiplicity of layers, and then you'll begin the process of putting in transitions and moving from an assembly, to a rough cut, and then a fine cut, and ultimately a finished cut.

7. The Story Unfolds and Unfolds

Editing is a process of construction. A table is a good metaphor. You first get your individual pieces together (the legs and the top), and then you assemble them with glue and pegs or nails. Once the table is held together, you go through many steps of sanding, finishing, lacquering, and finishing some more, before it is ready to be used. Editing is about not only connecting images and cutting and then assembling clips, but also establishing the overall pacing and rhythm of a film or visual story. There is a cadence in successful pieces that is similar to the way particular songs catch our unconscious desire for musical patterns that touch a deep place in us. "We are all rhythmic creatures," said David Zieff, "even if we don't realize it."

Step back in the editing process and try to feel those rhythms. Often the soundtrack or even music that is playing in the room while you are cutting can help you find them—and trust your instincts. Walter Murch talked about the best cut coming at the point when the viewer would naturally blink. The French photographer Henri Cartier-Bresson talked about this as "the decisive moment" he was looking to capture in his still photographs. As Cariter-Bresson wrote in his 1952 book of photographs entitled *Images à la Sauvette*, "There is nothing in this world that does not have a decisive moment." Your job as editor is to identify these moments and use them to tell your larger story.

A Note on Technology: Don't Be Intimidated

Don't think that you need expensive, sophisticated gear. Several years ago I had the great pleasure of being invited to be one of seventeen people documenting the Dalai Lama's visit to Central Park. I was a less experienced shooter than the others and was intimidated when I saw many people showing up with big shoulder-mounted camera rigs. Then I met Rickie Leacock.

Rickie is a legend among documentary filmmakers, having worked with Robert Flaherty on *The Louisiana Story*, and Robert Drew on *Primary*. Leacock was one of the pioneers of the direct cinema approach to documentaries, which stressed an observational kind of shooting and constructed visual stories without the use of narration or interviews. He also was one of the founders of the film program at MIT—so it was easy to imagine him as a technologist. Yet here was this man approaching with an easy smile and a small consumer video camera in his hands that was at most a fifth the size of the cameras that I and everyone else was holding. We seventeen filmmakers had been given the same mission—go out and find whatever story you would like to tell, and then shoot it.

It was a magnificent day, with the park teeming with New York City's human fauna. Everything in sight seemed to call for the camera's attention. And the cameras were rolling like crazy, at anything that moved and a lot that didn't. By the end of the day, the seventeen of us had gathered together again. Everyone had shot hours of footage and was busy emptying their pockets of mini-DV cassettes. I approached Rickie as he was opening his camera to take out his tapes, to ask how his day had been. He held out what I saw was a single tape, holding a paltry nineteen minutes of footage. On it, he said, was a beautiful story. And it was.

I watched much of the footage that others had shot, and it was a mind-numbing cascade of images. Then I watched Rickie's. He had captured the entire day in brief: the sweetness of children with their families, the delight of the crowd in the day, and the Dalai Lama connecting with an adoring audience with his humor, humility, and wisdom. The images Rickie captured that day told a complete story—well beyond the hours and hours amassed by everyone else, with cameras that cost five times as much.

My point here is that it is not about the technology you use, but what you do with it.

Taking Your First Steps: or, Where Do I Go from Here?

This all may sound hard. It can be. It is one thing to be able to listen to a Mozart symphony and identify all the layered instruments, notes, and structure, and quite another to pick up each instrument and play it. Steven Spielberg, George Lucas, and Martin Scorsese have spent lifetimes honing their craft, and they have teams of professionals working with them on each aspect of their productions.

Yet this should not scare you away. For every Spielberg, there are scores of individuals just like you learning to use these new instruments of literacy to tell their stories with astounding success. Start with simple, direct, short pieces and get your feet under you, and your comfort and proficiency will grow. Once you sit down in front of your computer and editing software, you will find that the construction process that is editing is actually quite intuitive.

There are reasons for this. We have been viewing these things for a lifetime. To take the next step on the way to real visual literacy, both receptive and expressive, is to practice critical close viewing of a professional piece of media. Pick your favorite film and then turn the sound off. See how tension is established, how character is established, how place is established. See how the story is actually an amalgamation of shots that, when pushed together, create meaning. Pause on a crucial shot and study the composition. Think of where the camera is placed and how things are framed. Then turn on the sound again and see how it works to deepen or alter what is on the screen.

Let your children watch television, watch it with them, and then talk about what worked and why. Whether it is a feature film, a sitcom, or the seven o'clock news, you'll begin to see the patterns within a piece of media, and you will be more literate as a result.

Watch the commercials, too. Record them and watch them again. Slow them down and watch them again. The people who produce them are familiar with all the tricks I've just described, and they use them promiscuously to get you to buy companies' products.

Start small. If narrative filmmaking is what excites you, try to tell a small story, or create just a scene. If you are interested in documentaries, shoot an interview with a family member and then watch it to see how the choices you made impacted the footage. Try to construct simple digital stories the way we do with our students at the Media Arts Lab, using images that already exist in your family albums; or shoot new images for the piece and exercise new muscles of framing and composition. If you want to make a political commercial for a local candidate, study the multitude of pieces that exist on the Internet to understand the tropes that can be drawn on to make your piece more literate.

The language of filmmaking, like the English language itself, is not static but constantly evolving. The Internet can be a vast wasteland of badly told, ineffective stories—you can learn as much from what doesn't work as from what does—but it is also filled with examples of wonderful, powerful, compelling stories told by today's emerging culture of visual storytellers, and those storytellers look just like you and me.

■ TEACHING A NEW GENERATION

Dennis Maika has taught eleventh-grade American history for thirty-six years in Mount Kisco, New York, and he had seen a near-constant decline in the quality of term papers as the world of standardized testing and rote memorization took over our schools. Kids weren't engaged, and it seemed that sustained intellectual effort wasn't valued in our system anymore. There had to be another way to get his students at Fox Lane High School really interested in American history again.

Dozens of public school teachers had said much the same thing to me: they were hamstrung by the battery of No. 2 pencil tests the district was forcing on them. While they *knew* the students were quite smart and ready to throw themselves with vigor at a project that intrigued them, the structure of public schooling was unfriendly to such outbursts of creativity. I believed, as did many teachers, that students weren't failing the schools, but rather, the schools were failing the students.

We helped Maika respond to this problem. At our encouragement, he replaced the term paper with an eight-month-long intensive video project with the same level of scholarly rigor that the school would have had for a written submission.

The assignment didn't change—document the effects of a single presidential decision—but the students now had to do it in a visual-media-based format. They had to research, write, revise, edit, and then produce a ten-minute video, which is a lot harder than it sounds. They had to look for original archival source material and also produce their own. This requires a level of library skills that were much greater than I ever had to develop using the Dewey decimal system in the 1960s.

Maika has seen academic fads come and go. But his eyes light up when he talks about the impact of this approach. "This was one of the most exciting projects I have ever done in my history of teaching," he told me later. "Students explored topics with a seriousness and a depth that I had never seen before. And they went through multiple revisions as they thought about the audience that would eventually see this—and not just about handing in a term paper."

One group of students did their video about Truman's decision to drop the bomb on Hiroshima. For their ending, they wrote and recorded a rapper's poetic song that related this moment in American history to their world, and they asked hard questions about the modern use of weapons of mass destruction. Another group created a CNN-style newscast and delivered the assignment in modern news vernacular. The projects took enormous commitment and follow-through from the students, but they said it didn't feel like work. One of them told Maika that he had checked a book out of the library for the first time in his academic career. Maika had never seen students prouder of their efforts and their work.

This story is being repeated with increasing frequency at some of the most forward-looking school districts, and it presents us with a national choice. There are two basic paths we can follow in an age of visual literacy. The public schools can decide to confront the reality of twenty-first-century communication and develop simple programs that teach students not only how to read and write, but also how to listen and speak, in all the media that really matter. Or they can let the inevitable forces of change get in front of them, and then attempt to cobble together a response years down the road, when the total obsolescence of their curricula becomes apparent.

I know this is phrased in a stark and uncompromising way, but I believe it to be one of the critical choices our nation faces in the next decade. And having spent the last ten years studying the academic regimens of public schools—while developing our own educational programs—I have seen the painfully obvious gaps in our system.

One of the biggest deficiencies is the way we measure whether our children are actually learning something, or wasting their days bored in a classroom absorbing stuff that won't make a difference in their lives and won't help them in their future careers. We are not only story animals; we are also reward-driven in a way that harkens back to Pavlov's canines. Show us a carrot, and we'll doggedly work our way toward it. So it is no surprise that human nature suggests that *what* we measure and *how* we measure it will dictate *what* we choose to focus on and *how* we go about it along the way.

We need a rethinking of how we measure both literacy and progress in this new sphere of literacy. Education has always been focused on preparing people for the workforce and creating citizens who are fully able to participate in society. The skills needed to compete fully in the global economy are quite different now from what they were even a few decades ago, yet our schools are stuck in a mentality from a different era.

The Massachusetts Institute of Technology says that part of its mission is "preparing students for jobs that don't exist yet." The noted educator Sir Ken Robinson, who led a national commission on creativity, education, and the economy in the United Kingdom and is the author of *Out of Our Minds: Learning to Be Creative*, suggests that we need to be graduating children who will have the skills necessary to solve the unanticipated problems of the future. Both MIT's and Robinson's points revolve around skills such as creativity, innovation, problem solving, cross-cultural understanding, and communication. In fact, throughout the history of education, communication has been at the center of the experience, regardless of subject matter. We can't learn (or teach) what we can't communicate—and, increasingly, that communication is being done through visual media.

In today's world, the skills our children require are about not just the kind of rote memorization of facts that can be best measured by standardized tests, but the ability to take in information critically, analyze and synthesize that information, and express oneself effectively.

I am not suggesting that we throw everything out about public schools, but we need to view our current system through the lens of visual communication. When we look closely at the art of media making, we see that it goes a long way toward developing those life skills that are increasingly valued in the workplace.

If we can combine this emphasis on a changing literacy with deep and rich math, science, social studies, language arts, and other skills, we might get there.

Still, a problem must be acknowledged up front. *How* to measure is as important as *what* to measure, and assessment drives our educational agenda—as it should.

The staggering size of our modern educational bureaucracies and the ungovernable nature of public school quality control mean that we have fallen in love with the idea of quantification. If we can't measure it by numbers, it must not exist. The end result of the 2001 education reform known as No Child Left Behind was that our schools were put even more firmly on the footing of the "scientific management" principles first articulated in 1911 by Frederick Winslow Taylor, which divided factory jobs into precisely calculated motions of repetitive action to maximize output. This did indeed result in greater American productivity—Joseph Stalin was said to be a great fan of Taylor's ideas—but it elevated the role of the drone worker and diminished the role of the master craftsman who had an organic and even emotional connection to his work.

President Obama and Secretary of Education Arne Duncan tried to move beyond the largely ineffective education policies of the previous administration with their Race to the Top program, which offered up billions of dollars as incentives to states to start creative educational strategies. What they failed to take into account, however, were the outdated standards used to measure success.

We are left with the same metrics—but now with more pressure for teachers to reach those metrics. This will lead to the inevitable result of less creative space for teachers to teach and students to learn and express themselves, and we'll likely fall farther behind in what really matters: the ability to think critically, communicate effectively, analyze and solve problems creatively, and collaborate.

A book called *The Global Achievement Gap*, published in 2008, cuts through the muddy thinking and administrative sediment that tend to choke any discussion of the best ways to reform our broken schools. The author, Tony Wagner, is the codirector of the

Change Leadership Group at the Harvard Graduate School of Education. He says flatly that "an endless battery of state tests is neither the most effective nor the most efficient way to hold individuals accountable, and they undermine the morale of both students and teachers." Some teachers report having to administer up to fifteen standardized tests per year to their students, and many of these are for useless administrative feel-good purposes, or are dry runs for the actual state test. These are torture for the students, who never see any point or reward. Frankly, I don't blame them.

What Wagner suggests instead is a real test that measures the variety of skills that students will actually need to develop in the global market—tasks that demonstrate critical thinking, problem solving, analysis, and creative expression. He believes, as does the educational guru Robert Sternberg, that our current array of computerized multiple-choice drills (including the vaunted SAT) provides only a poor glimpse into a single area of a student's aptitude: that of analytic capability.

Yet we all know that the kid who gets into an Ivy League school on stellar SAT scores isn't necessarily educated in the ways that matter. And even if a school district manages to produce acceptable test scores, it still may provide a poor view of whether its kids are ready to be full participating members of society. It's like trying to measure rainfall with a thermometer.

Another aspect of visual literacy that does not fit into a conventional rubric: the *performativity* of the visual medium, which is a priceless motivator of young people. Here is a time-tested way to draw shy kids out of their shells. I have seen many times how the prospect of having one's work shown publicly—and even performing in front of the camera—draws forth from kids a creative expression that the kids themselves did not know existed.

Visual media are much more effective than sports at creating friendships across social boundaries—make that social *canyons*. We all remember how going to school with more than ten people always involves a sorting out of popular kids from dorks. There is a rancid element in the human character that insists on creating in-groups and out-groups, and one traditional ticket into the in-group has been sports. Excelling at athletic competition will probably always be a way of getting the girls to like you and being invited to the coolest parties. Being into movies, let's face it, often earned you a place in social Siberia, and maybe a spot as vice president of the AV Club and master of the projection cart. All you needed were glasses with tape on them to make the picture complete.

The new visual literacy is going to change social boundaries and scramble the playing field a bit. Films are always fun to watch, and when the rewards go to the kids who show the most flair and creativity (and technical savvy) with the medium, there's going to be a shift in the standards of what makes a kid socially accepted. One of the many things I love about the 2011 J. J. Abrams homage to Steven Spielberg, *Super 8*, is the fact that the leader of the gang of kids is not the toughest or the most charismatic. He is, in fact, overweight and otherwise physically unappealing in terms of our popular culture. But he is the director of the little home movie the kids are setting out to make, which makes him the default alpha male.

Ron Howard is one of the few people who have successfully navigated the transition from child actor to healthy adult still working in the medium—now mostly behind the camera. Through his company, Imagine Entertainment, he has been responsible for creating TV shows such as *24*, *Parenthood*, and *Friday Night Lights*. When Ron was a young actor on *The Andy Griffith Show*, his off-screen time was spent largely on the basketball court and other playing fields. He was an athletic, team-sports kid. He is still competitive on the court, and strongly believes in the importance of sports in developing children, yet after decades of filmmaking, he has come to appreciate not only the creativity that is fostered in children through filmmaking, but the life skills that are developed.

Howard says that while he still values team sports, he has recognized that they mostly teach children how to react quickly. Yet the skills that seem to be most important in our adult life, regardless of profession, are centered more on slower decision making, collaborative problem solving, planning, and communication—in short, skills emphasized in the experience of filmmaking.

The inclusion of visual fluency in a core educational experience is about more than the acquisition of communication skills. It could be a catalyst for the development of critical life skills and the kind of social and emotional learning our schools do not provide.

Our modern school curricula are not set up to enable such an experience. In this sense, they are not modern, but instead, dangerously behind the times. The competencies they demand—in math, languages, and sciences—are good and necessary, but the means of communicating that knowledge is about to become seriously retrograde.

"I often wonder," writes the educational theorist Heidi Hayes Jacobs, "if many of our students feel like they are time traveling as they walk through the school door each morning. As they cross the threshold, do they feel as if they are entering a simulation of life in the 1980s? Then at the end of the school day, do they feel that they have returned to the twenty-first century?"

The weak methods of evaluating talent in visual literacy would make you think that our standards were located even farther back than the Reagan era (Calvin Coolidge would be more like it). The time has come for an updating of the curricula to reflect the new literacy and to include a new set of standards on which kids could be judged.

The irony here is that our basic school curriculum—the one divided into English, math, history, biology, chemistry, and physics— was *itself* the result of a great reform that took place in our country not so far back in the past. This division of disciplines that we all take for granted was actually regarded as cutting-edge reform back in 1892 at the annual conference of the National Education Association. This was a time when the frontier was barely considered "closed" and when rural schoolhouses often taught whatever the local schoolmaster thought appropriate, whether it was the plays of Shakespeare or the biological observations of Alexander von Humboldt. Standards varied wildly from town to town, and state to state, and publishers competed, as they do now, to supply all those kids with textbooks and readers.

A group formed by the NEA called the Committee of Ten—it sounds like a religious tribunal, or a superhero league for middle managers—had been appointed, with the Harvard president Charles Eliot as chair, to settle a philosophical divide between educators of the day. One faction felt that college-bound students ought to have more education in classical Greek and Latin languages and literature, while students for whom high school was the final stop ought to be introduced to vocational training, to be more effective craftsmen and industrial workers. This would reinforce a crude kind of class system within schools, labeling some as thickheaded bolt pounders and others as Cicero-spouting aesthetes.

The Committee of Ten offered a compromise, suggesting a standard of eight years of elementary education, followed by four years of secondary, and a common curriculum of English, math, biology, civics, and a foreign language. So, what we learned in public school did not come descended untainted from the Temple of Diana; it was the result of national reforms conducted by progressive educators trying to retool an educational system in a state of mild chaos in an era of technological and social change.

Sound familiar? We're at a point today when we need to have a similar shift in the way we measure the literacy and competence of all our students. The suggestion I'm making is that we not throw away the basics of the common curriculum advocated by the NEA more than a hundred years ago. These remain solid pillars of what was once the greatest educational system in the world, and they helped usher in what Henry Luce memorably called the American Century of national achievement and prestige. To that end, my suggestion for reform is one predicated on *enhancing* the value of what we already have in place.

Every student in a public high school in the twenty-first century should not be permitted to graduate until he or she has mastered the following:

- Be able to write a script for a short video segment.
- Be able to shoot a coherent piece of film narrative with the correct literate elements of expression.
- Be able to edit video out of raw material into a persuasive argument.
- Be able to access channels of distribution, including the Internet.
- Be able to critically understand and deconstruct visual media.

I believe that requiring these modest competencies would do a great deal to rescue many of our public schools from the depths of mediocrity into which they have sunk—and I am not alone. The National Council of Teachers of English, with its more than thirty-five thousand member teachers, is focused on supporting and advancing language arts instruction and learning and literacy. It has adopted an addendum to its core definition of literacy in 2008:

> Literacy has always been a collection of cultural and communicative practices shared among members of particular groups. As society and technology change, so does literacy. Because technology has increased the intensity and complexity of literate environments, the twenty-first century demands that a literate person possess a wide range of abilities and competencies, many literacies. These literacies—from reading online newspapers to participating in virtual classrooms—are multiple, dynamic, and malleable. As in the past, they are inextricably linked with particular histories, life possibilities, and social trajectories of individuals and groups. Twenty-first century readers and writers need to

> - Develop proficiency with the tools of technology;
> - Build relationships with others to pose and solve problems collaboratively and cross-culturally;
> - Design and share information for global communities to meet a variety of purposes;
> - Manage, analyze, and synthesize multiple streams of simultaneous information;
> - Create, critique, analyze, and evaluate multimedia texts; and
> - Attend to the ethical responsibilities required by these complex environments.

Patricia Edwards is a professor of teacher education at Michigan State University and a recent president of the International Reading Association, the largest global network of literacy professionals. In her first annual statement as head of this organization, entitled "Reconceptualizing Literacy," she laid out what she saw as the critical issues that educators must rethink for literacy in the twenty-first century:

> Perhaps one of the first steps for expanding our views of literacy learning would be to start with visual literacy. Visual literacy stems from the notion of images and symbols that can be read. Meaning is communicated through image more readily than print, which makes visual literacy a powerful teaching tool. Instructional approaches that make use of visual and digital media will better prepare students for their futures in a rapidly changing world . . .
>
> Therefore, we must expand our notion of literacy beyond reading and writing printed text to include interpreting visual and digital texts . . . Teachers will help students empower themselves with the necessary tools to thrive in increasingly media-varied environments.
>
> The definition of literacy as decoding print is outdated, and our new definitions must account for not only changing demographics but also the challenge of a technologically evolving landscape. If students are to successfully meet the social, political, and economic demands of their futures, they must be able to adapt and reinvent the ways that they read and write the world.

While our teachers understand what is needed, our education system has yet to listen. Much criticism has emerged from the last major attempt at overhauling our schools. This was the No Child Left Behind Act made law in 2001 with the enthusiastic support of President George W. Bush and most of Congress. It promised more federal money for funding education, but required schools to give standardized tests, formulated by each state, to all children to measure progress, with increasingly strict penalties meted out to administrators if the test results were not up to snuff. One of the really laudable aims of the law was to try to bust through the nearly impenetrable wall of teachers' unions and complacent administrative desk jockeys; to establish some hard quantitative data for whether kids were learning; and to figure out which schools were so dysfunctional as to need complete overhauling.

One of the weakest parts of the law, the focus on the standardized test, says a lot about the ways we have used an ineffective yardstick to measure the value of education. Such tests tend to suck all the creativity and improvisation out of the classroom and bring what is taught more in line with the rote memorization skills popular in nineteenth-century France, when the minister of education could look at his desk clock and tell a visitor exactly what page of Virgil the nation's schoolchildren were looking at in that very moment. Under No Child Left Behind, the test became the coin of the realm.

Teachers complained vigorously about being rewarded solely on test scores, and "teaching to the test" became an unavoidable classroom practice. Some districts even encouraged cheating, so as not to lose their federal funding. Disciplines not suited to testing—at least not by the rigid math of multiple-choice quizzes—such as art and music, took a huge hit, as the emphasis shifted to English and math. It was as if the spectrum of colors in the palette of knowledge were shrunk to just red and yellow. This is the best we can do?

I've seen better things happen at the Jacob Burns Film Center, where I think we can find excellent parables for this question of how we begin to assess learning in the coming century.

We offer courses in all aspects of animation, documentary, and narrative filmmaking, as well as in other forms of visual media. One of our teachers, Michael C. Williams, specializes in teaching elementary and junior high schoolers the art of hands-on film-making.

For one exercise, he wrote a bare-bones script open to infer-ence and interpretation. Student teams were assigned to create a short film around it. This script is a masterpiece worthy of Beckett, but it could be played for comedy, tragedy, existential angst, sus-pense, embarrassment, or any type of mood the student teams wished to channel through lighting, acting, and sound:

Person A: *Where are you going?*
Person B: *None of your business.*
A: *Yes it is.*
B: *No it isn't.*
A: *It is if you're going to tell him.*
B: *I'm not. I told you I'm not going to tell him. Why won't you believe me?*
A: *You've lied to me before.*
B: *That was a long time ago.*
A: *You better not tell him.*
B: *I won't.*
A: *You better not.*

Simple words, simple scenario. But a huge range of possibility waiting to be exploited.

"There's an inherent conflict there," said Mike. "And they can come up with the circumstances behind it." The interpretation—trying to find the meaning of what the text does not say—is part of the literary adventure of the filmmaking process. "For these kids there's a whole new literacy going on," he said. "I didn't know a third of what they knew."

A word of background on Mike. He knows what he's talking about. He was born in the Bronx and attended the State University of New York at New Paltz before getting a role in the smash hit movie of 1999, *The Blair Witch Project*. He plays the slightly overweight cameraman who deliberately throws a map away and succeeds in getting a trio of student filmmakers even more lost in a haunted wood outside Burkittsville, Maryland. The acting job was famously grueling—the filmmakers made their three actors camp in the woods for days, to give them a realistically haggard look, and kept them largely in the dark about plot twists. It is Mike we see in the film's last horrifying visual, one of the biggest intellectual shocks ever depicted on film, in my opinion—though I won't give it away here. After a brief stint on *Law & Order*, Mike mostly retired from the acting business. He now works as a school counselor in a local district and teaches for us in the summer. We're tremendously lucky to have him.

Two of his students, Alex and Evelyn, went to great lengths to weave a story around Mike's minimalist dialogue. Alex explained: "The lie I'm telling is that I'm going to the bathroom, but really I was going to film a scene for a movie. We're both child actors, but I'm more successful and I don't want to offend her." The future twist is that she is not only jealous of the other actor, but she has a crush on him, although she but does not want to say anything for fear of looking unprofessional. Two other students were nearby, filming the two actors in a sophisticated blocking technique, over the shoulder of one of them. When edited, the footage would be arranged in a way that would capture the casual conversational pose of both actors, as well as the facial expressions and body language that would hint at deeper waters. "This is hard work," said Evelyn. "But it's fun."

This was an exercise in which nine-year-olds were learning intricacies of dialogue and character motivation that might have come in a high school English literature class, or even later. But because the medium encouraged them to experiment with ambiguities and use visual means of framing a story, with the Raymond Carver–like understatement of dialogue to prompt the viewer, their appreciation for what it meant to create a work of literate art was coming to them earlier.

There is an oft-repeated story about the magic of technological education, but it is repeated so often because it is so instructive. Bill Gates, the founder of Microsoft and one of the most successful entrepreneurs ever to have lived, has credited his early interest in computers to one single event: the decision of Seattle's Lakeside School in 1967 to buy some remote time on a General Electric DEC PDP-10 computer, on which Lakeside students could dial in and write their own programs. These were some of the earliest days of nonprofessionals using computers, and Gates and his friend Paul Allen became obsessed with the tool. They spent hours and hours writing code, and even went so far as to hack into the computer and change the number of hours Lakeside was using the computer so the school wouldn't go over its allocation. They later made an agreement with Centre Computer Corporation that gave them unlimited time on the school's computer in exchange for their work trying to find bugs in the company's software. It was the tech equivalent of being able to use the swimming pool at all hours in exchange for chlorination and scrubbing. They weren't merely being educated; they were being hooked on a pattern of creativity that would later go on to change our world in incalculable ways, and create one of the mammoth corporations of American business.

There was resistance to computer education in Gates and Allen's day, just as there is to media education in our day. I can understand why. To the uninitiated outsider, it may seem like wasteful play. And without the right guidance, or done poorly, it can indeed lead to pointless games and diversionary nonsense. But the right encouragement can unlock enormous founts of intellectual energy inside children who are unmoved by more traditional forms of literacy. It is also a sneaky way to draw the inhibited child out of her shell.

"My goal," said Williams, "is to give them a sense of what actors do when they're working, which is primarily to connect with other people. There's a relationship going on."

Williams watched as Anthony, an outgoing kid wearing a T-shirt depicting a checkered necktie, played the same minimalist dialogue with Elijah, a more introverted fellow, wearing an orange shirt. They were playing the script less like a *New Yorker* story and more like an outtake from *Dude, Where's My Car?*

"Where are you going?" Anthony wanted to know.

"None of your *biz*-ness!" Elijah was supposed to snap back, with a little bit of street sass, but he was fidgety and nervous before the camera. In take one, he delivered the line flat, and the director was forced to call for another take. Williams gave him a bit of gentle coaching. Take two was also a flop. Williams told him Elijah was looking at the assembled crew instead of at Anthony, where the statement should have been directed. Another take was necessary.

"Sound check B," the assistant director called out.

"Camera rolling," someone else called out.

"Action!" the director called out.

On this third try, even with his eyes darting back and forth a bit, Elijah pulled off his lines to everyone's satisfaction. The routine was complete.

Williams went up to him with a high-five and a fist pump. "How'd that feel?" he asked, and Elijah grinned sheepishly. He was clearly going through a period of preadolescent awkwardness, but there, in this room, he was performing for his peers, and nobody was making fun of him. He was part of a team, and their success depended on him as much as on their own abilities.

Reflecting on what the students had gained from a few months of writing scripts, giving and taking orders, learning how to use cameras, and making a whole project come together, Williams said, "They felt like they were kings for a summer."

Consider this statement: "I believe that the motion picture is destined to revolutionize our educational system and that in a few years it will supplant largely, if not entirely, the use of textbooks."

Who said this and when? None other than Thomas Edison, the inventor of the motion picture camera, and he said it in 1922.

"I should say," he went on, "that on average we get about two-percent efficiency out of schoolbooks as they are written today. The education of the future, as I see it, will be conducted through the medium of the motion picture . . . where it should be possible to obtain one hundred percent efficiency."

Edison, an inventor par excellence, was, of course, also an unparalleled promoter of his own creations. And he did have a commercial interest in his prognostication. But what he said should not be ignored. In his day, while factories were being retooled to boost productivity, schools were looking to new technologies. And motion pictures were viewed as authoritative representations of history and the world around us.

The preeminent example is *The Birth of a Nation*, the D. W. Griffith film released in 1915, half a century after the end of the Civil War and the assassination of Abraham Lincoln. President Woodrow Wilson screened this bigoted version of Reconstruction at the White House and was supposed to have said, "It is like writing history with lightning, and my only regret is that it is all so true."

What is more likely is that this quote was manufactured as more promotional efforts from Griffith and his partner, Thomas Dixon, but it played on the seeming realism of this first feature film, which in many ways was the father to all narrative films to follow.

A closer look at the reality of film in the classroom reveals something entirely different from Edison's promise. It is not surprising that some critics are skeptical when they hear about new tools and technology being introduced in the classroom amid boasts of revolutionary education reform. They've seen this movie before and are ready reflexively to trash it.

By 1910, only a few years after films had been introduced, reformers and entrepreneurs were offering them for educational use, with George Kleine publishing a 336-page *Catalogue of Educational Motion Pictures*, offering more than one thousand titles for schools to rent. This was before World War I. In 1913, Edison said in an article in the *Dramatic Mirror*, "Books will soon be obsolete in the schools. Scholars will soon be instructed through the eye. It is possible to touch every branch of human knowledge with the motion picture." In 1917, the Chicago schools created a visual education department, and by 1931, twenty-five states had visual units within their departments of education.

But by the mid-1950s, it was clear that film had not taken firm hold of classrooms, let alone changed the basic method of teaching. Obstacles cited in National Education Association reports on the matter included: teachers' lack of skill in using equipment and film; cost of films, equipment, and upkeep; inaccessibility of equipment when it is needed; and the need to find and fit a film's to a given course.

What people were missing was that not only could film be instructional in the subjects it portrayed, but that it was a whole new language that needed to be understood to be properly contextualized and evaluated in the classroom. Hollywood editing was meant to have us not *see* the construction. Film was good for supplementing traditional teachings in history and the sciences, but it fell short of transforming the classroom, because teachers lacked the tools and the skills to help students critically read these texts and to teach students to make films themselves.

That has all changed. One thing we've seen at the Jacob Burns Film Center in recent years is the increasing ease of teaching our new "screenagers" in the language of film. They've always been comfortable with images, not just because they were raised on television, but also because they've been making little videos and texting one another pictures since grade school. They don't think of electronic imaging tools as anything to be afraid of—in fact, they barely think of them at all. This may sound paradoxical. Yet these digital natives may be less likely to be fascinated with technology than my siblings and I were with the black-and-white television our parents brought home in the 1960s.

"It is an almost instinctive assumption to believe that Net Gen students will want to use IT heavily in their education; they certainly do in their personal lives," write Diana and James Oblinger in *Educating the Net Generation*. But if you ask the students what technology they're using, "you will often get a blank stare." The iPods and cameras and software are a matter of only passing interest. What is far more important is the quality of results that these tools deliver.

Again, we come back to the home truth that *stuff doesn't matter*. It's what you teach yourself to do with the stuff that does. I have always believed that the primary—maybe the only—valuable delivery to the average person through this "stuff" is the transmission of stories.

Albert Maysles said the following, which I have tacked above my computer: "The stories people tell have a way of taking care of them. If stories come to you, care for them. And learn to give them away when they are needed. Sometimes a person needs a story more than food to stay alive. That is why we put these stories in each other's memory. This is how people care for themselves."

There's another component to measuring success, and that's being able to teach students the inner nature of the messages they've been taking in for most of their lives.

One thing that making small movies will help teach you is how all the little tricks work together to create a unified emotional effect. This, in turn, makes you a more intelligent watcher of all the visual messages you are bombarded with every day—both the good stuff and the garbage. But extra attention needs to be brought to the art of understanding what a filmmaker is trying to achieve and, in some sense, how he or she is trying to manipulate you. A sense of *media literacy*—a term that first came into vogue in the mid-1970s—ought to be part of any yardstick for how we measure competency in this arena. Educating children on the purposes and the "tricks" behind television, it was thought, would give them the tools necessary to decode much of what was being thrown at them. Curricula with roots in this era still exist in many public schools today, and they provided inspiration for college programs in filmmaking. The more we can bridge that to include the art of making films, the better off our children will be.

The public schools consultant Frank W. Baker has cited five core concepts for media literacy that he believes all students should be required to understand. They are:

- All media messages are constructed.
- Media messages are constructed using a creative language with its own rules.
- Different people experience media messages differently.
- Media have embedded values and points of view.
- Most media messages are organized to gain profit and/or power.

He further argues that media messages have cultural "codes" written into them that cue viewers—at least those viewers who have been passively inhaling the oxygen of Western media for a few years—to respond in a certain way. Remember how political advertisements tend to play soft, upbeat piano music and show bright (often red-white-and-blue) visuals when depicting the favored candidate, and use growling music and gloomy visuals when depicting the opponent? This is but one example of embedded codes that are useful to recognize and, when appropriate, dismiss in response to a message.

It is noteworthy that everything that Baker says about media messages is applicable to reading and writing as well, and has been ever since the first Sumerian merchant inscribed an ideogram into wet clay. The very etching of a letter or a word or a paragraph involves a point of view and a shared understanding of what that language means to a particular group of readers. Without shared cultural understanding, language is a meaningless gong sounding in the wind.

This is why the new literacy of the electronic age is more important than ever. Because those who are able not just to understand and pick apart what the language is saying (and not saying) are going to be able to command the means of expression, especially if they are *doing it themselves*. This is why I believe media literacy programs need to be updated and married to filmmaking classes. There is no better way to critically appraise the message of others than to speak one's own message.

Being able to assess and create literate works of filmic art, especially in this new century of visual communication, has educational value in and of itself—a critical life skill. My idea involves a standardized test of sorts. Within the next ten years, in order to graduate from a public high school in this country, a student ought to be able to make a film of about five minutes in length that demonstrates a definite story arc, a mastery of camera angles, a sense of proper editing, and a demonstration of literacy. These are criteria that will be judged by a faculty panel. Some of our most challenging secondary schools already require a senior project for their students to qualify for graduation.

We should never assume that a developmentally normal kid of any socioeconomic level is incapable of mastering a five-minute film, and I would expect that it would probably be a highlight of his school experience—being able to create and perform instead of being drilled on rote tasks and the litany of No Child Left Behind standardized tests that now pass for higher education achievement.

George Lucas, who knows the visual grammar of film better than just about anyone, said that the gap in opportunity will not necessarily be economic. "When people talk about the digital divide, I think of it not being so much about who has access to what technology as who knows how to create and express themselves in this new language of the screen. If students aren't taught the language of sound and images, shouldn't they be considered as illiterate as if they left college without being able to read and write?"

There is no reason for our schools to be so impoverished. Beeban Kidron is the director of *Bridget Jones: The Edge of Reason*. In 2008, she cofounded the charity Filmclub, which donates movies to schools all over Britain and encourages kids to think critically about the materials and review them in after-school programs. Her rationale is pragmatic.

"I think that stories, and the telling of stories, are the foundations of human communication and understanding," she told an interviewer from *The Guardian*. "If children all over the country are watching films, asking questions and telling their stories, then the world will eventually be a better place. It will not fix all the ills of modern society, but we have absolute evidence that kids go in, they go to Filmclub and they say it gives them confidence. We've had children that have had a difficult time at school, who say, 'I like school a bit better.'"

Kidron is right that bringing filmmaking skills into the public schools is not going to save democracy on its own, or create an intellectual paradise. But I am convinced it will take us leagues farther than the current state of affairs. Film works as a motivator. Film is fun. And film is the rising language of the twenty-first century, whether we want it to be or not. We might as well start embracing it now. There's a simple place to begin.

Teachers are not the problem. I've heard the worst about them: lazy, incompetent, slow to change, union goons—name your pejorative. But they are only as good as their job descriptions. Public school teachers are generally decent people of average intelligence who are trained to work within a particular system, one that is designed to create a certain output, and is as rigid and unfeeling as any machine.

With such severe constraints on what can be taught, how to teach it, and how it (and the teachers) will be measured, there is no breathing room to think about what skills are *actually* needed in today's world and how best to deliver them. We can't dismantle the machine entirely, but we might at least reprogram it to put out a better product.

At the Jacob Burns Film Center and Media Arts Lab, we have a commitment, first of all, to story. The heart of our experience of the world is organizing input into a coherent narrative—we do this every second. School systems have neglected this concept at their own peril. While the technology of communication has evolved and become more democratic, our schools have completely failed to keep up. At the end of 2006, *Time* magazine published a report on education entitled "How to Bring Our Schools Out of the 20th Century," which started with a look at the evolution of the classroom:

> There's a dark little joke exchanged by educators with a dissident streak: Rip Van Winkle awakens in the 21st century after a hundred-year snooze and is, of course, utterly bewildered by what he sees. Men and women dash about, talking to small metal devices pinned to their ears. Young people sit at home on sofas, moving miniature athletes around on electronic screens. Older folk defy death and disability with metronomes in their chests and with hips made of metal and plastic. Airports, hospitals, shopping malls—every place Rip goes just baffles him. But when he finally walks into a schoolroom, the old man knows exactly where he is. "This is a school," he declares. "We used to have these back in 1906. Only now the blackboards are green."

The author goes on to say:

> Kids spend much of the day as their great-grandparents once did: sitting in rows, listening to teachers lecture, scribbling notes by hand, reading from textbooks that are out of date by the time they are printed. A yawning chasm (with an emphasis on yawning) separates the world inside the schoolhouse from the world outside.

This analysis may be a little *too* simplistic. While classrooms haven't changed measurably in appearance or culture, they have made some attempts to evolve in response to changing technologies, but with limited success, because the "innovations" that were often sold to gullible school boards had a price tag attached and were far too married to a specific machine that would soon become dated and obsolete. It would take a very large landfill to hold all the computers bought by the taxpayers and then junked within a few years because the software was limited and the maintenance flawed.

Apple finally got it right in the 1990s, aggressively wooing school districts and sometimes offering gifts of free computers, in the hope that habits would be formed and big orders would be forthcoming—which they were. By 1995, about 56 percent of educational computers being bought were Apples, and a generation of children was taught to work with the versatile package Apple offered: a tool for many subjects.

Familiarity with the *intellectual possibilities* of the technology was the important thing, not the technology itself. E-mails, spreadsheets, websites, PowerPoint—all these are necessary things to master, whatever the enabling program may be. PCs can do it just as well; the hardware itself is almost beside the point.

Visual education certainly isn't about "the stuff." If our educators spend too much of their time training students on one particular type of video camera, or on operating a specific brand of video software, it will be wasting everyone's time. What is needed instead is a commitment to the basics of telling a smart story, which will be relevant many years into the future without regard to the exact means of the story's production.

Minor innovations in technology will continue to roll off the factory lines and into the big-box stores on a semiannual basis; as I write this, the tools in our schools are already becoming obsolete. What will never wear out or get moth-eaten is the talent for using this technology in creative and thoughtful ways. And that takes us back to the roots of public education in the United States, which are often misunderstood.

Benjamin Franklin wrote in 1749 that "questions of right and wrong, justice and injustice, will naturally arise" as students debate historical issues "in conversation and in writing." Franklin insisted that students should read newspapers and discuss current controversies, thereby developing their logic and reasoning. George Washington took up this emphasis in a democratic citizenry in his Farewell Address as president. He urged, "Promote, then, as an object of primary importance, institutions for the general diffusion of knowledge. In proportion as the structure of a government gives force to public opinion, it is essential that public opinion should be enlightened." If he had given this speech today, he would have done it as a multimedia presentation.

Thomas Jefferson proposed a public education system for Virginia in 1779, only three years after the establishment of the United States. Though the language is wordy, his prescription seems modern:

> To give to every citizen the information he needs for the transaction of his own business; to enable him to calculate for himself, and to express and preserve his ideas, his contracts and accounts in writing; to improve, by reading, his morals and faculties; to understand his duties to his neighbors and country, and to discharge with competence the functions confided to him by either; to know his rights; to exercise with order and justice those he retains, to choose with discretion the fiduciary of those he delegates; and to notice their conduct with diligence, with candor and judgment; and in general, to observe with intelligence and faithfulness all the social relations under which he shall be placed.

There is not a single attribute on this list that today does not have a relationship with the ability to think visually and express oneself digitally. To these men of the Enlightenment, the goal of education was to create a population of students able to understand their role and support a burgeoning system of government. The job remains the same today.

In an influential book called *The Creation of the Media*, Paul Starr argues that it was the confluence of three factors—an emphasis on freedom of the press, the creation of the post office, and the literacy of the population—that ensured the success of the American project: our economic and even diplomatic and military dominance in the world.

In 1837, half a century after the Revolution, Horace Mann became the first secretary of the Massachusetts Board of Education. The devoutly religious Mann, living in a New England still dominated by its Protestant settlers, believed that the development of moral character was paramount. But he also began to lay out the case for understanding texts and expressing oneself in the plainest language of the day. He wrote in his *Annual Report* of 1839, "If the most distinguished authors desire to consult books before they attempt the discussion of great subjects, then to require children to write composition, without supplying them with some resources whence to draw their materials, is absurdly to suppose, not only that they are masters of a select and appropriate diction in which to clothe their thoughts and feelings, but also that they possess a degree of originality which even the ablest writers do not claim."

Mann favored originality of expression instead of rote memorization. The act of taking pen to paper is a fairly simple motor skill that can be mastered at a young age. But the value of what one is communicating is the key.

No one would argue that we live—or should live—in a society dominated by a class of professional scribes. The expression of ideas in a clear, crisp way lies at the core of our ability to work and do business together. Can you imagine a doctor who can't write a cogent medical history? Or a lawyer who can't write a brief, or even an electrician who can't read a manual for a new device or appliance? And this is only in their professional capacity. Without these skills, they also couldn't participate in society in any real way.

One November morning in Vermont a few years ago, Jay Hoffman, a teacher at the Frederick H. Tuttle Middle School in South Burlington, woke up early. It was Election Day and he planned to stop by his local polling place before going to school as usual.

When he entered the voting booth, his cell phone started to ring. One of his young students was on the other end with an urgent question: "When will you be at school, Mr. Hoffman?"

A group of kids was already massing in front of Hoffman's classroom, at the ungodly hour of 7:00 a.m. Hoffman told the kid on the phone to calm down, that he was voting and that he would be there in an hour, when school actually started.

When he got to school at the appointed hour, he saw that the lights in the classroom were already on and that the kids had found a way to get into the room before school was scheduled to start and were already engaged in their schoolwork. This was consistent with what had happened earlier in the term. His students had already persuaded him to let them use the classroom after the school days were over, and even during their lunch periods. He had told them that he couldn't just let them into the classroom before the school day, but they'd shown up anyway and—after the failed plea to him in the voting booth—had roamed the hallways until they found a janitor and persuaded him to use his master key to open their classroom so they could get to work.

What would inspire a group of ordinary kids to force their way into a classroom—in effect, to break in—to get about the business of learning? Sounds like a parent's fantasy, but it actually happened.

This kind of deep engagement is similarly happening in other schools that have embraced film production as part of the core educational experience in a smart way. The Tuttle students were working on an Election Day broadcast for their news program, *SBNN News*—"The News Kids Choose." Their work was important to them; they were nearly obsessed with it. The janitors at the Frederick H. Tuttle Middle School have since come to expect this kind of request from Jay Hoffman's students.

These students' efforts paid off in ways they didn't expect. In 2008, they won the eSchool News Empowered Education Award and were honored in Washington, D.C. The following year, they won third place in C-SPAN's StudentCam 2009 competition, with a segment that discussed the U.S. economy as the most pressing issue of President Obama's early presidency. But these awards are only markers of the real learning experience going on, which far exceeds the traditional curriculum in getting the students to engage in the act of creation and of working together as a team—a critical skill for the workplace. Hoffman's classes continue to be among the most popular in school and are routinely oversubscribed. The students' news broadcasts are followed not only within their school, but also through a local cable channel that allows them to reach more than thirty thousand viewers.

All the stories are chosen by the students, something Hoffman believes is one of the secrets to the success of the program. "There are no make-believe situations, and the kids are excited about being empowered." Politicians have learned to call them. Senators Patrick Leahy and Bernie Sanders are frequent guests on their show. A company called Green Mountain Power asked if a remote team from the school could cover the opening of the first electric car charging location in Burlington. That coverage was featured on the University of Vermont's website.

To be sure, this outsize influence wielded by middle-schoolers can be partly credited to the small-town nature of the state of Vermont, but such achievements in new literacy are possible anywhere—as is the power to get otherwise dull-eyed preadolescents excited about "building something."

Hoffman used to teach wood shop and once ran a small construction business in Poughkeepsie, New York, so he has always believed in the importance of kids using their hands to make things. With a master's degree in technology education, he also believed that "making" wasn't limited to wood and steel. One day, he held a big garage sale and sold many of the school's carpentry tools to clear out space and make room for a television studio in the old wood shop. He brought in a local cable access station to help with the infrastructure, and found grants to wire up the school and place television monitors in every classroom. And he'd saved enough of the woodshop tools to be able to build sets for the studio.

It turned out, of course, that the work being done in the television studio had many parallels to the craftsmanship skills taught in woodshop, which have been recognized since the dawn of public education in the United States. The careful planning, research, and preproduction are akin to the blueprints of a construction project; the interviewing and shooting, akin to construction; and the editing and postproduction, akin to the finishing of a wood project.

The programs took off. The students are now in the process of doing a cooking show with a local organic restaurant—a promotion of healthy eating and nutrition, shot in the kitchen of the restaurant. They have also tackled tough subjects such as educating teens on how to avoid being victimized by sexual predators.

Hoffman continues to be inspired by the passion these young students bring to this work, and explains that he wants to create a new position within the school faculty—"community integrator," recognizing the power of media and the opportunity to use this tool of new literacy and storytelling to bring people together. In the course of this work, Hoffman has recognized that the children are not only acquiring these hard skills, but are also learning some of the skills most important to their future success—both as potential political activists and as fully participating members of their community. While not all his students want to become hard-news journalists like Christiane Amanpour or Anderson Cooper, they all take away the immersive educational experience that speaks to the way they understand the world.

Hoffman has some advice for any educator who wants to make moving pictures a part of the learning experience: Do it deliberately. Do more than just show films and sit back. Be sure to learn it yourself along the way, as you guide the creation of your students, and then eventually be able to explain the tropes of filmic literacy, in the same way you'd be able to explain how to solve a quadratic equation or explicate a poem by Edna St. Vincent Millay.

Pockets of teachers across the country are leading the way in developing innovative curricula and introducing visual literacy into their classrooms, and they are finding their students more engaged in every aspect of their educational experience. This is the kind of school that as a young student I'd have wanted to break into as well.

Let's draw the camera back. We now have a democratic reach of media on a level never before possible in human history. A lone thinker or performer in Jakarta, Buenos Aires, or Novosibirsk, or in the middle of the Sudanese desert, or perhaps even an unhappy United Airlines customer from Nova Scotia, can post an idea in the new worldwide marketplace of the moving image and quickly command an audience that would fill dozens of sports stadiums.

The global spread of a single idea has been possible since the first flattening of papyrus on the banks of the Nile, of course, and the printing press made it possible in great volumes. But several new factors are in play in our era that will change the very definition of literacy, and we must pay attention.

The first is, of course, the sheer speed at which ideas and images can now be circulated. Users of YouTube who understand the intrinsic languages of the medium have learned that a successful video can get three million hits within a twenty-four-hour period. That's an astonishing number of human beings to touch in so short a time frame, and with such a cheap set of tools. Access to a book contract, a television studio, or a huge national newspaper used to come between the average person and the masses. Now it takes only a great concept, a cell phone camera, and an Internet hookup.

The second factor that will change the definition of literacy is the way that the simplest of images need not be translated. The ability to appreciate a soundless movie is innate in almost every culture. It takes no knowledge of English (or any language) to appreciate the quirky genius of Matt Harding's "dancing guy" videos, in which he performs the same strange Irish jig in front of hundreds of landmarks around the world—from a bridge in Venice, to a jungle in the Galapagos Islands, to a sand dune in Namibia—all to the electronic notes of "Sweet Lullaby," a song that samples sound clips from a dying language indigenous to the Solomon Islands. The sounds were recorded on tape in 1971 by French researchers, and then rediscovered and popularized by the band Deep Forest, and then rediscovered and popularized to a massive degree by Harding and his silly dance. A follow-up video was even more successful, because Harding had persuaded people around the world to join him in the goofiness. He was at first dancing by himself in front of these landmarks, and then realized, while in the town of Mulindi, Rwanda, with a group of curious children, that it was much more fun to make the dancing a group experience.

These images are quintessentially literate, I believe, because Harding seized upon a simple wordless message: dance transcends language. He put out a call for helpers via the e-mails he received from around the world because of his previous dancing videos, and set dates when he would be in a particular city. The video of forty sites is a colorful canvas of world diversity, and also of monoculture. Thirty million people have watched it.

The video revolution is going to unlock unexpected creativity and energy like this from millions of unexpected and heretofore obscure places. Record companies and television stations are disappearing filters. The only "master curator" will be the instant human response. And the sharing is going to create a cumulative effect of creativity as people who don't know one another, and who would never have met one another, will begin to build on one another's work.

Here's an interesting object example. The filmmaker Jon Chu directed *The Legion of Extraordinary Dancers*, a Web-based show about a team of "good" dancers who fight a team of "evil" dancers with the energy of their moves. Chu began to notice a remarkable phenomenon unfolding. Fans of the show began to post videos of their friends improvising the steps and developing entire new routines, which were then imitated and further reified by the principals of the show. The dance was being organically evolved by strangers from all corners of the globe, which never would have been possible in an age before file sharing.

"Dancers have created a whole global laboratory online," Chu has said. "Kids in Japan are taking moves from a YouTube video created in Detroit, building on it within days, and releasing a new video, while teenagers in California are taking the Japanese video and remixing it to create a whole new dance style."

Chris Anderson, curator of the visionary TED Conferences, calls this effect "crowd-accelerated innovation." The collective shaping of what we believe and read and watch is going to be done more and more by nonprofessionals with a visual message. Computerized video has become part of the massive evolving cloud of ideas that constitutes what we call "world culture," always in dialogue, changing shape as it pushes and pulls against itself, and every voice that contributes to it is like a small little breath of its own. We will see more growing clouds like this, and not just in the arts. Academics have begun to make a slow embrace of digital scholarship. More conference papers are now being supplemented by video presentations, which are easier to absorb by laypeople, and have the added benefit of being easily transmitted for com-ment and discussion.

The dissemination speed of video content is creating its own language, as amateur filmmakers repeat one another's tropes, in both earnestness and parody. Let's look at one of the most popular videos of 2011, one that was widely maligned for its stupidity—but it was stupidity of only the most ingenious, improvisational sort. A Dallas, Texas, man named Christopher Torres was work-ing on a Red Cross fund drive when a few people on a live com-puter chat suggested he come up with a drawing of a Pop-Tart and a cat. It was meant to be a punchy suggestion, but Torres took a few minutes and created a crude drawing of a cat with a cherry Pop-Tart for a torso. He then pictured the cat flying through space trailing a rainbow, and set it to the soundtrack of an annoying Japanese electronic song whose lyrics can best be rendered as *nyannyannyannyan,* on an endless loop. The thing went viral, and the Internet was soon rife with culturally specific imitations, in-cluding Mexican Nyan Cat, who is wearing a sombrero and flying over cactus; Rasta Nyan Cat, who is wearing dreadlocks, smoking a joint, and trailing the Jamaican colors; and Heavy Metal Nyan Cat, who is flying through a landscape of skulls to a harsh, sped-up soundtrack.

The trope is ridiculous, but it is literate because the imitations, first of all, build on what came before them, and second of all, make a whole new joke in which the reader's sense of the absurd provides the humor. The whole piece is weirdly compelling for this reason.

These humorous rip-offs are part of what is called an Internet meme—meaning an evolving concept or image spread from person to person, with improvements and quotation along the way. The term *meme* was coined in 1976 by the biologist Richard Dawkins, who defined the term as a self-replicating unit of cultural transmission (by imitation, mutation, and replication) that plays a role in cultural evolution analogous to that played by the gene in biological evolution (examples are melodies, fashions, skills, and even built structures such as limited-exit highways). It is probably as close to a spiritual concept as this famous atheist has ever promulgated.

The future of the world is not assured because of memes such as Nyan Cat. But this video is one example of how the electronic moving image is a tool for unlocking enormous creativity from unforeseen corners of the world, as people are rapidly exposed to new storytelling tropes and formulas.

Here's a more adult and productive, yet still humorous, example. On March 31, 2008, a musician named Dave Carroll boarded a United Airlines flight to Chicago from his home in Halifax, Nova Scotia. He was going to Nebraska with members of his folk-rock band to play a week's worth of concerts. When the plane landed in Chicago, Carroll was surprised to hear a woman in the seat behind him murmur, "My God, they're throwing guitars out there." When he opened his guitar case in Nebraska, he discovered that his $3,500 guitar had indeed been smashed at the neck.

This was only the beginning of his problem. When Carroll took the logical step of filing a claim for compensation, he was taken on an epic runaround by the airline, a familiar journey to anyone who has ever tried to raise a problem with a big company. Carroll persisted for nine months before a customer service representative, Ms. Irlweg, finally e-mailed him to deny his claim because, among other reasons, he hadn't reported the damage to the Omaha airport within twenty-four hours. This was to be the last communication the airline would have on the matter, she explained.

But it was certainly not to be Carroll's last communication. A song was already knitting itself together in his mind, a bouncy Johnny Cash–style heartbreaker with, as he put it, "a train

groove—that boom-chick-a-boom sound." The title and the cho-
rus were straight up and unapologetic subject, verb, and object:
"United Breaks Guitars." It was like a cleaner version of a phrase
you'd see scrawled on a bathroom stall.

As Carroll was writing this revenge song, he was also thinking
visually. He could see baggage handlers amusing themselves playing catch with his precious cargo, and the film noir chalk outline
of his dead guitar on the tarmac. The visual wordplay kept accu-
mulating in his mind, and Carroll realized he'd have a good time
shooting a video of his gripe with United Airlines. So he gathered
some friends, including two from a production company, at the
firehouse in the village of Waverley, near Halifax, where he works
as a volunteer firefighter.

They had fun. Three friends dressed up as ridiculous-looking
mariachis, with mustaches and sombreros, to play the band members. Two of Carroll's fellow firefighters put on reflector vests and
headsets to portray oafish baggage handlers. In a flash of inspiration, somebody cut some holes out of a foam board to make it look
like windows in the fuselage of an airplane. "The props don't look
too good," Carroll acknowledged. And the performers were less
than professional. "What you don't see was that the camera cuts
away just before we start laughing ourselves silly." This wasn't Hollywood, and more important, it didn't have to be. The end result
was a playful bargain-basement video that accompanied Carroll's
four-minute-and-fifteen-second musical story of what happened to
his guitar and the gauntlet of corporate ineptitude that followed.
Total cost: $150, and most of that was spent on lunch for the crew.

Carroll uploaded the video to YouTube shortly thereafter. By
the first evening, July 6, 2009, six people had watched it. But by the
end of the next day, that number had rocketed to 333,000 views as
the video spread by Facebook and e-mail. Within three days, a
million people had seen it.

As you might predict, United was shamed into responding. They called Carroll with an apologetic tone and an offer to "make this right"; one of its spokesmen diplomatically called the situation "a unique learning and training opportunity to ensure that all our customers receive better service." Three months later, Dave Carroll became one of the only witnesses before a congressional panel ever to sing his testimony. He and the band members performed a noninstrumental version of "United Breaks Guitars" to a U.S. Senate hearing on travelers' rights.

This is a story about many things: the power of social media, the dishonesty of corporate customer service and PR, and a guy who used his creative prowess to get results. But it would have been about none of these things, and Carroll would never have heard from United again, if it hadn't been for one critical quality: the extremely *literate* nature of his video. This was the only reason, in fact, that his message broke out from any of the hundreds of thousands of anticorporate rants that saturate the Internet.

The video, both cheap and charming, looked like the improvised special effect a band of junior high school kids would have cooked up for their play. But it drove home one of its unspoken messages: Dave Carroll was a little guy fighting big interests. "If I had access to CGI or other kinds of computer graphics, I might not have even used them," he said. "It was important to show 'this person had no resources.'" This is all part of a visual story that is successful because of the integrity of all of its elements.

"I think visually and I know I'm not alone," said Carroll. "If you wrote a book or a speech, it takes a long time to get it out. There's a whole other level to it when you add images."

One thing will never change, no matter what kind of new technology emerges in the coming century: we are story animals. And we need to tell our stories in as direct, as unmediated, and as emotionally resonant a way as possible.

The development of communication, language, and technology—and the evolving nature of literacy that follows—needs to be seen not just as a natural evolution to spur commercial interests, but rather as a way to quench this insatiable thirst for story. The new way to tell our stories is like a meme itself.

As we have seen from our look inside the brain, visual stories resonate and communicate in a more primal and prelingual way than words. Human biology is such that we experience visual images and stories in as close a way as possible to actually *having the experience*. This is the power of the mirror neurons that makes us think we are eating an apple when we watch a video of such, or that we are being chased, or are doing the pursuing, when we see those images on the screen. Vision is at its core a creative act, and we combine visual stimuli from what we see with an ever-growing database of visual understanding from our experiences. The database is already there to be accessed. We who grew up in the age of the moving image are already wired to be literate. There is therefore little to fear in the new arena—except for one thing.

America runs the risk of falling behind other industrialized nations in this vital method of spreading ideas. Our public schools are still drawing with sticks in the dirt when they should be using calculators. Power in the information age is primarily about the spread of ideas, and any look at the way ideas are now spread around the globe leads to the inescapable conclusion that the power to persuade has become primarily a visual game. It is more than an illustration; it is primary text.

We are not talking here about just receiving information and entertainment. That's been the case since the dawn of television in the 1940s, or even the birth of the cinema in the 1910s. We're now talking about each and every human being as a creator of information and entertainment, about a wide democratization of the medium. Unless we grasp hold of the potential of visual media now, we will be second-rate storytellers.

Literacy has always been the barrier between the haves and the have-nots in our society, and in the larger global society and economy. Anyone angling for a computer job today has to be literate in the language of mainframe coding, just as anyone who wanted to be a merchant in Ur needed to know the rudiments of cuneiform. Visual literacy is the new frontier, one not limited to scribes, but open to all of us. And for the first time in the history of the planet, it has an instant global reach. It will not wait for the sluggards. We *must* adapt with the changing times and acquire the necessary skills in order to have full access to this opportunity—to remain competitive and engaged. Because, ultimately, one of the most rewarding things we can do is tell our stories and hear the stories of others. It is one of the fundamental cures for loneliness throughout time, a means of human connection.

The novelist David Foster Wallace once said this about the written language of novels:

> I guess a big part of serious fiction's purpose is to give the reader, who like all of us is sort of marooned in her own skull, to give her imaginative access to other selves. Since an ineluctable part of being a human self is suffering, part of what we humans come to art for is an experience of suffering, necessarily a vicarious experience, more like a sort of "generalization" of suffering. Does this make sense? We all suffer alone in the real world; true empathy's impossible. But if a piece of fiction can allow us imaginatively to identify with a character's pain, we might then also more easily conceive of others identifying with our own. This is nourishing,

redemptive; we become less alone inside. It might just be that simple.

Stories, then, are a way to relieve the inevitable suffering that is part of the human experience of being inside a walled-off body, unable truly to experience the pain or joy of another person. The mirror neurons are—biologically speaking, at least—the best tools we've got in this department, and visual media are the key that opens the toolbox.

Wallace was no big fan of TV and the movies—he called them "low art" and a "lazy" experience for the viewer. I agree that they can be if all you do is sit and let yourself be filled with visual drivel and never really engage with what you're seeing. The best way to engage and be in dialogue with these media, of course, is to be a participant and start making stories yourself.

Those who decide to tell their own stories—even something as seemingly trivial as a cartoon cat flying through the air, or something as vital as the story of their grandmother's fight against Alzheimer's or the investigation of a soldier's death in Afghanistan—are like the poets of the nineteenth century competing with one another to find the best metaphors for the ocean, or the most tightly linked couplets. They're like painters copying and improving one another's visions of a biblical scene. This is the enormous web of culture weaving itself forward. And this is attainable by everyone. While we haven't been taught this kind of literacy, we have been exposed to it all our lives—from the first time we were set in front of a television set.

Many thousands of years ago, stories were told on cave walls and in words and songs by people sitting around campfires. Papyrus and paper allowed us to share stories across space and time, and opened up opportunities as well as the need for literacy. We are now returning to that campfire of flickering images and stories, this time one transportable across time and space. But we must move in that direction in a smart and literate way—and we will be the better for it. We can thrive in the age of the image.

As the old Chinese saying goes, the best time to plant a tree that will grow for a hundred years was a hundred years ago. The second-best time is right now. We must begin to *see* what the future holds for us.

NOTES ON SOURCES

ACKNOWLEDGMENTS

Although the subject of this book is the influence of visual media, it would be impossible to research, chart, or describe fully its effects without the immense recording power of the written word. If anything, my respect for the sanctity of printed material only grew as a result of my research. I drew upon multiple volumes that informed the factual content and conclusions of this narrative. The most important are highlighted here.

Perhaps the most influential book on my thinking about the hidden structure of wordless images is Leonard Shlain's *The Alphabet Versus the Goddess: The Conflict Between Word and Image* (New York: Penguin Compass, 1998). Irving Fang's *Alphabet to Internet: Mediated Communication in Our Lives* (St. Paul, MN: Rada Press, 2008) is an excellent source of historical material. This is supplemented by Dietrich Scheunemann, ed., *Orality, Literacy, and Modern Media* (Elizabethtown, NY: Camden House, 1996), and Stanley Cavell's *The World Viewed: Reflections on the Ontology of Film* (Cambridge, MA: Harvard University Press, 1971). Jerry Mander's *Four Arguments for the Elimination of Television* (New York: HarperCollins, 1978) is a book that made me laugh and think. Information about the Chauvet caves is in Stephen Jay Gould's *Leonardo's Mountain of Clams and the Diet of Worms* (New York: Three Rivers Press, 1998). While focused on print texts, Marjorie Garber's *The Use and Abuse of Literature* (New York: Pantheon, 2011) goes beyond discussing definitions of literature and also addresses what it means to read in a "literary" way, which is easily applicable to close viewing of visual texts. The most compelling book about the emergence of language and its connection to the natural world is David Abram's

The Spell of the Sensuous: Perception and Language in a More-Than-Human World (New York: Vintage, 1997).

The development of movies—and the implications for a new method of literacy—was covered in a series of books, including Charles Musser, *The Emergence of the Cinema: The American Screen to 1907* (History of the American Cinema series) (New York: Scribner, 1990); A. R. Fulton, *Motion Pictures: The Development of an Art from Silent Films to the Age of Television* (Norman: University of Oklahoma Press, 1960); Jonathan Auerbach, *Body Shots: Early Cinema's Incarnations* (Berkeley: University of California Press, 2007); Rebecca Solnit, *River of Shadows: Eadweard Muybridge and the Technological Wild West* (New York: Penguin, 2004); John Freeman, *The Tyranny of Email* (New York: Scribner, 2009); and Paul Starr, *The Creation of the Media: Political Origins of Modern Communication* (New York: Basic Books, 2004). A seminal work of visual images that I keep returning to is Eadweard Muybridge's *Muybridge's Complete Human and Animal Locomotion* (1887; reprint, Mineola, NY: Dover Publications, 1997).

Two distinguished philosophical tomes must be mentioned: Susan Sontag's *On Photography* (New York: Farrar, Straus and Giroux, 1973) is an unforgettable analysis of what the reproduction of images has done to our collective notions of reality; and Marshall McLuhan's *Understanding Media: The Extensions of Man* (New York: McGraw-Hill, 1964) is a multidimensional look at "reading" that goes far beyond any one aphorism.

The best description yet of the neurological impact of the image can be found in Marco Iacoboni's *Mirroring People: The Science of Empathy and How We Connect with Others* (New York: Farrar, Straus and Giroux, 2008). A comical and effective summary is Jeffrey Goldberg's piece for *The Atlantic* magazine, titled "Rethinking Jeffrey Goldberg," in the July/August 2008 issue. The German pornography study, titled "A Functional Endophenotype for Sexual Orientation in Humans," can be found in the journal *NeuroImage*, November 2006. Sigmund Freud's 1935 essay "A Note Upon the 'Mystic Writing Pad'" presents an interesting model for thinking about the connections between sensory intake, memory, perception, and consciousness.

The pragmatic language of cinema has been explained in thousands of film textbooks, none so clear as David Bordwell and Kristin Thompson's *Film Art: An Introduction* (New York: McGraw-Hill, 2009). I also found the following most helpful: Jennifer Van Sijll, *Cinematic Storytelling: The 100 Most Powerful Film Conventions Every Filmmaker Must Know* (Studio City, CA: Michael Wiese Productions, 2005); Gustavo Mercado, *The Filmmaker's Eye: Learning (and Breaking) the Rules of Cinematic Composition* (London: Focal Press, 2011); Dan Auiler, *Hitchcock's Secret Notebooks* (New York: Avon Books, 1999); Marcie

Begleiter, *From Word to Image: Storyboarding and the Filmmaking Process*, 2nd ed. (Studio City, CA: Michael Wiese Productions, 2010); Jeremy Vineyard, *Setting Up Your Shots: Great Camera Moves Every Filmmaker Should Know* (Studio City, CA: Michael Wiese Productions, 2000); Gabrielle Oldham, *First Cut: Conversations with Film Editors* (Berkeley: University of California Press, 1992); Lewis Cole, *Rethink–Reimagine: A Real Life Sketch of Composition* (Athens: Mediterranean Film Institute, 2004); and Walter Murch, *In the Blink of an Eye: A Perspective on Film Editing Revised*, 2nd ed. (Los Angeles: Silman-James Press, 2001). Documentary filmmaking is in many ways its own unique kind of art, and Michael Rabiger's *Directing the Documentary*, 5th ed. (Burlington, MA: Focal Press, 2009), provides an excellent overview. If you are inspired to begin understanding this mode of communication from within, these are great places to start, and they deserve some space on your bookshelf.

I am a student of the business of education, and found both Tony Wagner's *The Global Achievement Gap* (New York: Perseus Books, 2008) and Kathleen Tyner's *Literacy in a Digital World: Teaching and Learning in the Age of Information* (Mahwah, NJ: Lawrence Erlbaum Associates, 1998) provocative. Still relevant is Horace Mann's *On the Art of Teaching* (1840). I also referred to Larry Cuban's *Teachers and Machines: The Classroom Use of Technology Since 1920* (New York: Teachers College Press, 1986) and *Cardinal Principles of Secondary Education: A Report of the Commission on the Reorganization of Secondary Education, Appointed by the National Education Association* (Washington, D.C.: Department of the Interior, Government Printing Office, 1918). Heidi Hayes Jacobs, ed., *Curriculum 21: Essential Education for a Changing World* (Alexandria, VA: ASCD, 2010), is an engaging collection on the importance of rethinking our schools in order to embrace twenty-first-century communication skills.

Neal Feigenson and Christina Spiesel's *Law on Display: The Digital Transformation of Legal Persuasion and Judgment* (New York: NYU Press, 2009) is an excellent, uncommonly interesting book on what could be a dry topic. Paul Messaris's *Visual Persuasion: The Role of Images in Advertising* (Thousand Oaks, CA: Sage Publications, 1997) is a good overview of a complex business.

Henry Jenkins was good enough to lead me in person through some of the main points he covers in *Convergence Culture: Where Old and New Media Collide* (New York: NYU Press, 2006), and his *Spreadable Media: Creating Value and Meaning in a Networked Culture* (New York: NYU Press, 2013), written with Sam Ford and Joshua Green.

I need also to recognize the various visual media that influenced my thinking and understanding of this subject. Werner Herzog's *Cave of Forgotten Dreams* (IFC Films, 2011) allowed me access to the immense beauty of the paintings of

Chauvet. The German-produced documentary series *Automatic Brain* (European Broadcasting Union, 2011) provides a good explanation and presentation of the brain's visual processing. And of course the hundreds of films I have watched through the evolution of this project (together with the thousands before) have all played a part in my understanding of the language of cinema, and deserve to be mentioned by name—yet the space here is too limited to include them all.

■ ACKNOWLEDGMENTS

Thanks for helping bring this book to life begin with Tom Zoellner. He was willing to dive into the world of film and visual literacy with me and stayed in even when the waters got cold, and in the process helped me get my thoughts in order and my words in shape. He brought a writer's love of the word to this conversation about the power of visual images, and the book is better off for his support and I for his friendship.

I also had the opportunity to meet some inspiring people along the way, all enthusiastic and generous with their time and knowledge. Professors Rafi Malach of the Weizmann Institute, Uri Hasson of Princeton University, and Marco Iacoboni of UCLA helped me understand the neuroscience involved in processing visual images. Professor Henry Jenkins and Dean Elizabeth Daley of USC provided wisdom about the culture of media and its impact on education. Charles Musser of Yale shared his insights on the emergence of early cinema. Philip Carlsen of MindSign guided me into an fMRI tube and studied my "brain on video." Thanks also to Joe Lambert of the Center for Digital Storytelling, Brian Shin of Visible Measures, and the educators Dennis Maika and Jay Hoffman.

YouTubers Freddie Wong and brothers Benny and Rafi Fine welcomed me into their worlds, which were fascinating to see, as they represent the emergence of a whole new community of filmmakers. Thanks also to Dave Carroll, Liz OuYang, and ManSee Kong for sharing their stories of truly independent filmmaking.

I have had an opportunity to spend time with many filmmakers whose work continues to inspire me—none more so than Jonathan Demme, Ron Howard, and Steven Spielberg, and I am thankful for their leadership of the Jacob Burns Film Center and support for this project. Jonathan's close and thoughtful reading in particular made this a better book. Martin Scorsese is one of our greatest storytellers and his passion for the roots of world cinema is inspiring. He is a giant of cinema, and intuitively understands the power of visual images—whether on the big screen, in the classroom, or anywhere in our society. When he embraced this project and was willing to add his own words to the subject, I was beyond thrilled. I hope you are as well. One filmmaker I met along the way who has had an enormous impact on my understanding of documentary filmmaking is Albert Maysles. I also want to thank Paul Schrader, Debra Winger, Arliss Howard, Noah Hutton, Ido Haar, Andy Young, Susan Todd, David Zieff, and Simon Schama for their films and deep insight. I must extend a special note of thanks to the filmmaker, writer, and programmer Kent Jones, whose extraordinary cinematic knowledge is outdone only by his generosity of spirit.

As I mention in the Notes on Sources, one of the books that has had a real impact on me is *The Alphabet Versus the Goddess*, by Leonard Shlain. A few years ago, a mutual friend arranged an intimate dinner that would allow me to meet Shlain. The conversation that evening went on for hours. Only a few weeks later, I received a note from Leonard that he had just been diagnosed with a brain tumor, which ultimately took his life. In a Google search to clear the title of this book, the only reference I saw to "The Age of the Image" (aside from a song of that title) was a 2005 article in *Edutopia* magazine, written by Leonard. Needless to say, he was ahead of his time.

The entire Jacob Burns Film Center board and staff have contributed to this book in many ways that are visible and even more that would fall under the radar but need to be acknowledged. While listing everyone by name would take a chapter in itself, and at the risk of leaving anyone out, I want to specifically mention several people who have had a profound influence on my starting and finishing this book. I have learned so much and benefited greatly from the wisdom and friendship of Janet Maslin, Art Samberg, David Swope, Nancy Kohlberg, Gary Knell, Hugh Price, Esmeralda Santiago, Janet Benton, and Barry Shenkman. And I want to thank Kathryn Davis, Cindy George, Bob Bernstein, Ben Cheever, and Heidi Hayes Jacobs for their belief in me and in this book. Sabrina Coughlin is a dear friend and was a true partner in founding the JBFC.

The Jacob Burns Film Center and Media Arts Lab have been a wonderful home for the past twelve years, thanks to people such as my dear friend, and our director of programming, Brian Ackerman, whose deep wisdom and enthusiasm for film can be found in the pages of this book. I have learned so much from our extraordinary team of educators. I want to thank Emily Keating, Anne Marie Santoro, Joe Summerhays, Holen Kahn, Brady Shoemaker, Sean Weiner, Aaron Mace, Jessica Sucher, Adam Rokhsar, and the rest of the JBFC team for their contributions and insight. I also want to acknowledge and thank the tens of thousands of students and the countless teachers who have participated in our programs and been the guinea pigs for the development of our work and my thinking about this subject. Our art director, Susan Kineke, has been a constant and valued partner in all things visual; and Dominick Balletta helps keep it all going today, and for that I am thankful. I have often said to our team at the JBFC that our accomplishments are collective accomplishments, and this book is no different. Thanks to each of you for carrying a heavier load and allowing me to complete this project.

I need to acknowledge and thank each of the JBFC members who helped form and continue to maintain this great community. We began a dialogue many years ago that continues today and has informed this book in more ways than you can imagine. And thanks to our more than one hundred thousand students, who have been our laboratory animals *and* our teachers over the last decade.

The team at Local Projects, especially Jake Barton and Daniel Liss, provided a wonderful forum for exploration around image and visual literacy during the writing of this book, and our discussions are reflected in these pages.

The illustrator and storyboard artist Robin Richesson, who has created storyboards for movies such as *American Beauty*, put some of the key concepts in the Grammar, Rhythm, and Rhyme in the Age of the Image chapter into easily understood illustrations. Thanks also to Greg Nemec and Kenny Velez for getting things rolling in this regard, and to Lynda Curtis for her gift of friendship, photography, and a very kind presence behind the camera.

So many friends offered support and nourishment along this journey: Nancy and Keith Krakaur, Marvin Israelow, Dorian Goldman, Helen Bernstein, Bob Goldberg, Betsy MacIsaac, Keren Sharon, Brian Skarstad, Louise Beech, Lael Morgan, Heather Nicolson, Becky Samberg, Jeff Samberg, David Barber, Joe Cosgriff, John Pizzarelli, Todd Sandler, Nitzan Ofir, Sharon AvRutick, Joe Wallace, Peter and Jen Buffet, Bradley Thomason, Bob Dandrew, Amber Rubarth, Marcina Hale, and Roberto Cristobal—thanks! And to my dear friends Nancy and Jerry Kohlberg, your wisdom and support in my life, and in my pursuit of this work, are beyond anything I could hope for.

In many ways, the project became real when I began working with my literary agent, Gloria Loomis. I couldn't have been more fortunate than I was in meeting her—thanks, David Alexander and Ruth Mass!—and her interest in me and in the project has been beyond wonderful. She helped me refine my proposal and then guided me through the process and placed this book in the perfect hands. I also want to thank Julia Masnik for her always-enthusiastic support.

As for the perfect hands, Sean McDonald believed in this book from the beginning, and an *idea* for a book became reality when he took this on. He challenged me from the beginning, and at every step along the way made it better. He had great insight into the subject and was deeply engaged in the conversation that is reflected in the pages of this book. This book came to life because of his belief and guidance, and by the hard work of Emily Bell, Chris Peterson, and the rest of the Farrar, Straus and Giroux team. A special note of appreciation to Rodrigo Corral, who threw himself into the inspired design of the cover of this book.

My family has been an overwhelming fount of support and encouragement. The Apkon, Hertz, and Mass families have been constant supports, as have the Lazevnik and Itkis families. My parents instilled in me a sense of the possible, for which I am thankful. I have learned so much through the eyes and minds of my children, Talia, Ori, and Maayan, but I have learned even more from their hearts. They inspired this book. Talia was also my trusted reader and was quick to keep me in line when I strayed from the core of the work.

And to my wife, Lisa. She has put up with late nights and time away researching and writing, and has always done so with a smile and a gentle push forward. She listened as I read aloud early drafts of this manuscript and served as a patient and thoughtful audience. She believed in this adventure more than a decade ago and has believed in me even longer, and for this I am most fortunate. She is my true partner in life and in everything good.

A Final Note

My mother has been a constant source of encouragement and my father first inspired in me a love of image when he put a camera in my hands and took me on his early morning photo shoots and into the darkroom. It was his mother, my grandmother Dora Apkon, however, who has been with me most on the journey of this book.

She was born in Poland at the beginning of the 1900s and moved to Havana, Cuba, in the 1920s, when she was denied admittance to the United States, ultimately emigrating here in 1931. She spoke very little about her earlier years, other than her brief work as an actress in Havana. Sadly, she passed away in 1990, almost a decade before my work at the JBFC began. A year ago my father was going through some old boxes that contained her remaining possessions. He called me to say that he had come across an old passport-like document that shocked him when he opened it. It was an official student ID from the Warsaw Film School from 1925, with my grandmother's picture on it. Next to it he found her transcript listing the various cinematography, directing, and other classes she had taken. This was a story that, remarkably, she had never shared with anyone. Needless to say, she was ahead of her time as a woman filmmaker in Poland in the early 1900s. My father scanned the ID and transcript and sent them to me. They brought me to tears.

I had no idea of this part of her life, and she had no idea how I would choose to spend my life immersed in the world of film. I wish she had known my wife and children; they would have brought her much joy. When I found this long-hidden story, I wanted one more conversation with her to share our joint passion. I realize now that she was very present with me in the writing of this book, and this conversation is captured between the lines of these pages.